AXEL VERVOORDT
THE STORY OF A STYLE

© 2001 Assouline Publishing for the original edition
601 West 26th Street, 18th floor
New York, NY 10001, USA
Tel.: 212-989-6769   Fax: 212-647-0005
www.assouline.com

ISBN: 9782843232978
10 9 8 7 6 5 4 3

Layout design: Sébastien Ratto-Viviani

Color separation: Gravor (Switzerland)
Printed in China

All rights reserved. No part of this publication may be
reproduced or transmitted in any form or by any means,
electronic or otherwise, without prior
consent from the publisher.

AXEL VERVOORDT
THE STORY OF A STYLE

TEXT BY
MEREDITH ETHERINGTON-SMITH

PHOTOGRAPHS BY
LAZIZ HAMANI

ASSOULINE

*I dedicate this book to my wife, May,
and to my sons, Boris and Dicky.*

contents

introduction	8
memories	16
influences	30
métier	74
restoration	86
exhibitions	94
castle	110
kanaal	148
volledig	168
illustrations	181
photo credits	195
acknowledgments	195

"I consider myself a very eclectic collector and dealer. I treasure the timeless and disdain the trendy. My taste spans centuries, continents and economic strata. I love the tension between different objects and different cultures. And I always let the space I am restoring inspire me."

Axel Vervoordt

A backward glance at the history of interiors, their decoration and furnishings, reveals the importance of visual density. The overcrowded, over-upholstered, over-decorated rooms that please the eye of one generation are anathema twenty years later. The pendulum of style swings perpetually from the overstuffed to the understated.

In Axel Vervoordt's case, he is happy living in both densely furnished rooms, and in rooms of more severity and space. "I like to work, for instance, in a room that is richly furnished, like an English library; a beautiful desk, books, mahogany furniture. That sort of room suits a man's business life and gives me a lot of confidence. On the other hand, I like to spend my spare time in rooms which are very sparse and severe. Once I am in the room in the castle where I live that is furnished in this way, I really don't want to talk about business, I don't want to read about business, and I like to listen to contemporary music. Opera, which I also love, is for the library downstairs. It is yin and yang, and the contrast between the full library and the empty 'withdrawing' room is central to my thinking."

Early indications of new millennium styles suggest that the way forward is to pick and choose from all periods as Vervoordt does. "I feel I am making a trip around the world in my own home." Vervoordt's talent is in assembling interiors that look as if they had been there forever. Interiors that suggest humanity in their arrangement and in the burnish of their daily use, where nothing looks new except the way the furniture, pictures, and objets d'art are placed in the living space, in fresh contexts and juxtapositions of a visual density that suits the twenty-first-century eye and way of life.

This is the future in which Axel Vervoordt, heir to the Northern European aesthetic tradition, already lives. Vervoordt has spent most of his fifty-four years pursuing and capturing the evidence of human creativity. He discovers superb objects and works of art, both major and minor, from every archaic, antique, and contemporary culture. Whether they are found languishing in an attic, at a country auction, or during the dismantling of a great house, Vervoordt possesses these discoveries for a time, however brief, and then finds them new homes.

His voyages of discovery span three continents, and his daily existence is spent in the slipstream of the treasures he discovers. The date of each acquisition is carefully noted in a series of notebooks, with a little sketch and a brief description. Then, together with art historians and assistants, he spends time—months if necessary—researching the creator of the work, its past owners, the houses where it was displayed, its journey through history.

A native of Antwerp, Belgium, Vervoordt is a man of high and concentrated purpose, with the endless energy to achieve his aims. His face is of a type often seen in sixteenth-century Flemish and Dutch pictures. Alert. Astute. Genial. Outgoing. But there is also something of the orient, of the Buddha in the frequently contemplative gaze of his eyes. In Vervoordt's face may be observed the yang of his European baroque heritage and the yin of his attitude toward Zen and the silent power it invokes in him.

Vervoordt and his wife, May, inhabit an enchanting castle, reflected in a deep moat in the flat Flanders landscape near Antwerp. Their sons, Boris and Dick, have both followed their father into his business.

Kasteel van 's-Gravenwezel was first recorded in 1108. The oldest part of the present castle dates from the early fourteenth century; its rococo façade was added in 1729. In the large park, eighteenth-century sculptural fragments inspired by classical mythology by sculptor Michiel Van der Voordt lie partly hidden among fallen leaves. A flock of sheep grazes. Shaggy mountains of rhododendrons, clipped in cloud formations, rise like sculptures from the grass, concealing a lake. Clearings in the beech woods reveal stones set in sand to remind one of the sea. And behind the eighteenth-century orangery and conservatory—both still used as such—and the dependencies now used as libraries and studio offices, lies a vast formal garden of "rooms" whose walls are formed by geometrically clipped box hedges. There are stables for Vervoordt's horses and a pool overlooked by a tiny neoclassical pavilion full of pale, silvery Venetian grotto furniture.

Vervoordt's clients come from all over the world in search of the rare and the beautiful in the ever-changing arrangements of furniture, objects, and paintings in the high-ceilinged rooms of the castle's main floors. What awaits them is usually rather more than the average shopping trip. They might find Vervoordt in the library, deep in discussion with the members of an avant-garde musical ensemble. They might sit next to a major international sculptor, or a forensic psychologist, at one of May's famously delicious lunches or dinners.

From this happy hybrid of home, visual laboratory, and cultural happening, Axel Vervoordt's reputation as a leader of contemporary taste has spread throughout Europe and America. His avidly curious and far-ranging mind does not confine itself to his chosen aesthetic discipline. Weekend guests often find themselves dining by candlelight in the garden and engaging in impromptu seminars discussing questions that range from contemporary morality, via the best way to bake bread, to the design of grand opera. Twice a year, over weekends in spring and late autumn, he opens his doors to the public: more than 6,000 visitors might pause to admire May's exquisite displays of flowers from the gardens or Vervoordt's new arrangement of the library or drawing room.

Vervoordt often uses the Flemish word *volledig*—literally *vol,* meaning "full," and *ledig,* meaning "empty"—as shorthand for his philosophy of what constitutes the ideal surroundings for himself and for those he advises. To him, a room should be a series of visual adventures in space. Spatial planes should be interrupted by the conjunction of very different, almost opposing, objects. These juxtapositions should inspire contemplation and thus a certain type of mental liberty. His passion for space might seem paradoxical for a man who, from a very early age, has been obsessed—there is no other word for the depth of his concentration—with the works of art, furniture, and objects that have enriched human life since civilized time began.

Vervoordt cites three main strands of influence in his work. The first is that of contemporary and Oriental art, and *arte povera,* which to him signifies the importance of a life of meditation, empty space, a love and respect of nature and of human existence. The second is architecture, which represents proportion, balance, and harmony, such as one might find in an eighteenth-century library. The third strand is the baroque, either gilded and courtly, or more simple and countrified. To him, the baroque conjures up the good life of great food and entertaining, and wonderful conversation with friends.

Is Axel Vervoordt an antique dealer? He would more correctly be termed an antiquarian. Is he a furnisher? Yes, because he advises his clients on what to acquire and how to arrange these acquisitions in their own homes. Is he a decorator? He dislikes the word and is very uncomfortable when described as such, but he does have very strong views about the interiors in which objects can come triumphantly into their own, and he will advise his clients accordingly.

Vervoordt is not merely preoccupied with possessing, even for a brief moment, the things he finds beautiful. He is a true creator, a philosopher of the three dimensions whose dialectic is founded on the visual. His raw material, his vocabulary, is drawn from a vast array of works of art. With these elements he effects new compositions, putting them into new contexts to create a dynamic new harmony.

Axel Vervoordt choreographs objects in space. This is his métier and here is his story.

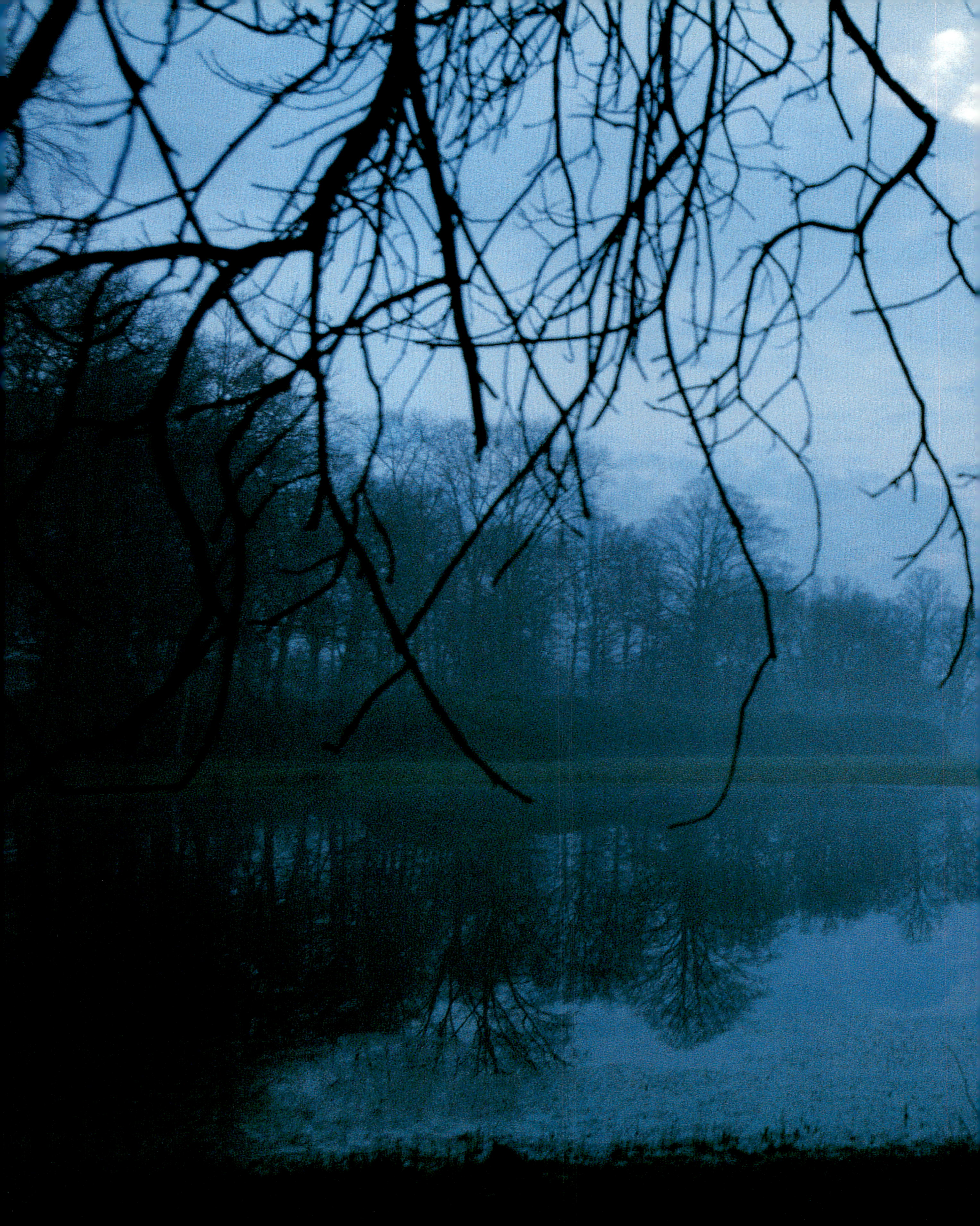

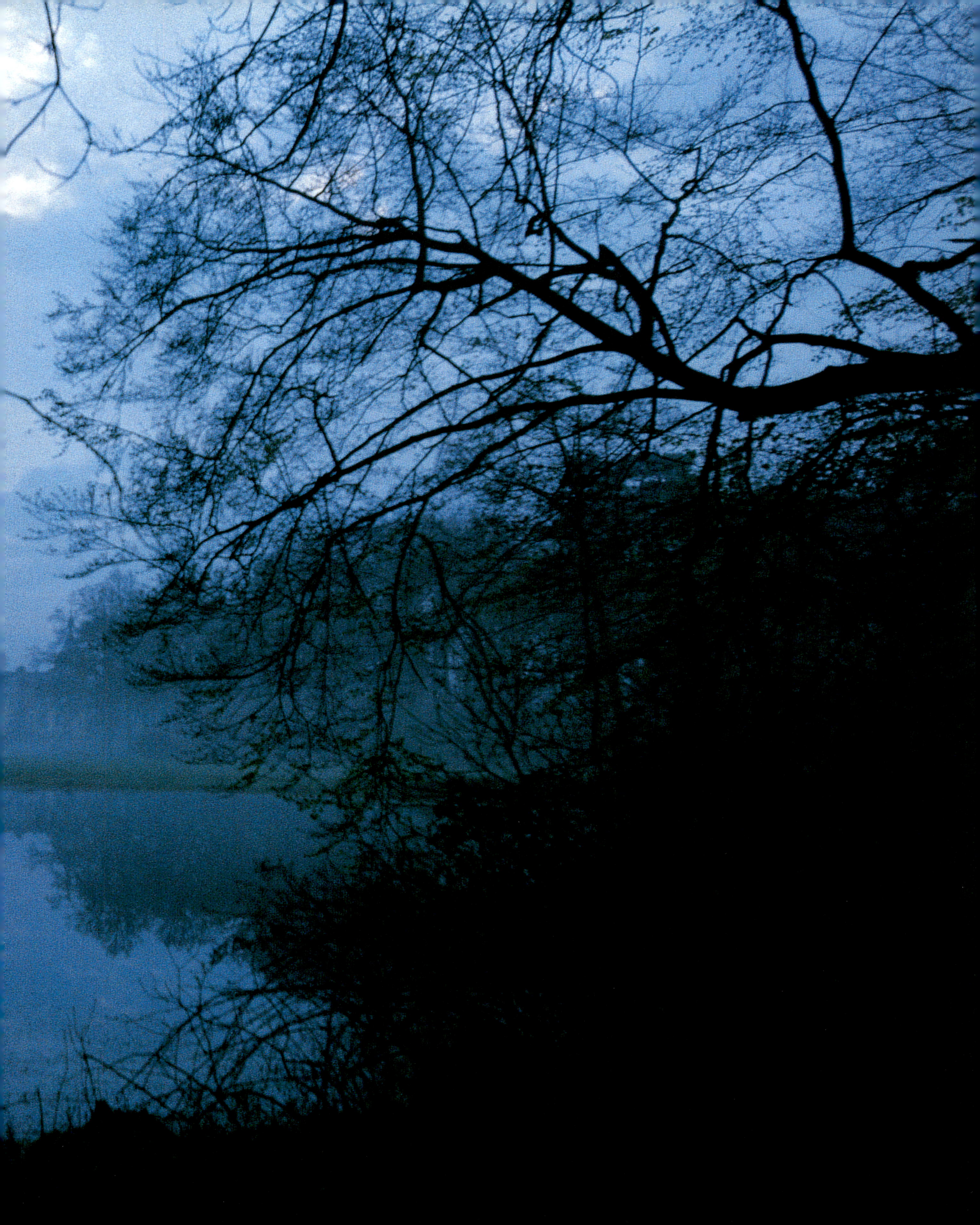

"The whole of art is an appeal to a reality which is not without us, but in our minds."

Desmond MacCarthy

1857

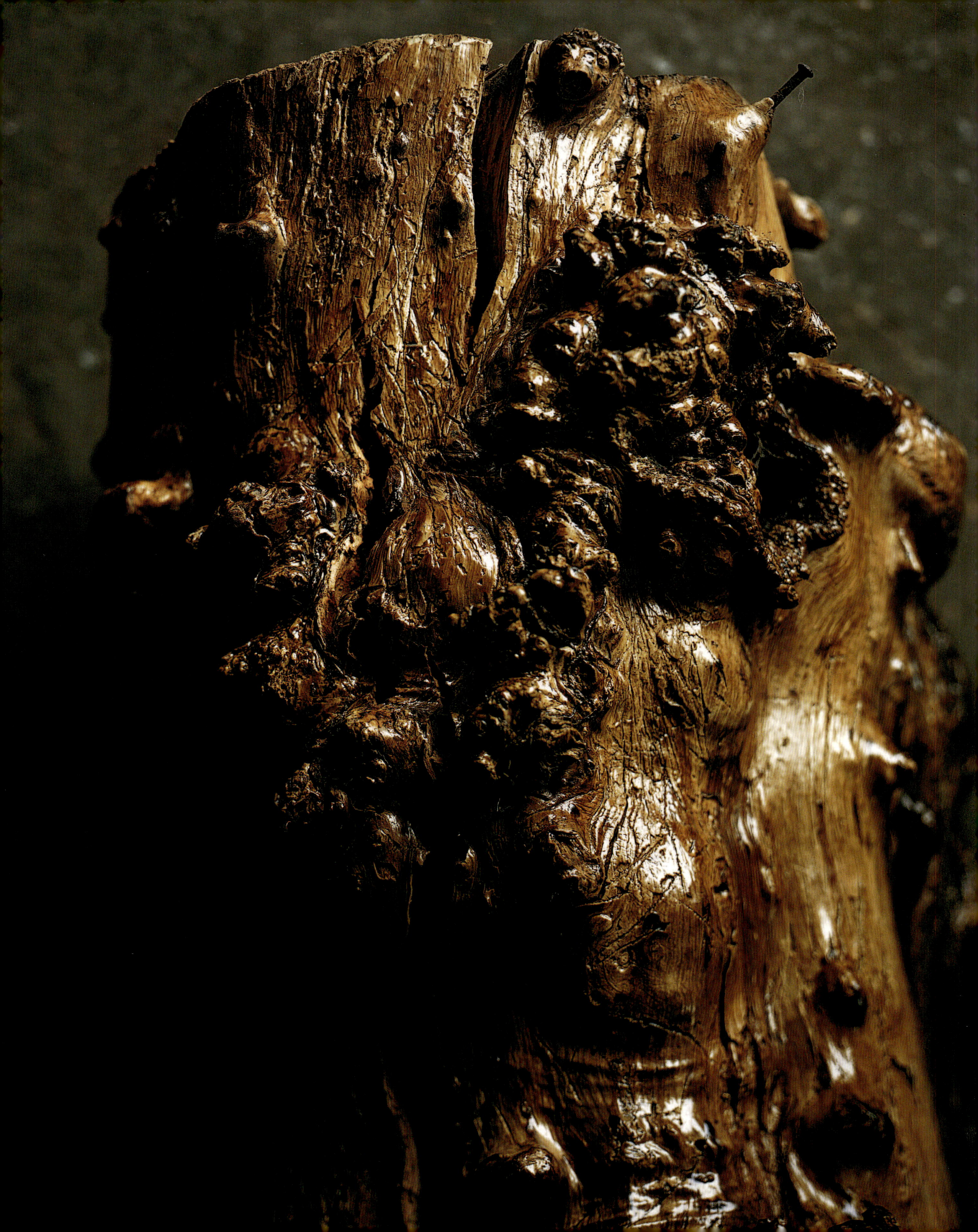

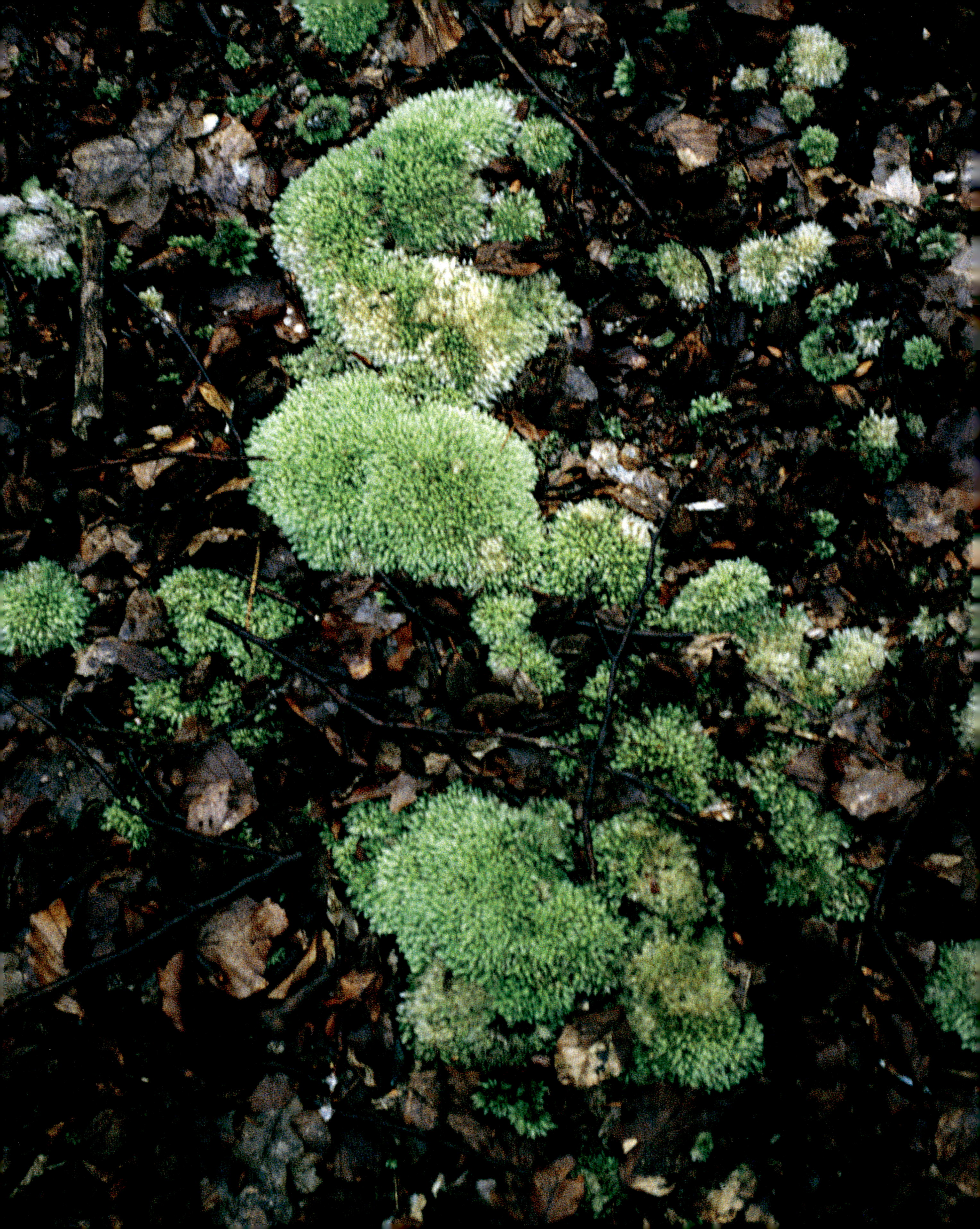

memories

I was born in Antwerp in 1947, and when I was very small indeed, perhaps five or six, I was taken for walks in the local park. It was a public park but almost nobody ever went there except my father who had grazing rights for over 100 horses. The park covered hundreds of acres; there were wild meadows, a river, lakes, and huge trees. No one else was allowed to keep horses on it, so in my mind it was like our own meadow, and here I learned all about wildflowers and sometimes picked them and arranged them in little bunches. We had some really old ladies as neighbors. They were very friendly and they loved me. I have loved old people ever since, for their knowledge and their memories. The old ladies played a game with me, ordering bunches of flowers and paying me for them. It was my first experience of making other people happy with the beautiful things I had found.

As the years went by and I ventured further afield, I began to explore the local antique and junk shops. I found curiosities and little treasures that intrigued my eye which I bought for myself.

It was just chance that I found I could perceive the beauty in objects that others might find ugly or strange. To me, some objects are very positive to the eye and others are very negative. Looking back, I ask myself, was I right in buying and selling at such an early age? I don't think I ever asked myself that question at the time, but now I believe that as long as I can give more value to a sad and neglected object by discovering its true and hidden glory, restoring it to life, putting it somewhere better, making people happy they own it and, at the same time, making money to find more beautiful and neglected works of art, this must always be a good thing.

My childhood was spent with my parents and older sister in a small house built by my uncle, who was an architect, close to the big park, the Rivierenhof, on the outskirts of Antwerp. It was a charming house of red brick and white paint with tracery windows. My father was a successful businessman. A dealer in horses, he imported more than a hundred animals a week from Poland, Ireland, and England, selecting with a sure eye those suitable for jumping, for dressage, for labor in the harbor, or for the abattoir. He was very knowledgeable indeed about horses and, through the horse world, had friends of all kinds, from princes to farmers, all of whom came to our house.

My mother was the first great influence on my life, and encouraged my early excursions into taste. She was very clever, read a great deal, and spent a lot of time discussing radical new ideas. She preferred the natural and the simple, and created a very special atmosphere

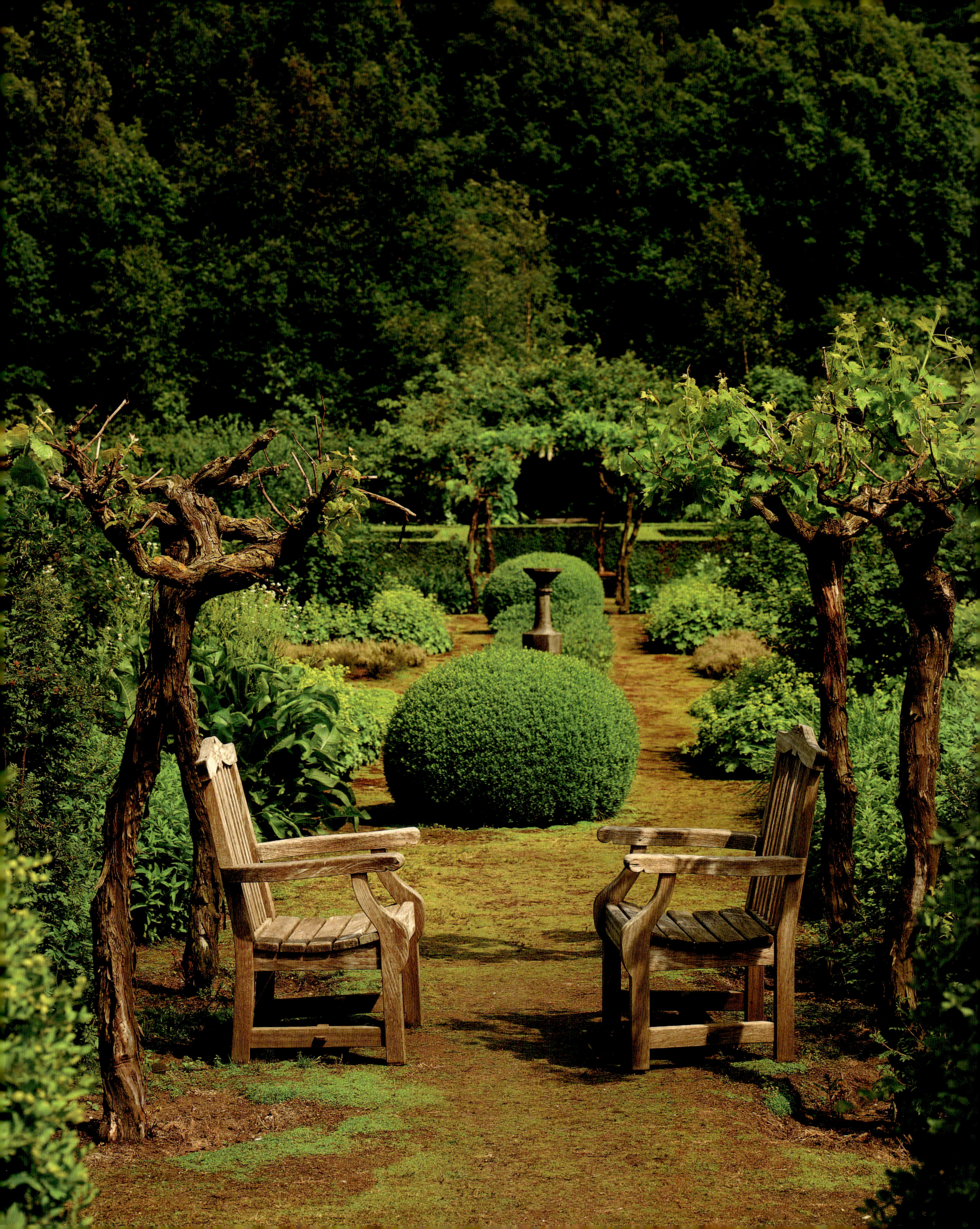

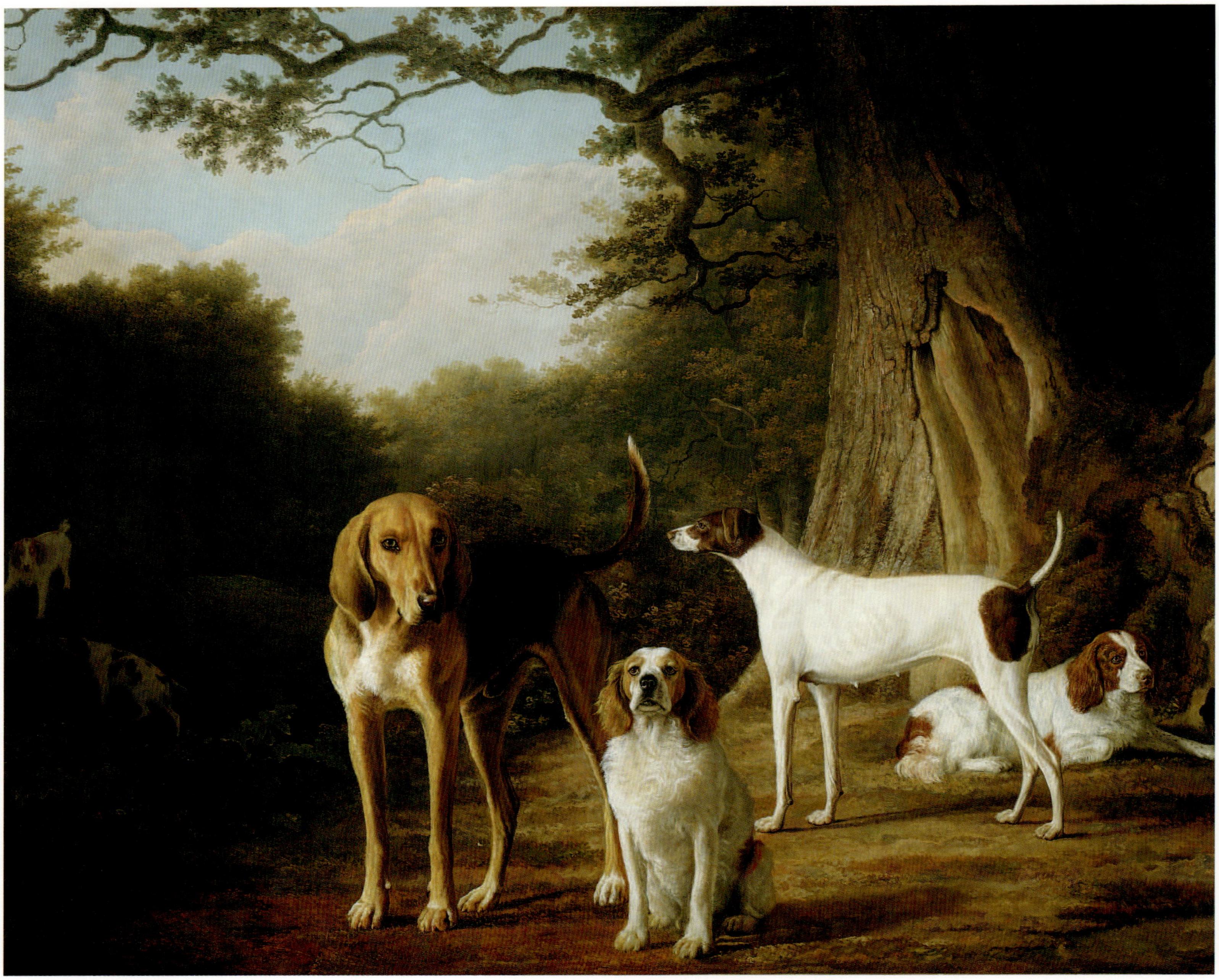

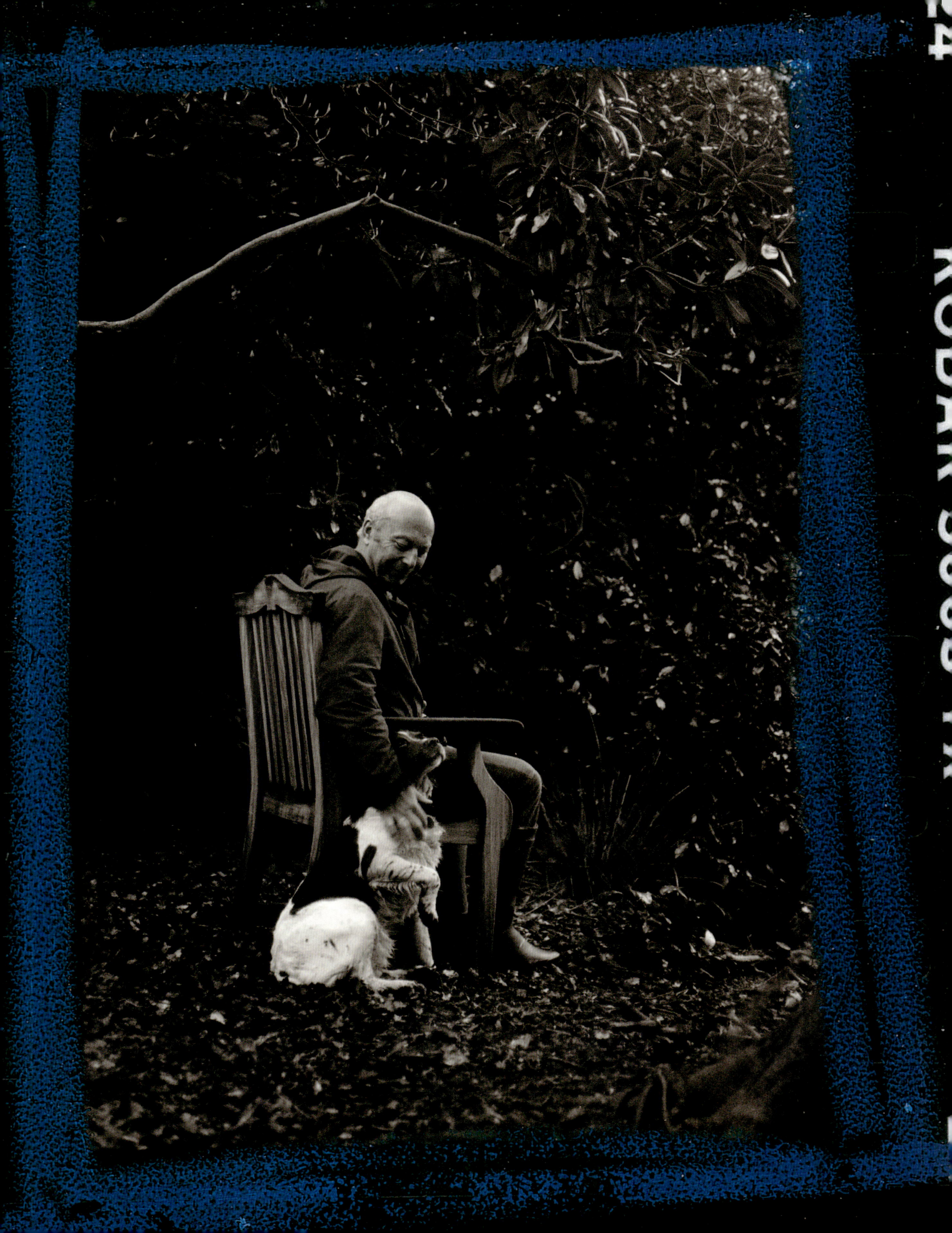
24
KODAK 5063 TX

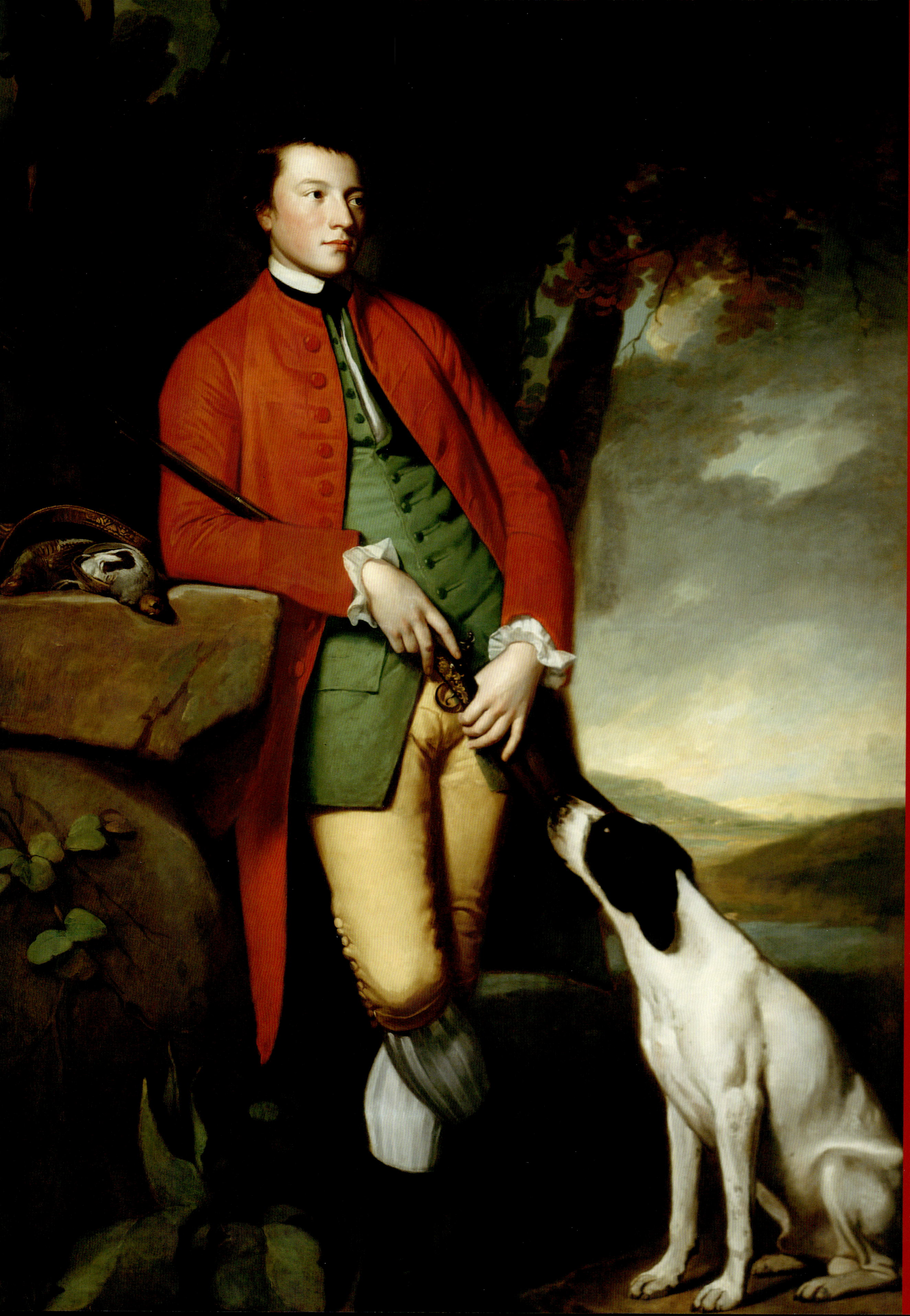

at home. She prepared wonderful food and the house was always full of friends, in a casual, informal way. She had fascinating and unusual friends, all of whom I met because we children were always with our parents, which was unusual then. Perhaps three times a week her friends would come round to make music. They would play Chopin, or even film music. Of course in those days there was no television and not much radio, so people had to make their own amusements. I look back on it now and realize what a wonderful, warm world it was.

I must have been about seven when I became interested in creating art myself. My sister had made terracotta figures at school and when I saw them I decided to make a figure of Christ on the cross, depicting Jesus as a king. I attended a Jesuit school and my schoolmasters were very impressed by the result. My mother found a local artist to make plaster molds of my crucifix to hang in all the classrooms. This convinced my mother that I should have extra tuition in art during my schooling with the Jesuits, and she immediately went around the artists' quarter in Antwerp looking for artists who could teach me painting and sculpture.

The tutors she found not only taught me about painting, drawing, and sculpture, they also took me to exhibitions and introduced me to contemporary artists and their work.

Throughout my adult life I have been friendly with contemporary artists such as Jef Verheyen, who introduced me to the works of Mark Rothko, Lucio Fontana, and Yves Klein, among others. Abstract art has helped me to better understand ancient art, because it is universal yet also represents the viewpoint of our own age.

My mother's visits to the artists' quarter in search of tutors had another rather unusual consequence which played a crucial role in my development—and still does. She fell in love with Antwerp's old sixteenth-century houses, which were in a very bad state after the war. Everyone wanted to live on the city outskirts or in the country. Nobody wanted to live in the center around the cathedral, so the area became very run-down; it had been grand, now it was a seedy district. Because of this, the houses were cheap.

It all started with the artist who my mother had commissioned to reproduce my terracotta crucifix. She lived in a virtually ruined sixteenth-century house and needed money to make a trip around the world. My mother fell in love with the house and bought it. When she told my father what she'd done, he was furious—partly because it was in the red-light district. But my mother was not to be deterred from her purpose, which was to restore the house and rent it to artists. This she did, and with so great a success that she soon bought more and more houses in the area, then rented them to artists and to restaurants to pay for yet more acquisitions. I am proud to say that my mother was extremely influential in saving for posterity part of the sixteenth-century center of Antwerp.

I became fascinated by the process of restoring these houses and, as I grew older, helped my mother. These restorations couldn't cost a great deal because she could not afford to spend too much, so we restored and decorated in the simplest manner, helped by artists who needed to make money. The restorations were appropriate to the original look of the houses, which taught me a great deal at an early age about how to bring new life to the beauty and simplicity of the past, and about the importance of space, proportion, and purity.

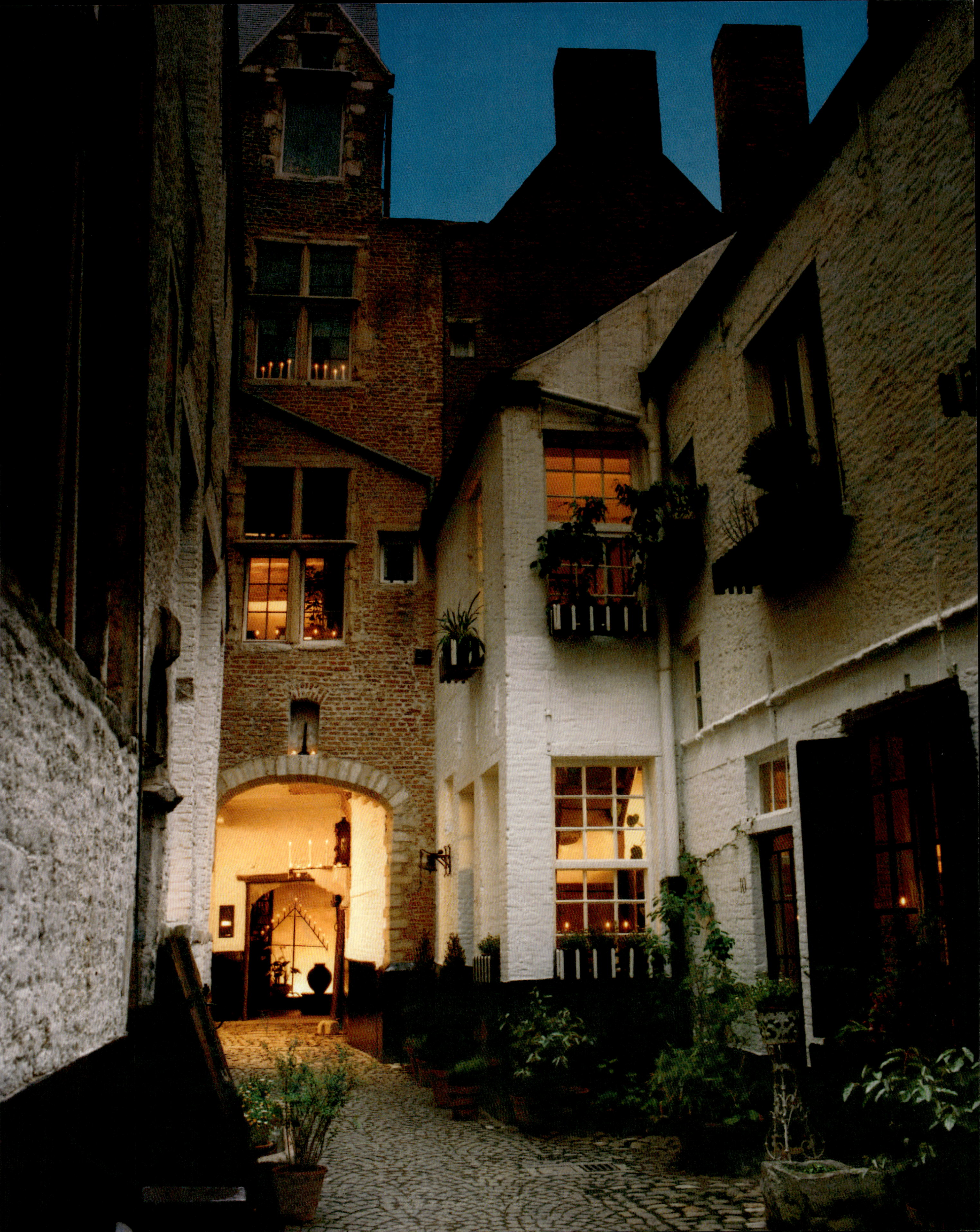
10

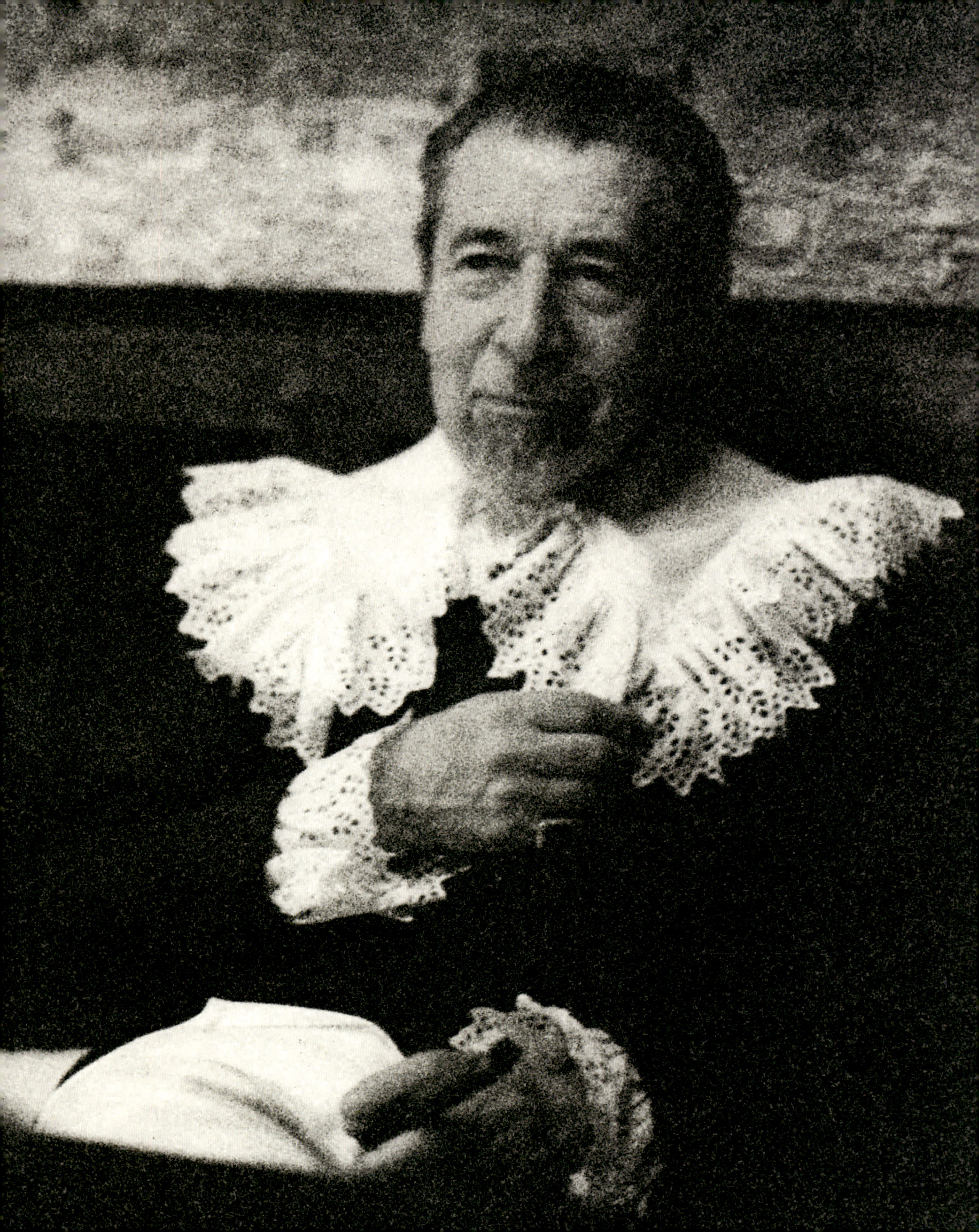

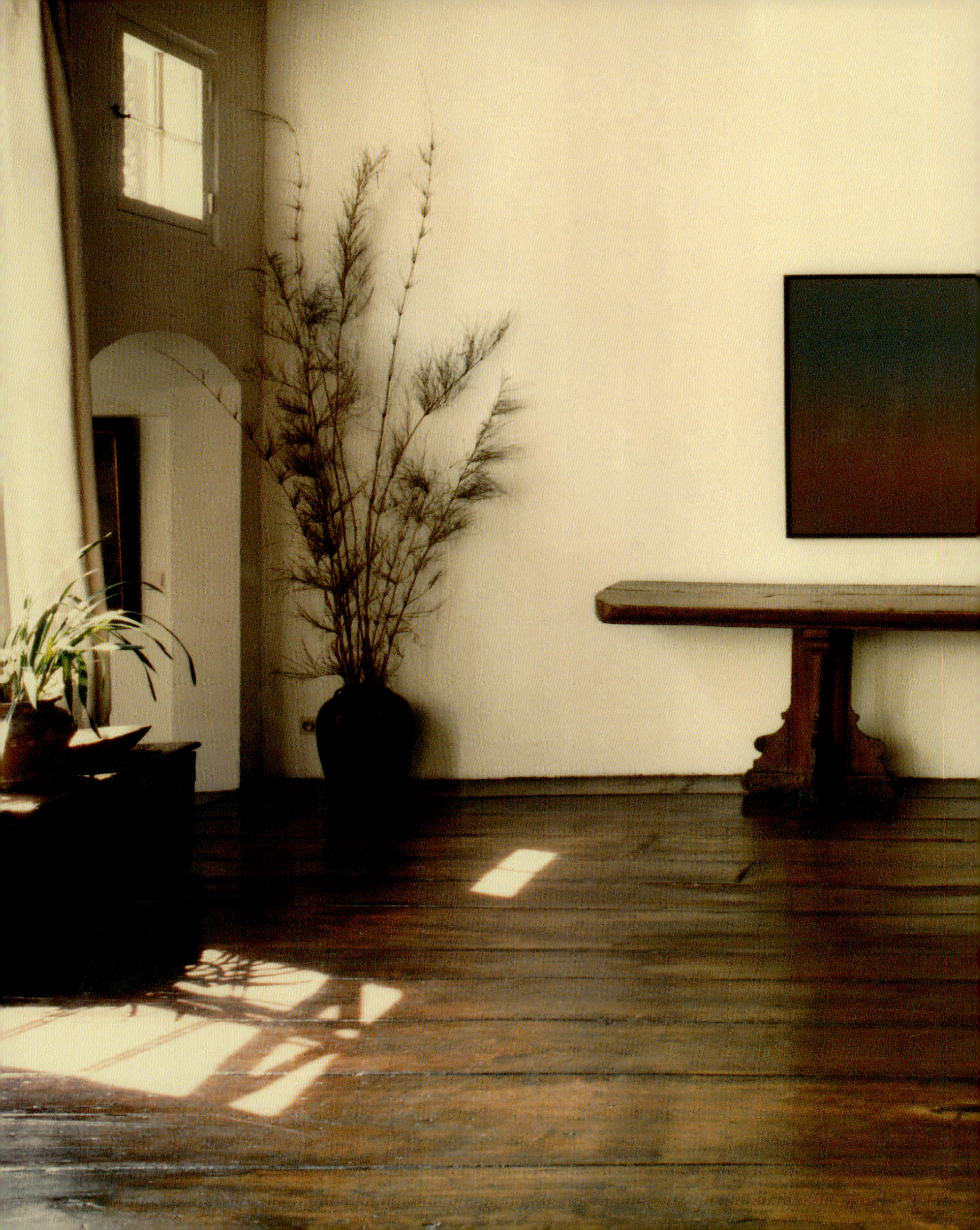

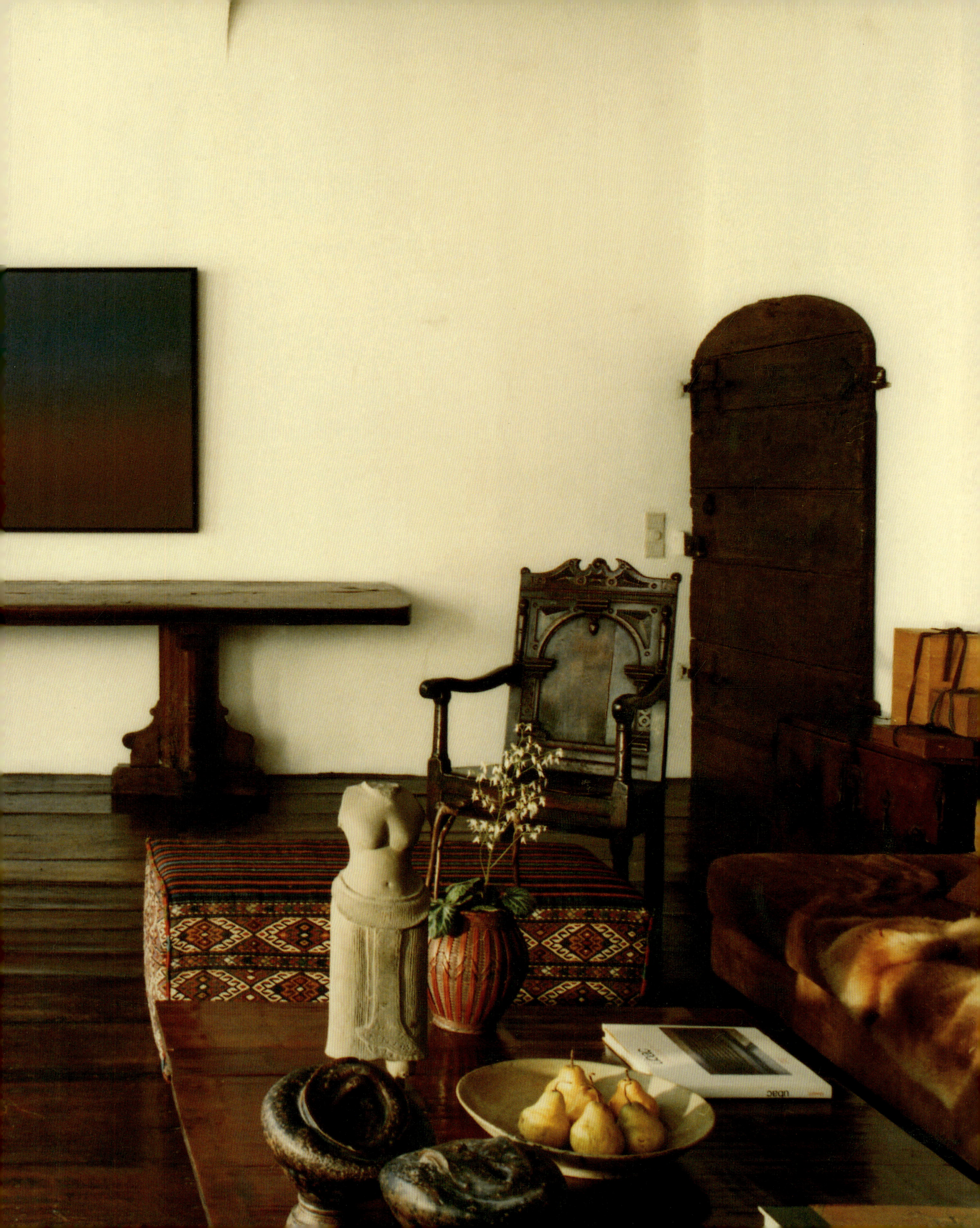

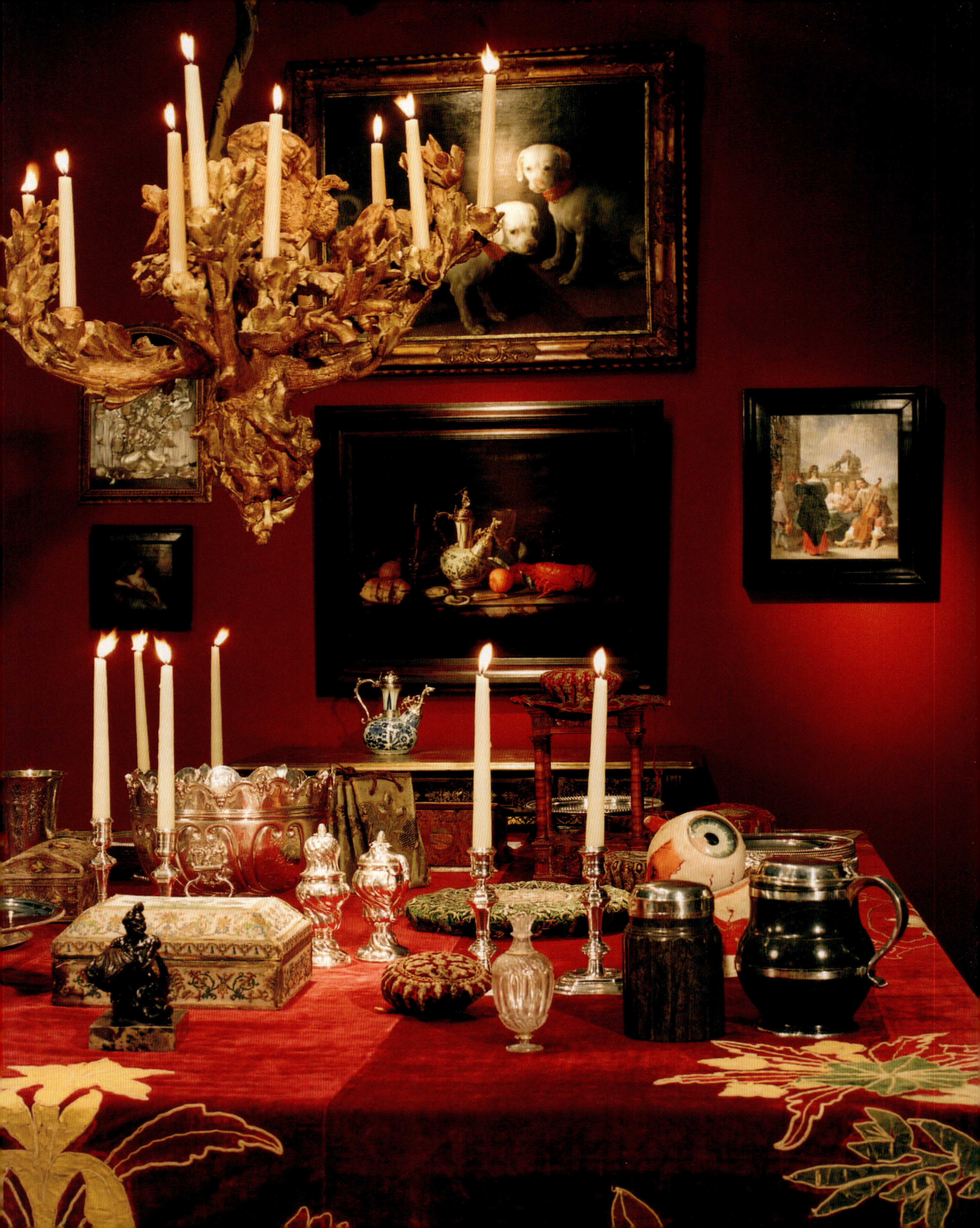

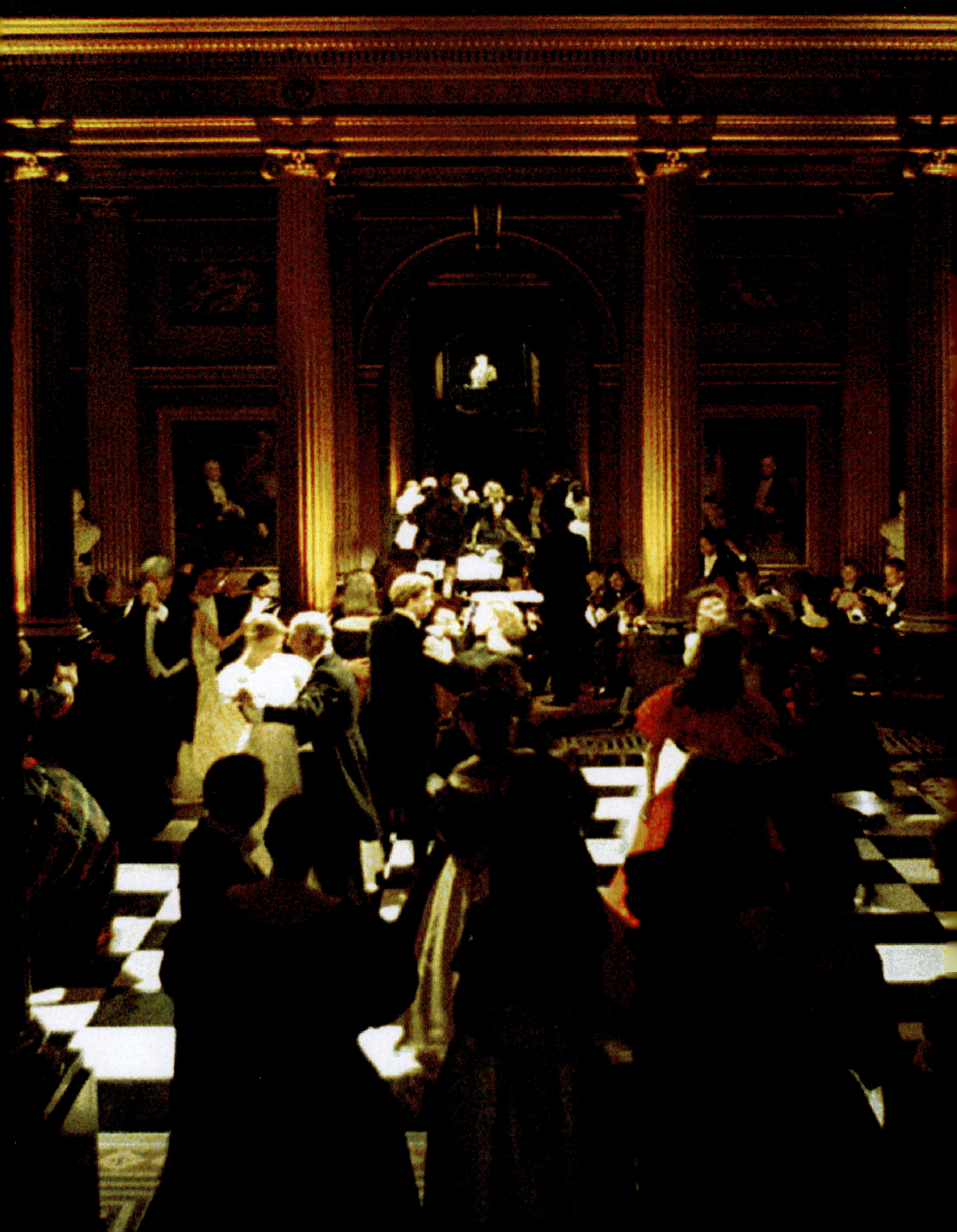

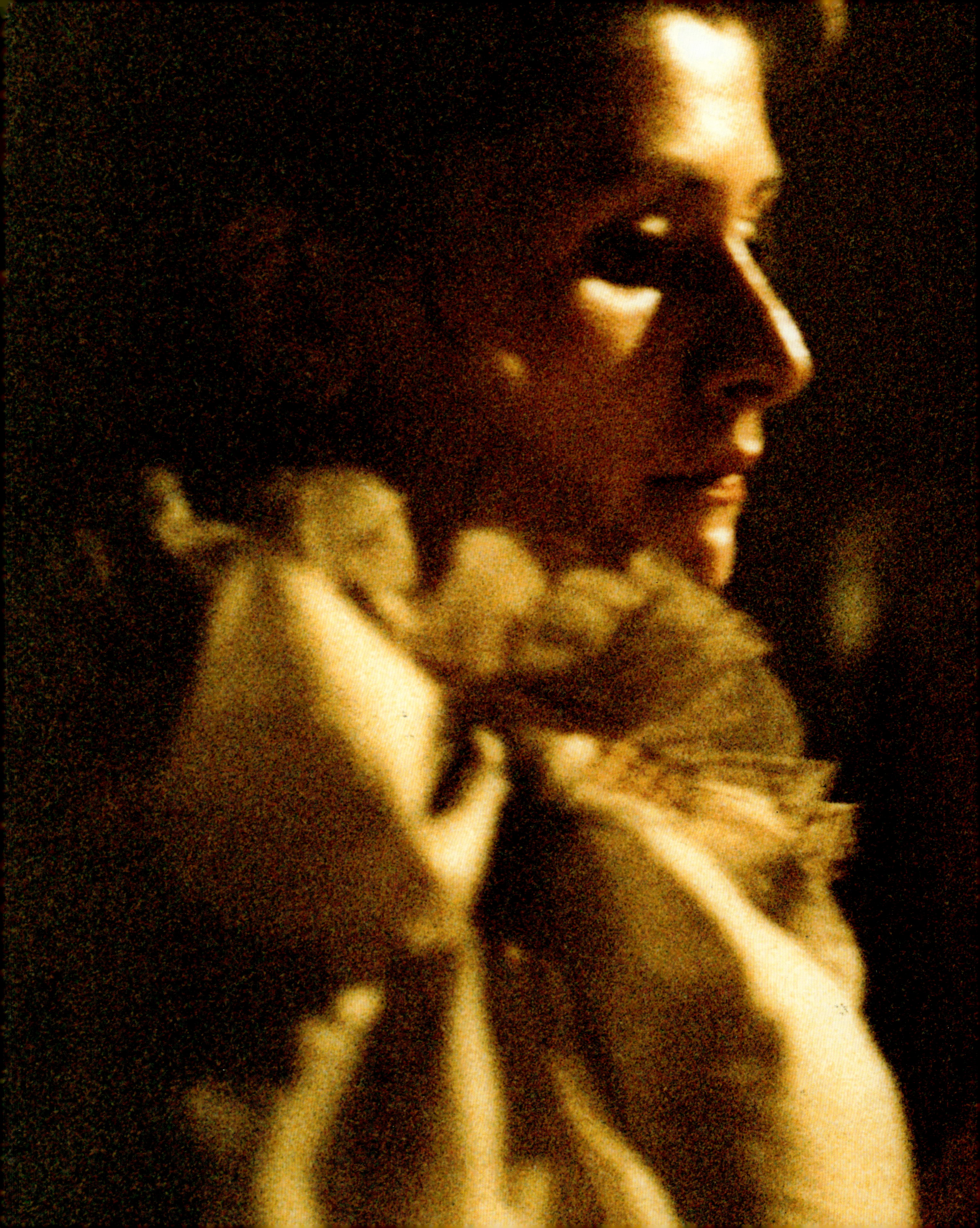

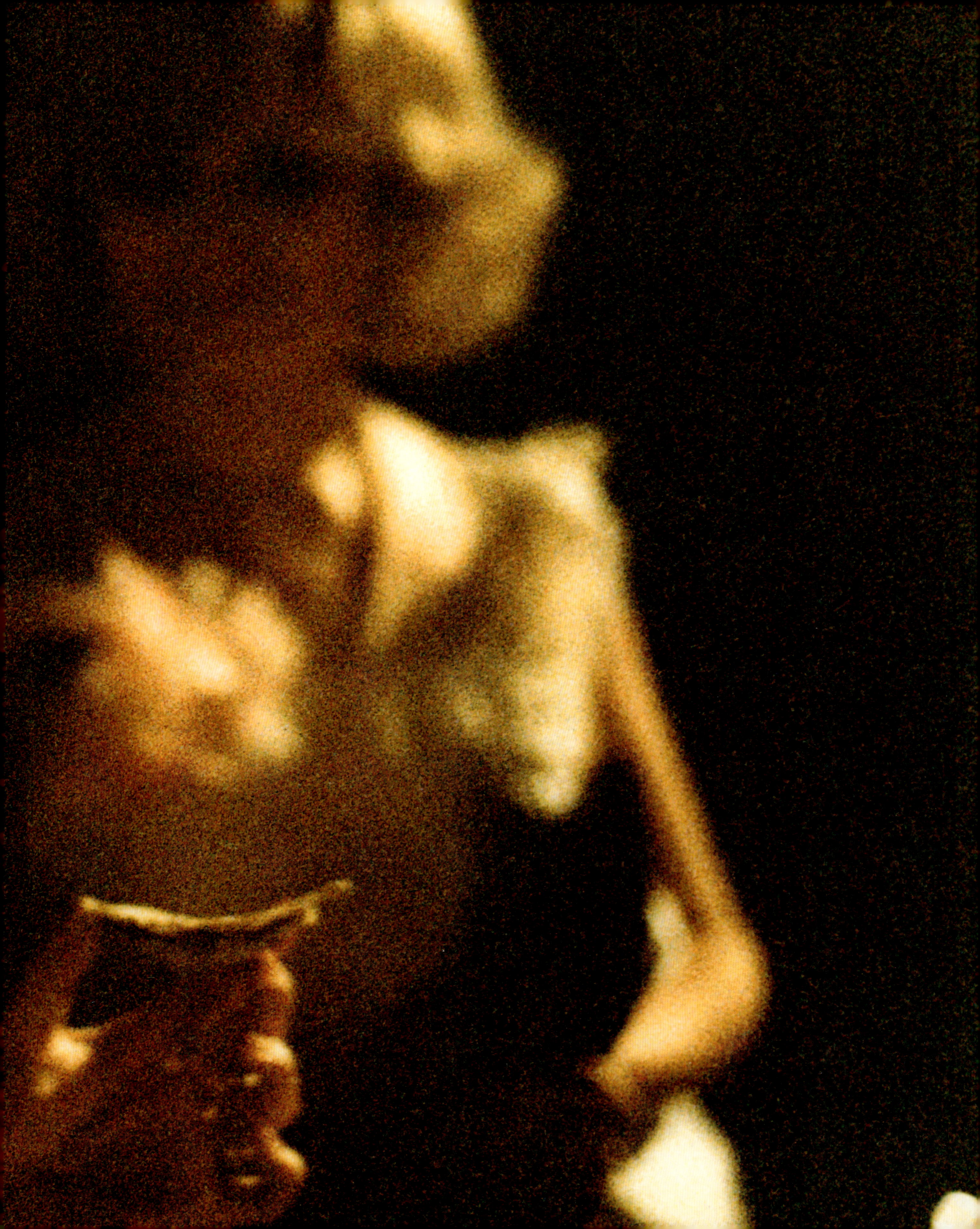

influences

A great many people have been important in my life to the development of my eye and therefore my métier. In terms of how to run my business, I learned a great deal from my father over the years, but in the beginning my strongest influence was quite definitely my mother. She had extremely good taste and created a gentle atmosphere in our house, where everyone was welcome. She was highly cultivated, a very modern person, always interested in new ideas, and I hope I am like her in that respect.

Once a week her uncle would come for tea and they'd avidly discuss ideas culled from books they'd read on philosophy and art. My sister and I always listened and learned from my parents' wide and eclectic circle of friends. Many of them shared their knowledge of a particular field of collecting and helped me in developing my eye. The origin of my appreciation and knowledge of all kinds of works of art came from looking and learning about their sometimes extraordinary collections and from their stories about individual objects, their history, provenance, and worth. It was the equivalent of being sent on an eighteenth-century grand tour through the art of old and contemporary culture.

Anything made of wood I love with a passion. This dates back to the influence of John Blanckaert, my parents' best friend. He was a wood merchant and he took me to the big forests in France where he bought his wood. He taught me to recognize different kinds of wood, to appreciate the different qualities of oak, yew, or pine, to love wood and its inherent warmth and depth. He was a very distinguished man—he looked very English. He also loved eating, so he took me to the best restaurants, which gave me an early love of good food and wine. He was childless and I think he thought I might take over his business one day.

This love of wood is evident in every room of the castle. I prefer plain, unadorned, architectural furniture from England, Ireland, or Northern Europe to the elaborate lines and details of French furniture.

And I also like and collect treen—turned wooden objects dating to the sixteenth century in *Lignum Vitae,* which were made at the court of Henry VIII and in other smaller royal courts in Germany and elsewhere.

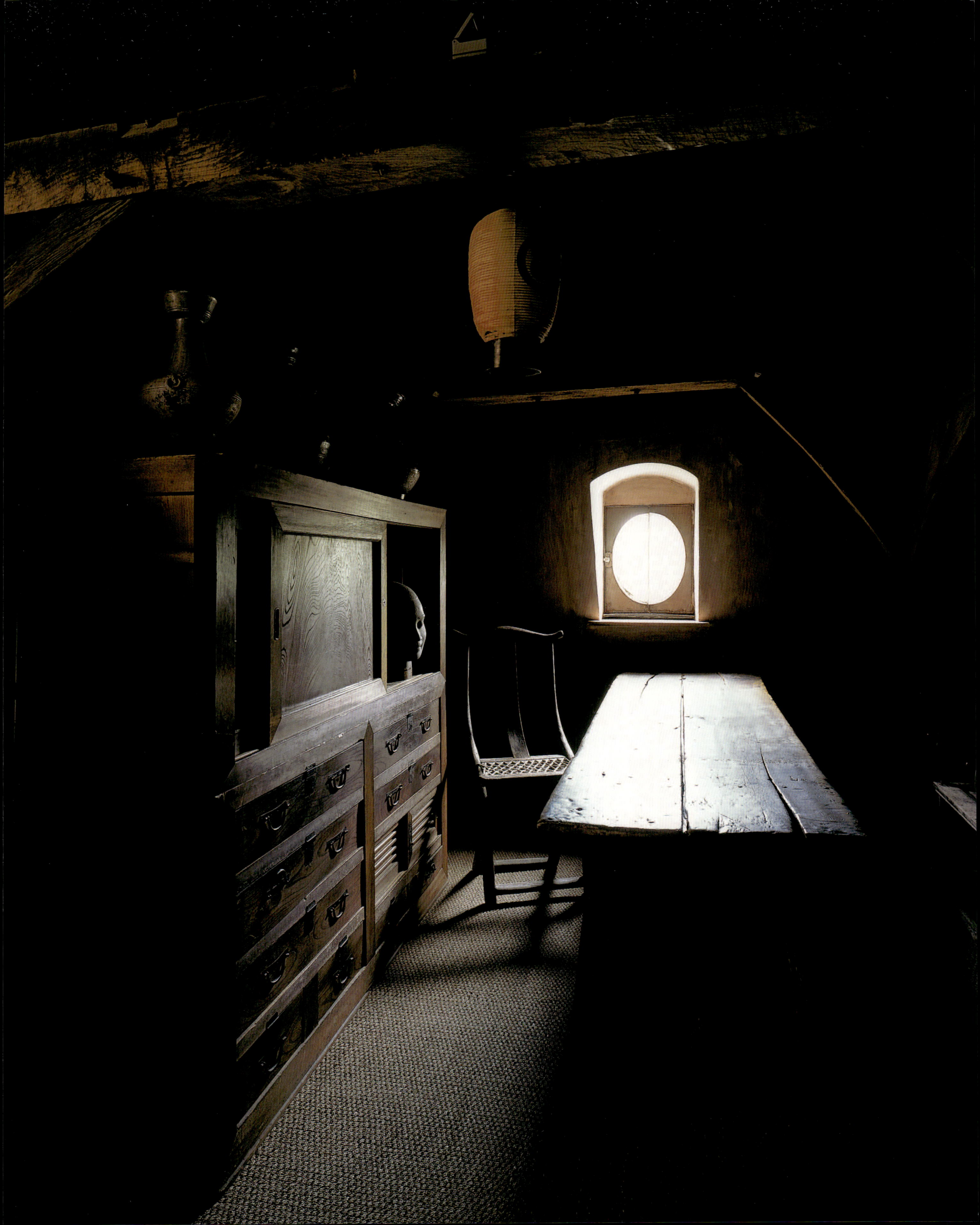

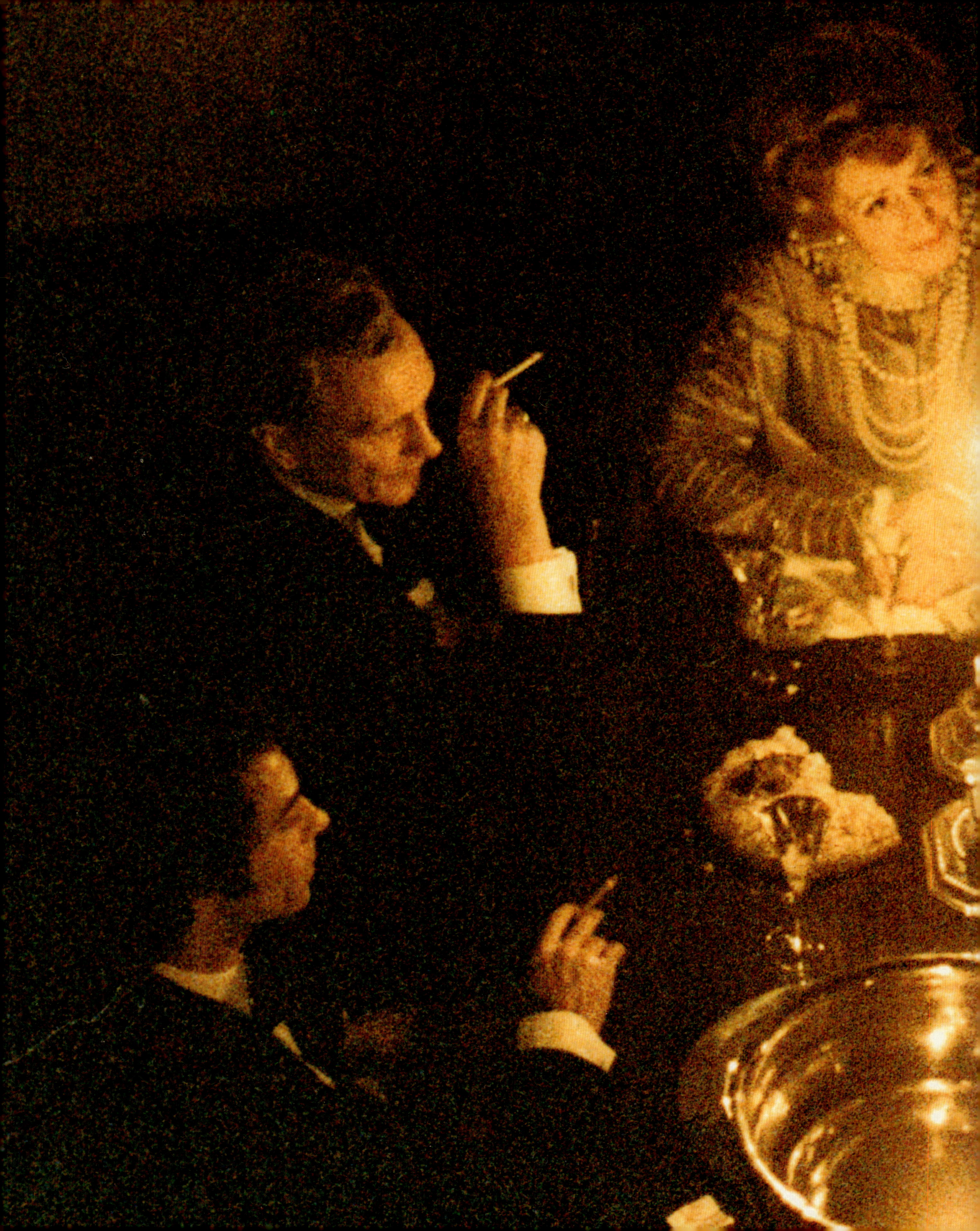

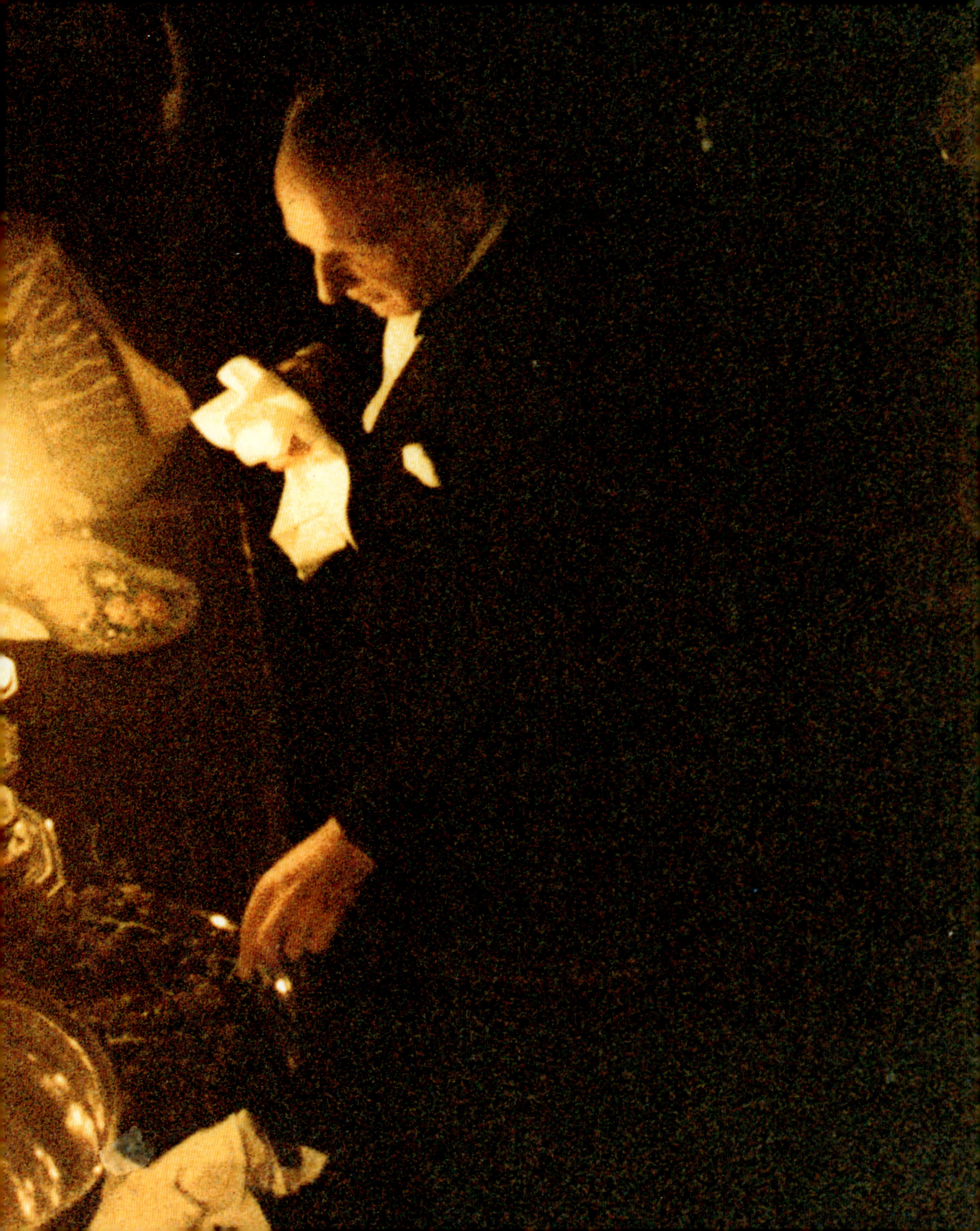

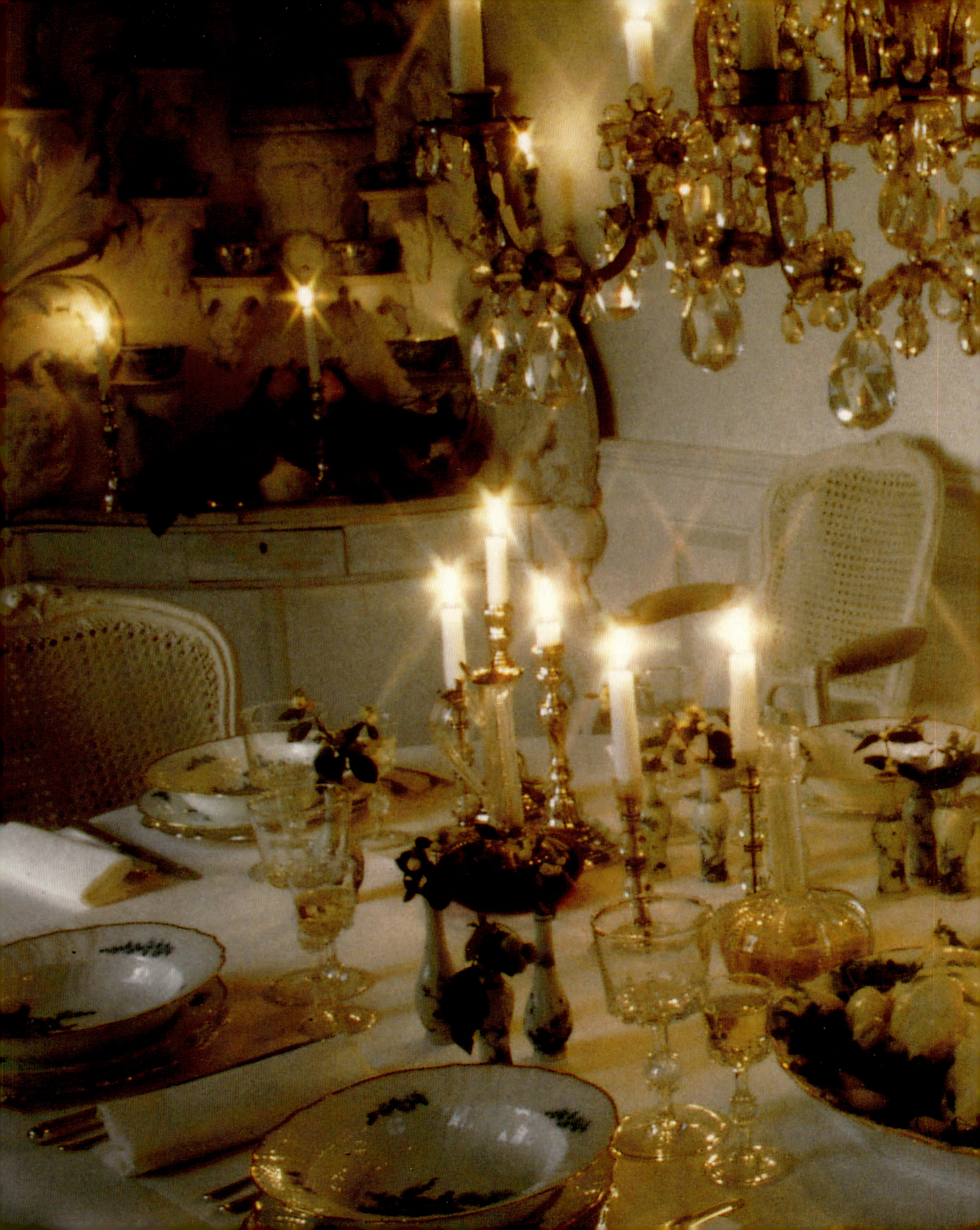

They also invented engines to achieve the most difficult of turning. I have many old books that explain how to make the turning engines; this was the beginning of the machine age in effect and so it is a very important part of social and cultural history. I delight in collecting miniature pieces of architecture, masterproofs made by apprentices to demonstrate their skills.

I was very lucky to grow up in Antwerp among a circle of connoisseurs from the interwar generation who were happy to show and explain their collections to me. A primitive art gallery in Antwerp also attracted my attention and led to my enduring interest in primitive art and how it influenced modern art.

I also vividly remember the magpie collection of my art teacher, Professor van der Spiet, who lived in an artist's studio with ancient plaster casts hanging on the walls and had filled his small house with the interesting and beautiful objects that caught his fancy. From him I learned how to draw and acquired a thorough knowledge of organic paints long before they became fashionable. He showed me how to mix "lost" paint recipes and taught me about fresco techniques. When I started to restore houses with my mother, and later for myself, and then to arrange houses for others, this knowledge of the techniques used in the northern mercantile interiors of the fifteenth and sixteenth centuries played an important part in the interior look I was developing.

I believe in the historical, not the merely decorative. I like depth, not superficiality—everything needs a deep human reason, and for me it is important to create something interesting, not just decorative. I find the spirit of things much more important than the look of things—I really don't mind if things are ugly. They have their own beauty, if only one looks hard enough.

Old Antwerp itself, in the period of Rubens, has inspired me greatly as well. The warm, stylish full interiors of the baroque have been a profound influence, containing as they did beautiful textiles, tooled leather on the walls, Renaissance bronzes and curiosities, and the spirit of collecting so typical of the time. Rubens collected, so did many of his contemporaries in Antwerp. The other day I saw a picture in Christie's of one such *Kunstkammer* and I was again amazed by the details of how they used carpets on the tables and how they arranged lots of fabulous objects.

I love rococo but I don't want to possess it as much as I do the baroque. I like the sweetness of the style, the sense of fun and playfulness but I wouldn't like it in every room—I like it in the dining room, or in a little room where you might have a glass of champagne, or in a ballroom.

Peace, contemplation, and serenity for me come from the Orient—and from the primitive farm furniture one finds in the mountains. I find this inspirational because it has extreme simplicity, and because it is the opposite of the destructive philosophy of a machine aesthetic. To me, *arte povera* artifacts show a gentle human respect of nature in the careful selection of humble materials chosen and worked to last for centuries. These primitive artifacts convey a warmth of spirit rather than a cold aggression. For me *arte povera* furniture and works of art from the Orient are linked through the poverty of materials and the idea of making the best of them into something that would last for an age.

I like to live in both these worlds, the warm, rich world of the baroque, and the serene, calm world of the Orient. I love Zen gardens and Zen houses and rural Japanese dwellings. I also admire Thai monasteries because even unrestored and empty they have a real aura of peace and beauty.

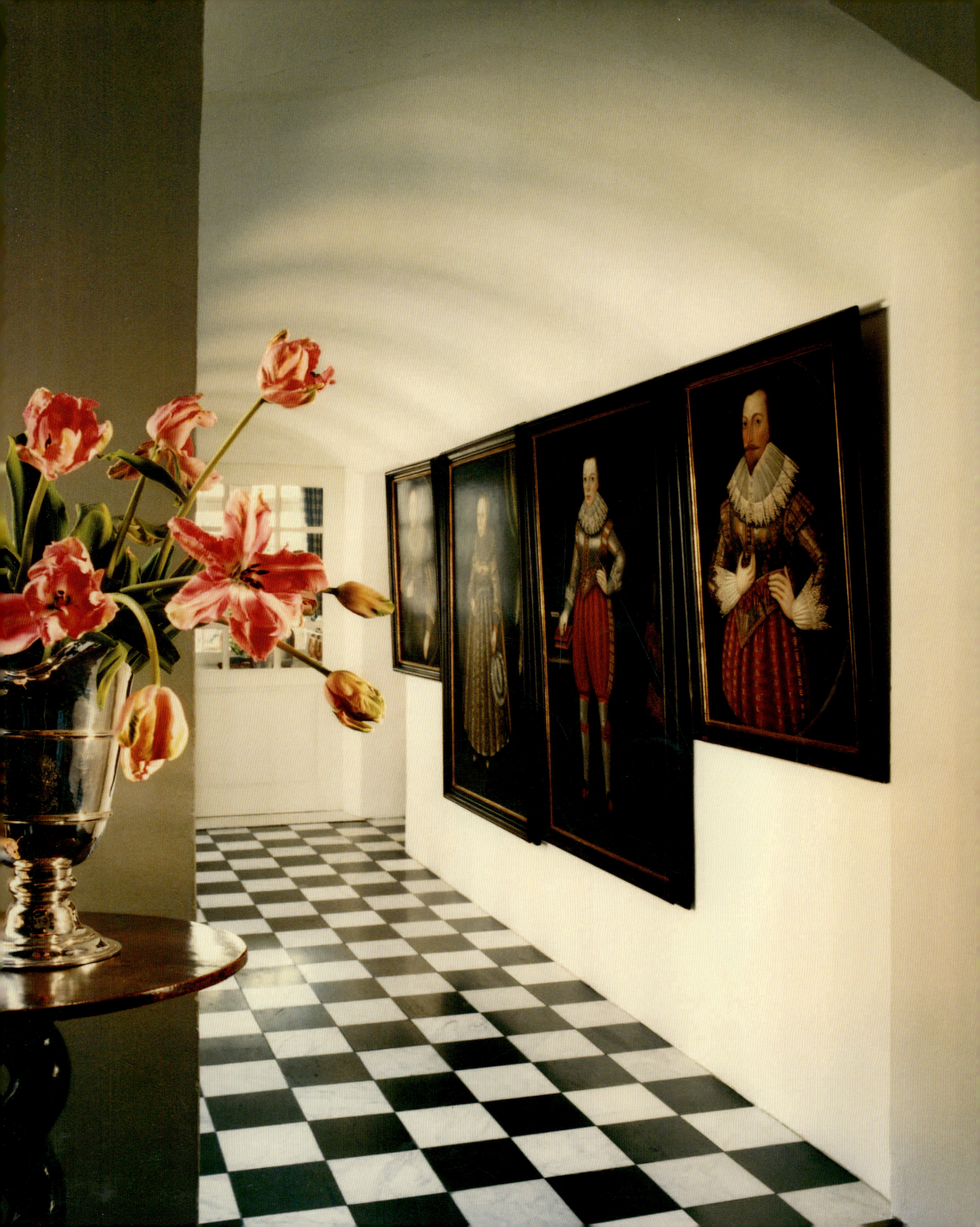

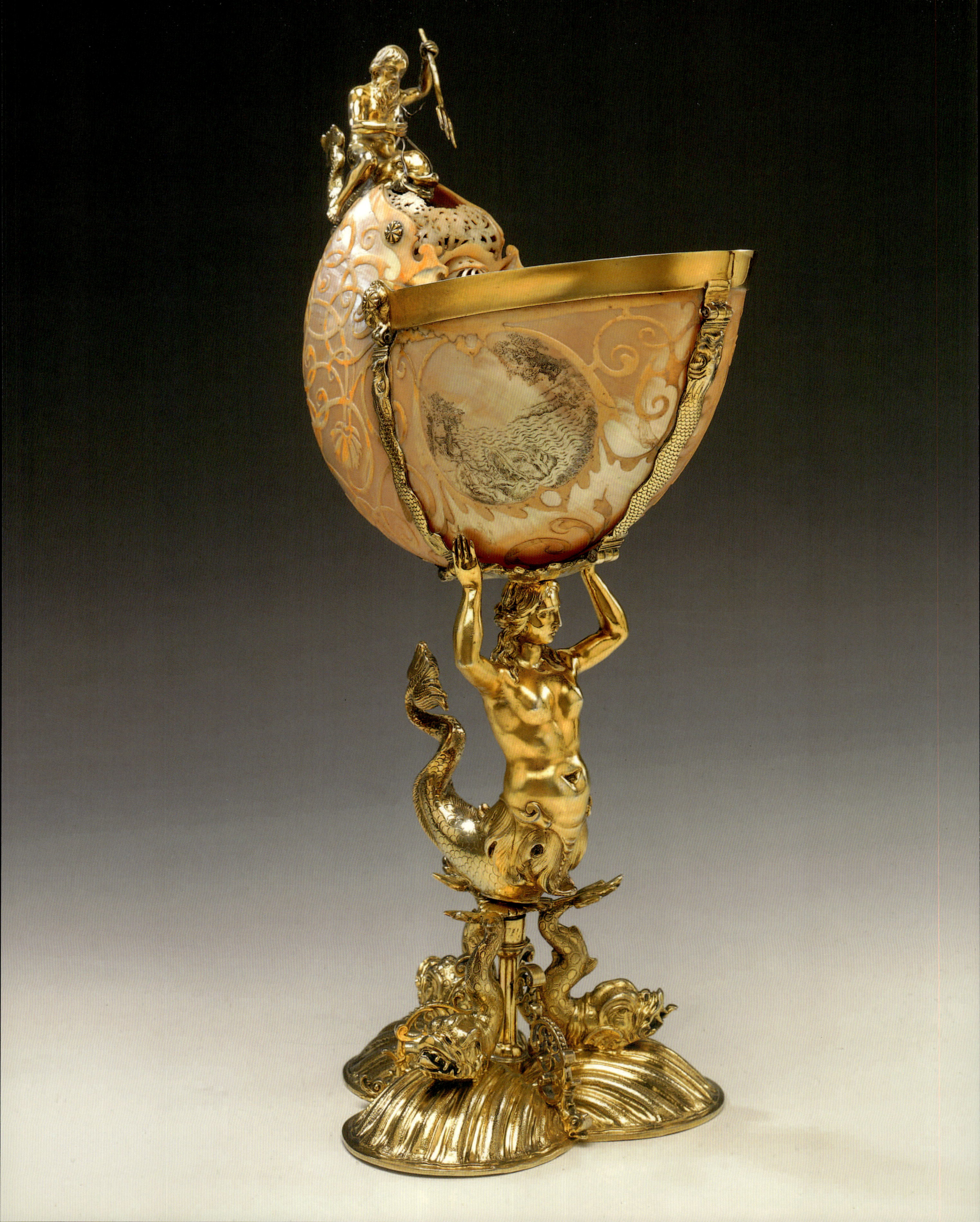

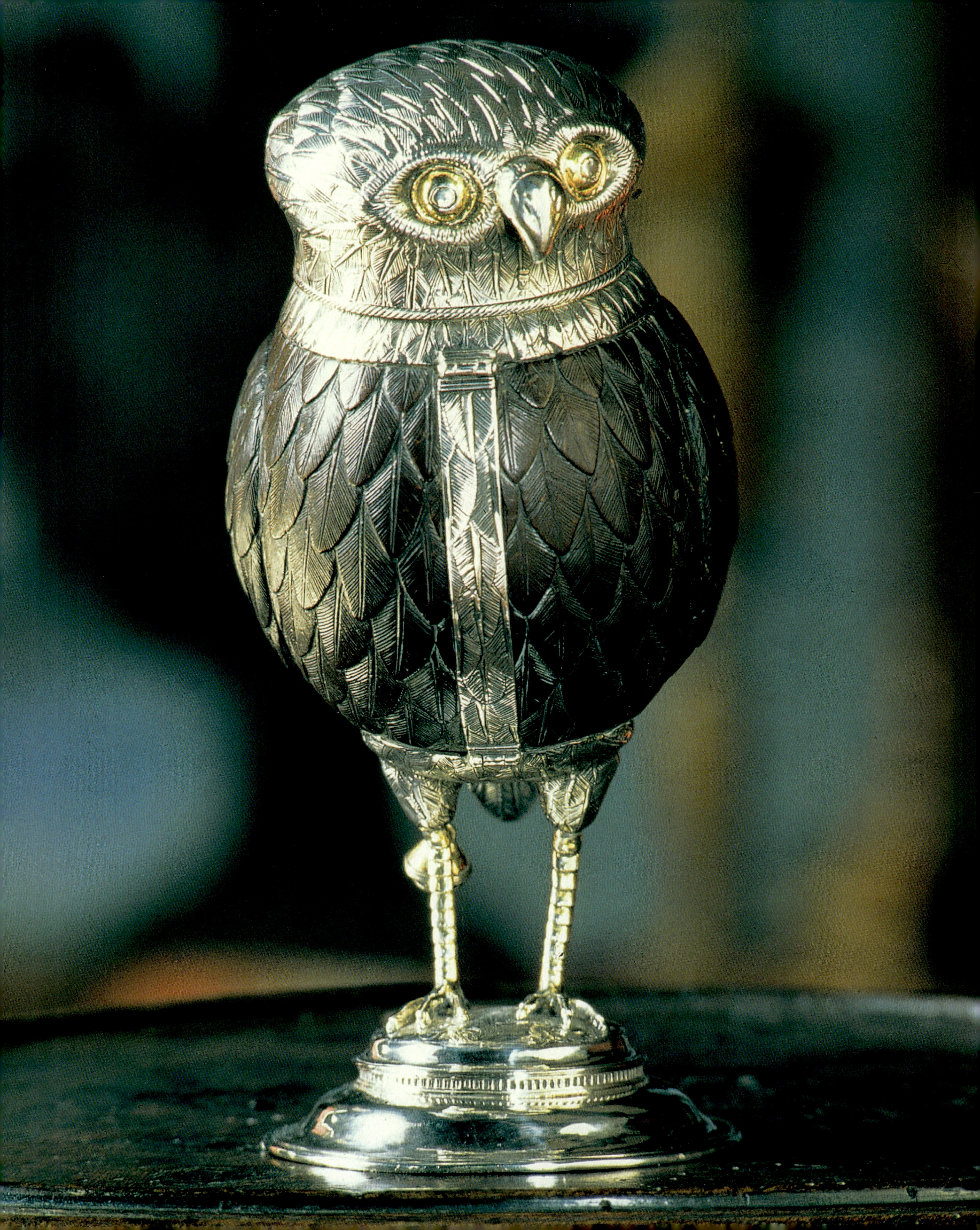

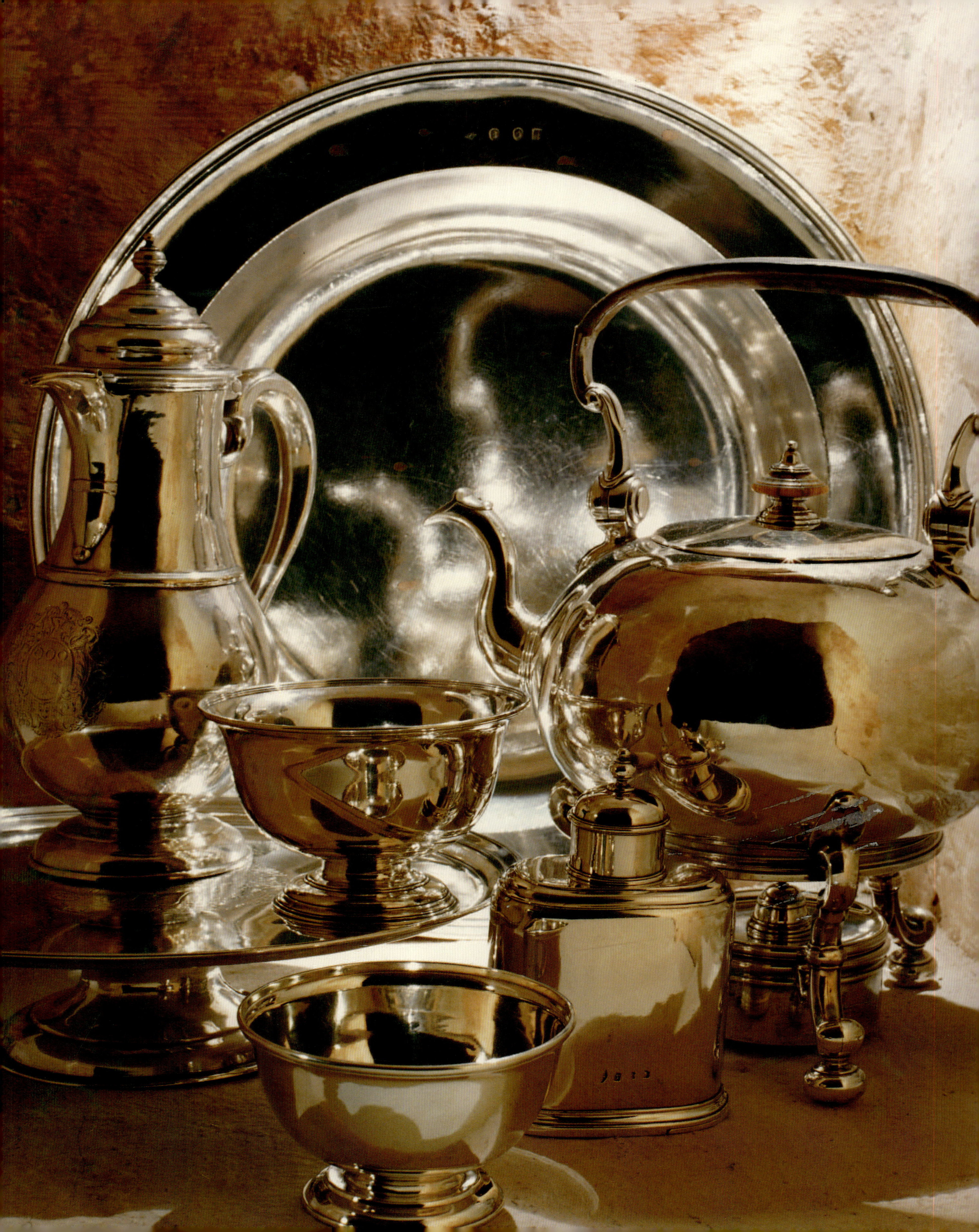

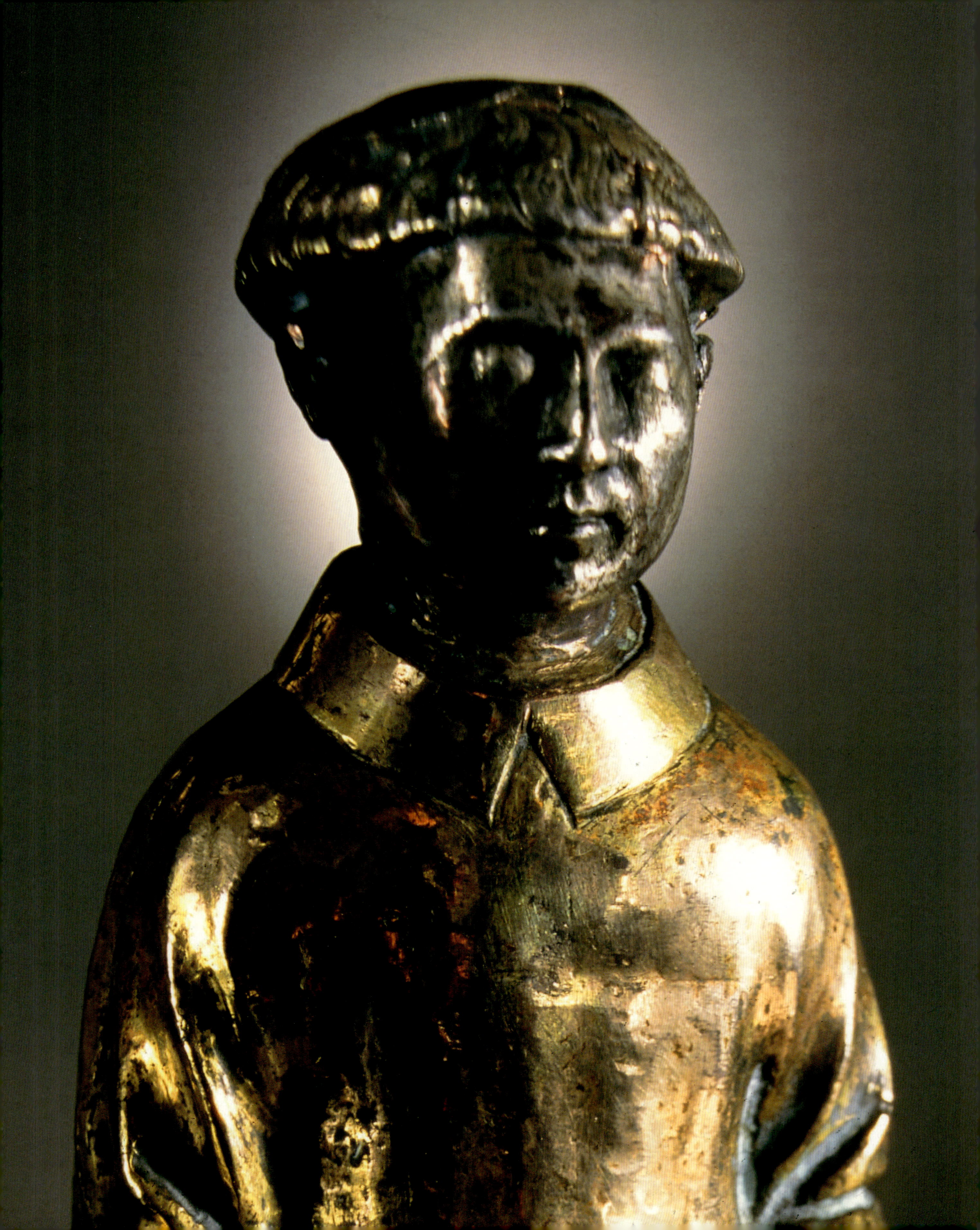

The first one I saw was a complete ruin with every bit of stone lying on the floor. Not one piece was whole yet they all had an aura. It really impressed upon me how incomplete things are also important.

Years ago, we visited the Forbidden City in China before it was restored, where I took pictures of the old paint on the doors which were like the most beautiful abstract paintings by Rothko. We have also been to Egypt several times, and have seen all the great temples. All these things are great influences on me—unbelievable spaces which are still on a human scale.

The point about influences, wherever they come from, is to use them where you need them. If you live in a big house, every room can have its own character and you can travel from one ambience to another. Where you choose to go in your house depends on your mood and the people you are with. I love libraries, like the one in the Reform Club in London, for instance. Libraries are always my favorite rooms.

But I don't just admire the historic and the old. My first art tutors encouraged my involvement with contemporary art. I remember when I was quite young visiting an important exhibition of works by Jean Tinguely and admiring them very much. I couldn't afford to buy one, but quite soon afterward I found a seventeenth-century chest with a lock so huge its wheels and cogs filled the inside of the lid. When one turned the key, the whole lock moved. I bought the chest because it reminded me of the Tinguelys; it is, in effect, a mobile of the seventeenth century.

I have always found it extremely stimulating to the eye to mix very abstract contemporary art with beautiful things from the distant past. In the library at home, a very pure *Concetto Spaziale* by Lucio Fontana hangs over the chimneypiece on which stands a jade Shang Tsung in a brownish color, representing the earth. A Pi of the Western Chou period in blue jade stands on the other end of the chimneypiece. It is very big and represents heaven and the cosmos of stars in the heavens. Over 4,000 years separate these three examples of man's creativity and yet one informs the others and they exist together in harmony.

My involvement with the art of my own time really started through my friendship with Jef Verheyen, the contemporary painter who published his manifesto *Essentialism* in 1958, dealing with the precise definition of painting, its limits, and the confinement of light. Verheyen exhibited abroad for the first time that same year and struck up friendships with Piero Manzoni and Fontana and also met Yves Klein. From 1960 on, Verheyen participated in all the important group exhibitions put on by Zero, a group opposed to tachism and emphasizing the importance of light. He was a great friend and influence. We would often stay up all night discussing philosophy, how to look at things, the importance of art. He taught me that the way one looked at things was of the utmost importance. That means you must feel something with your eyes, not just look at it. During these discussions I began to appreciate his notion of emptiness as the place where the essence reveals itself and where "nothing" means "everything."

It was through Verheyen that I met another extremely important influence, Dr. Jos Macken, a neurologist who helped awaken me to the spatial serenity of Zen art. A very clever person with a wonderful collection of Oriental art, he gave me my first book on Taoism and many Zen books, sparking a

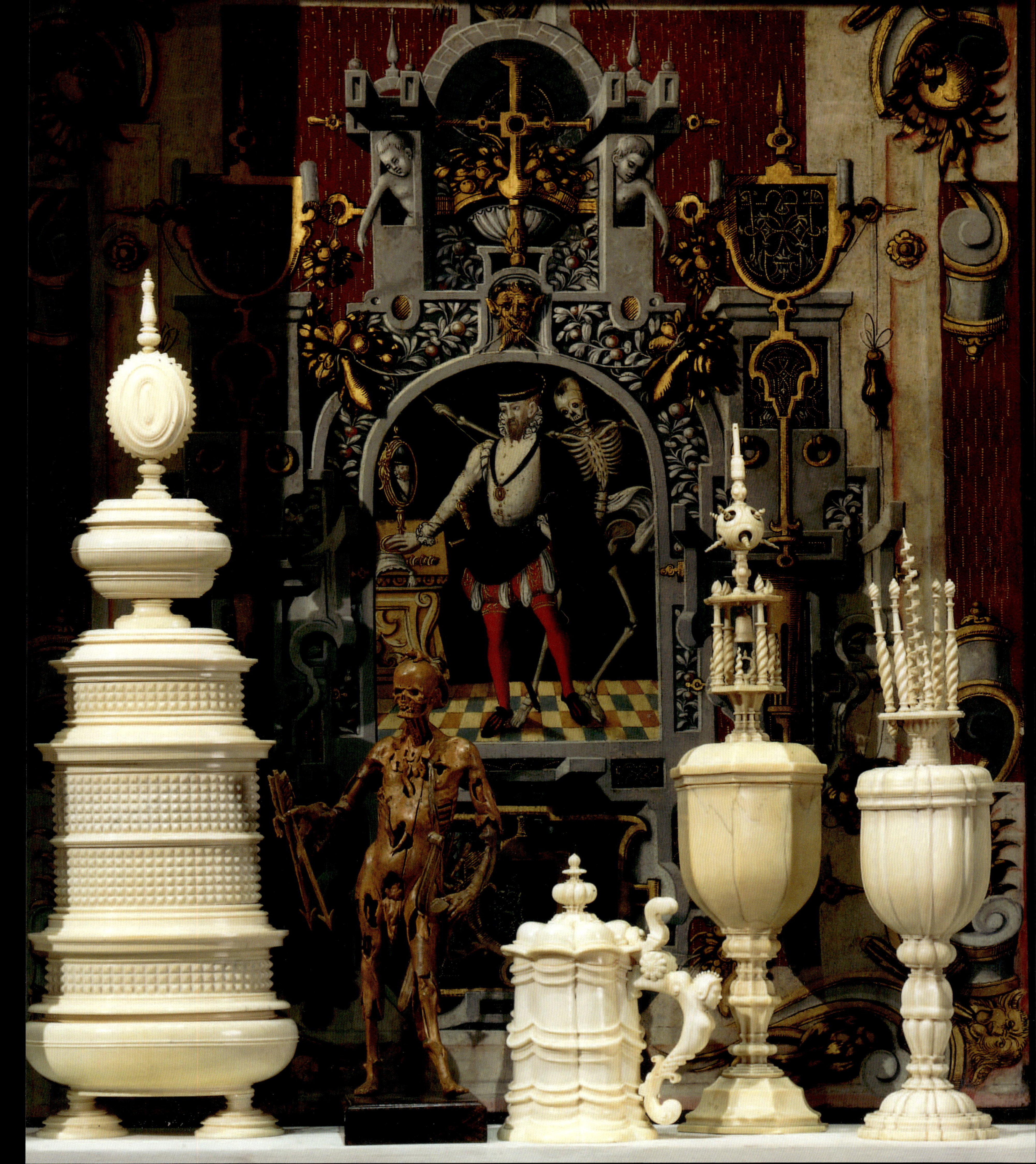

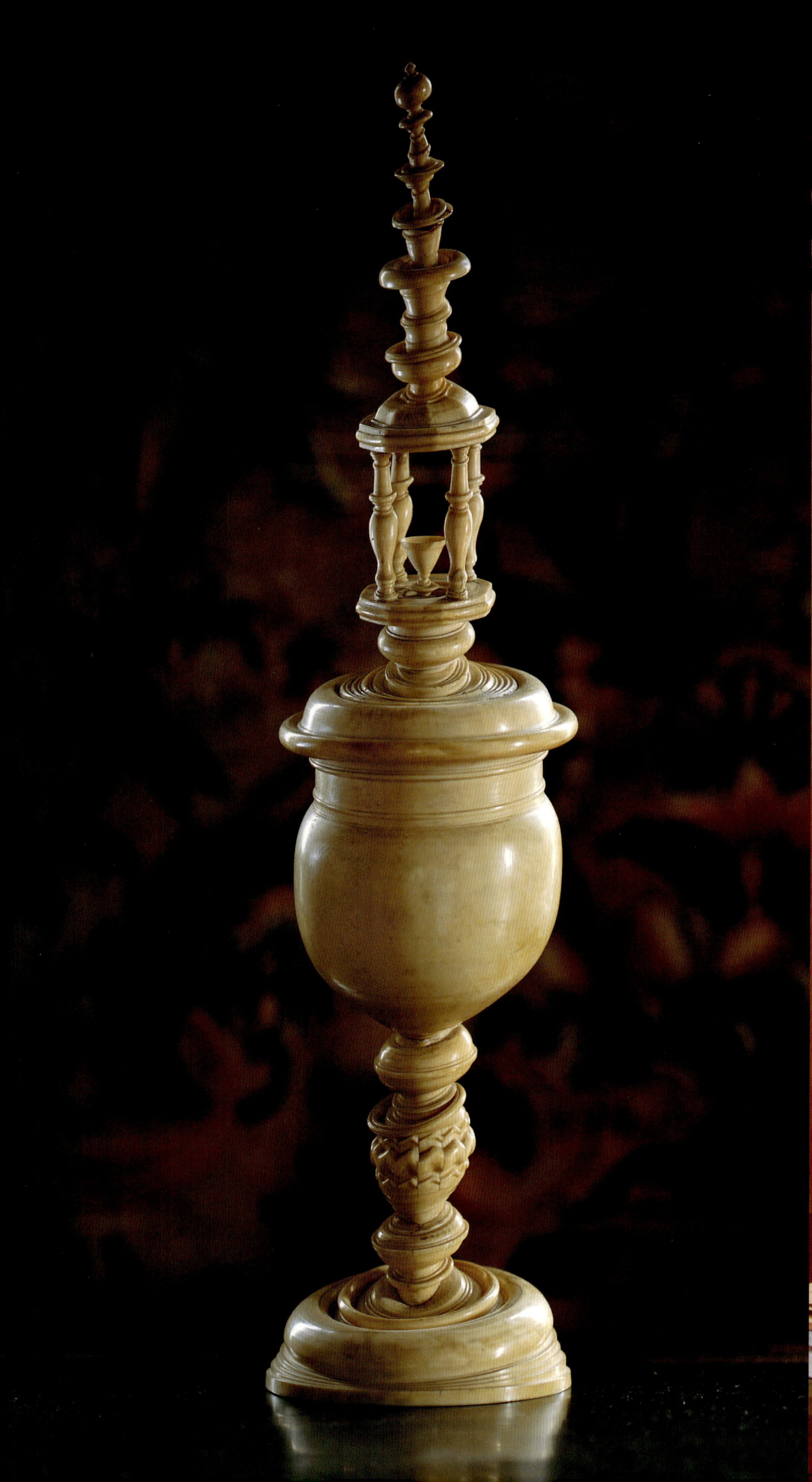

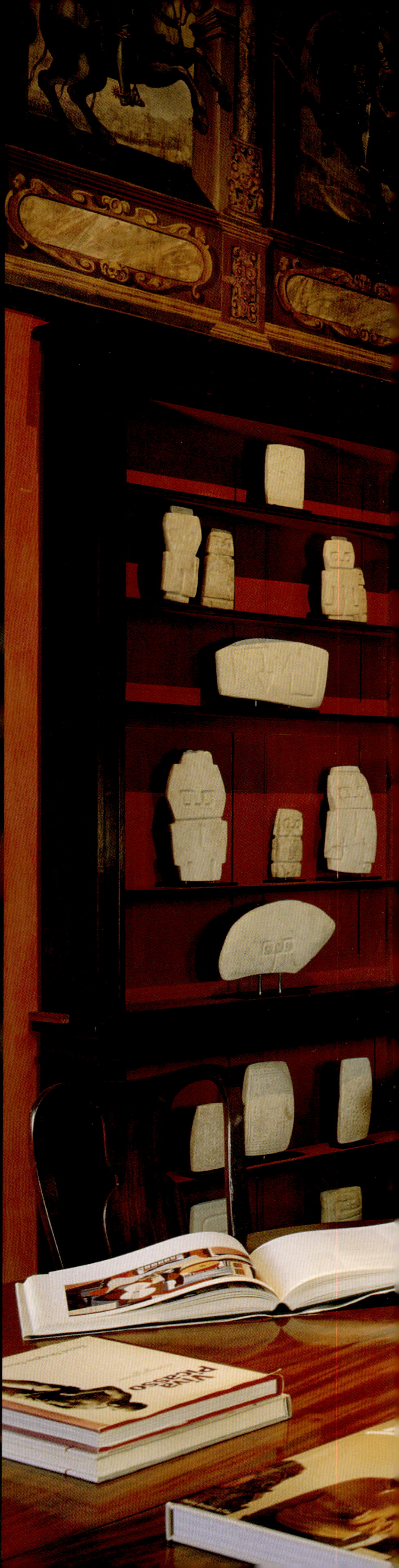

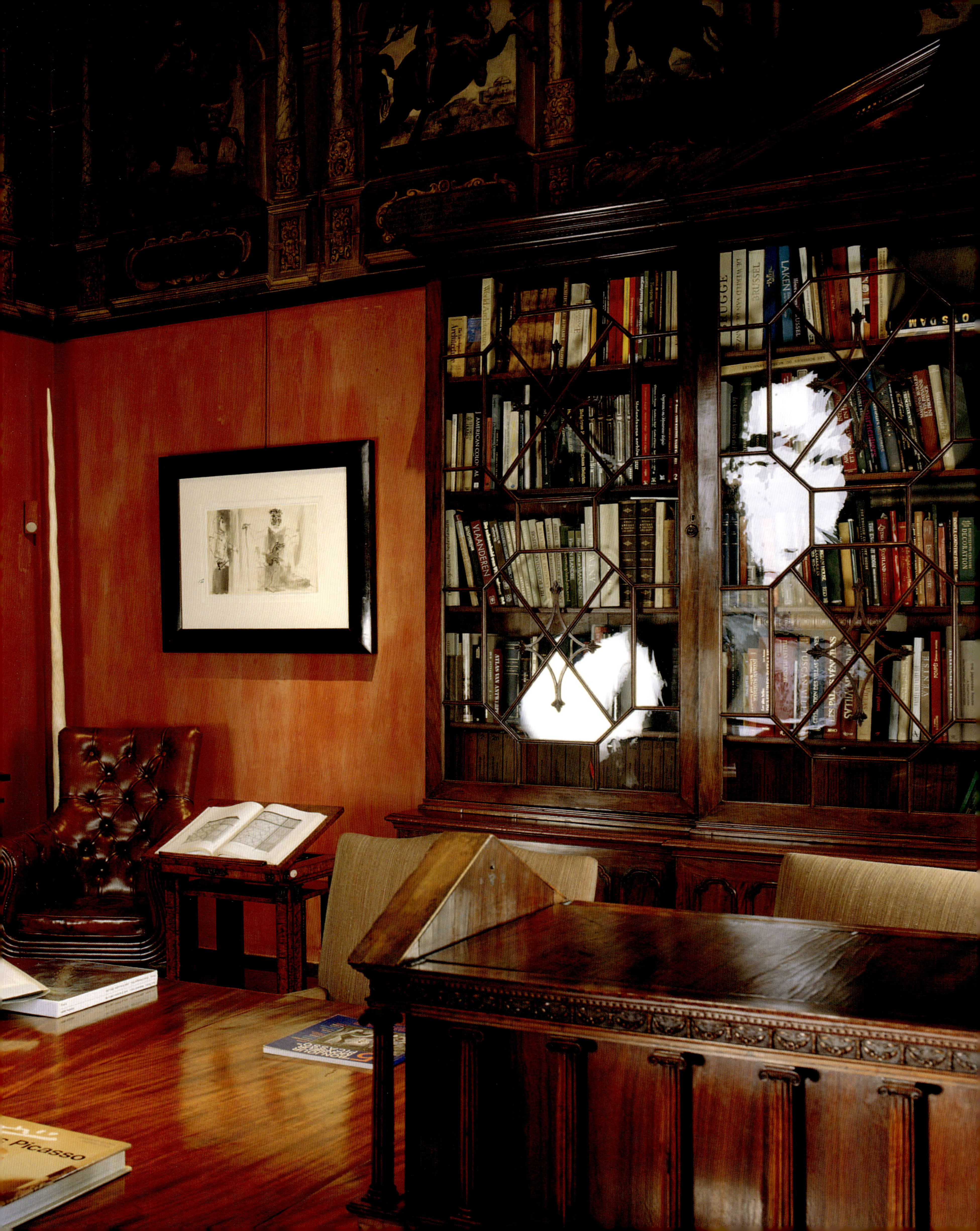
BRUGGE
BRUSSEL
LAKEN
VLAANDEREN
DECORATION
Picasso

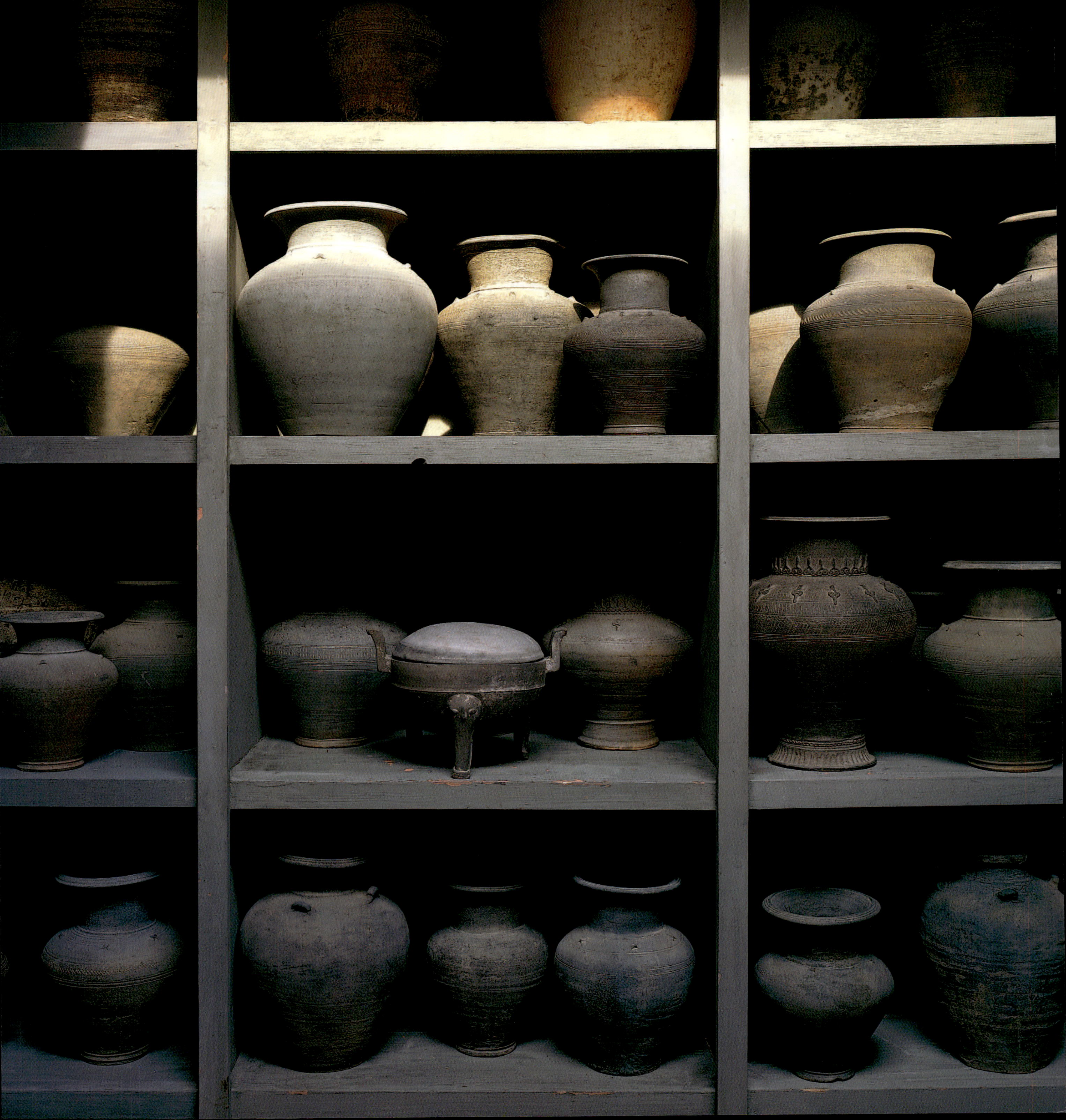

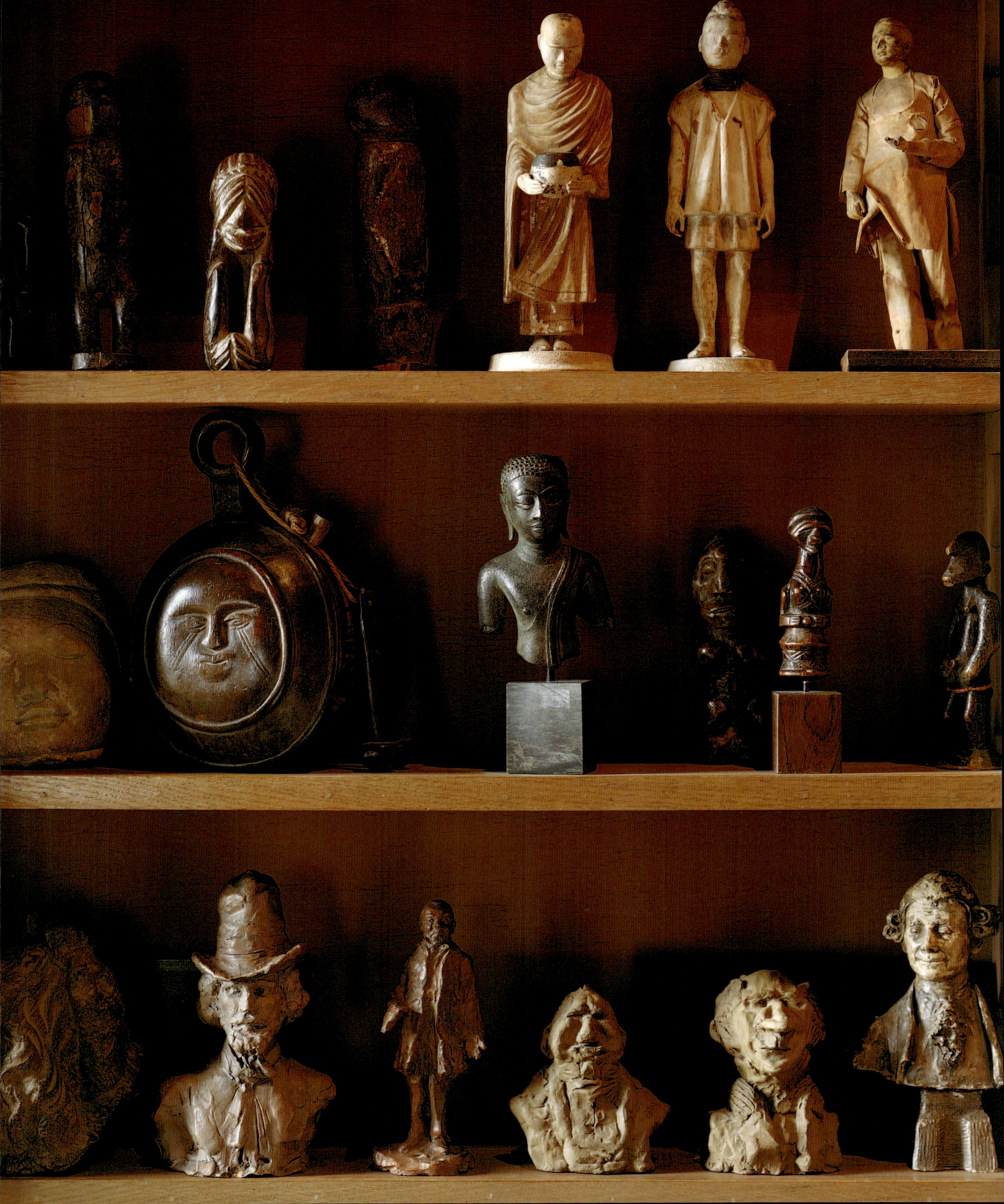

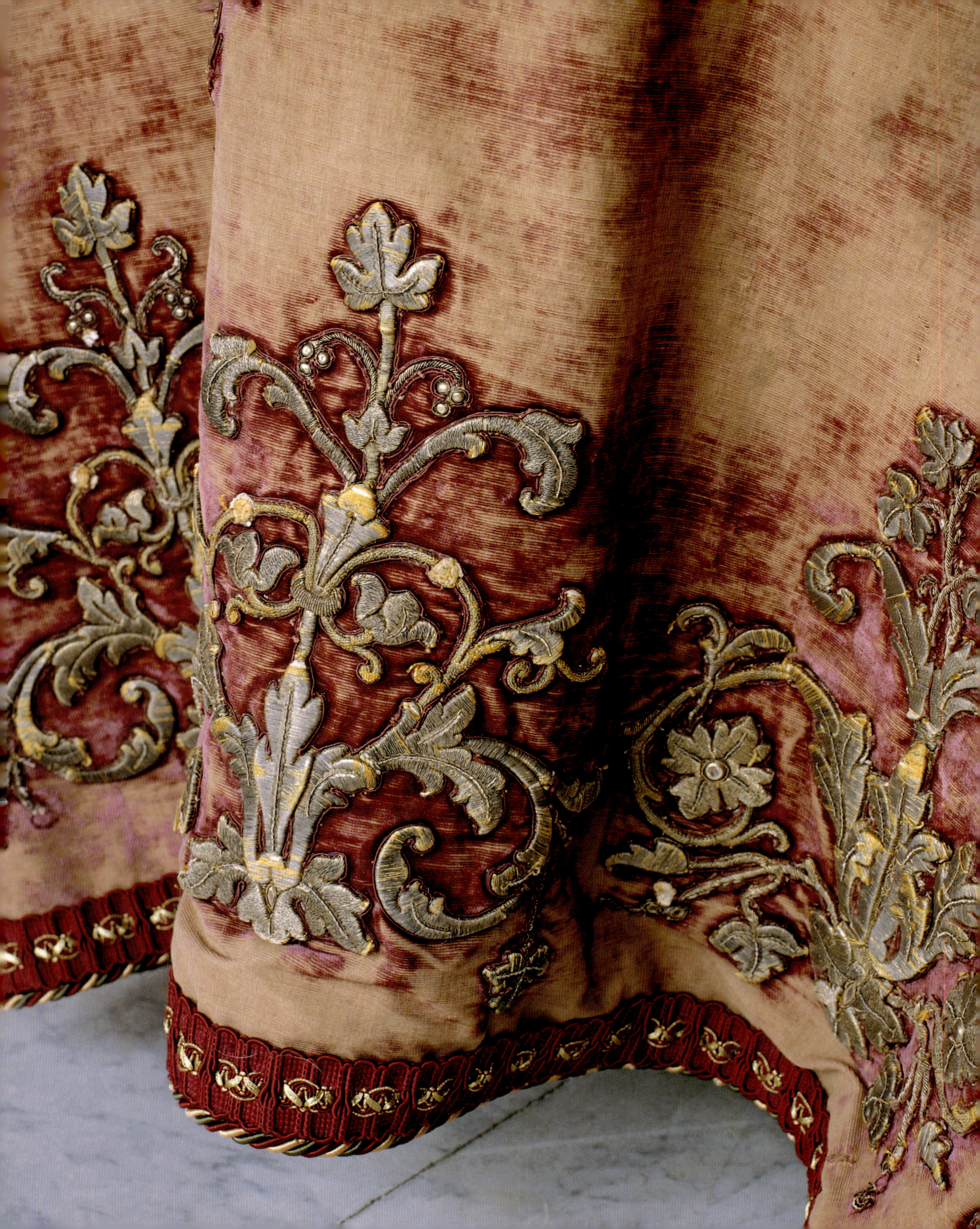

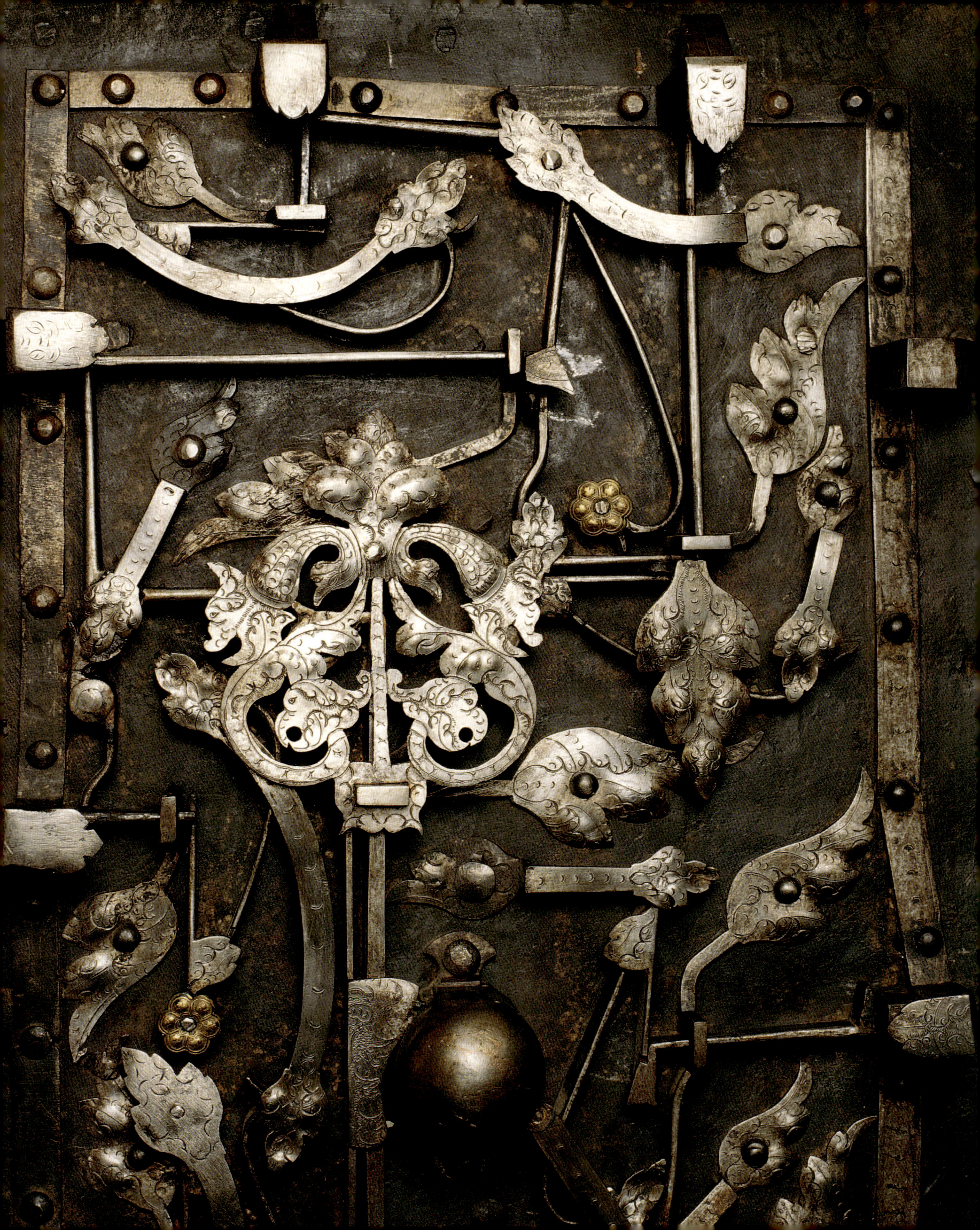

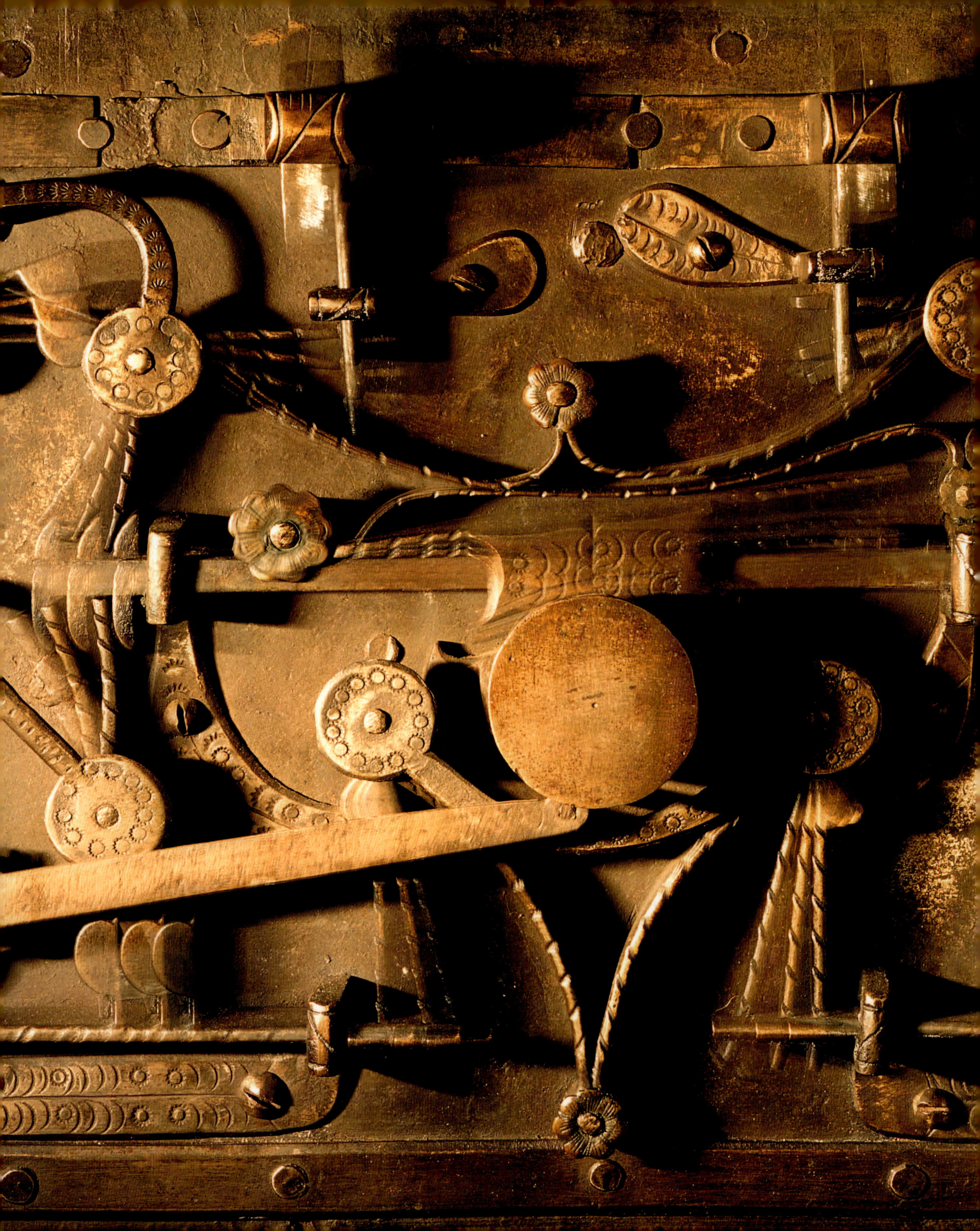

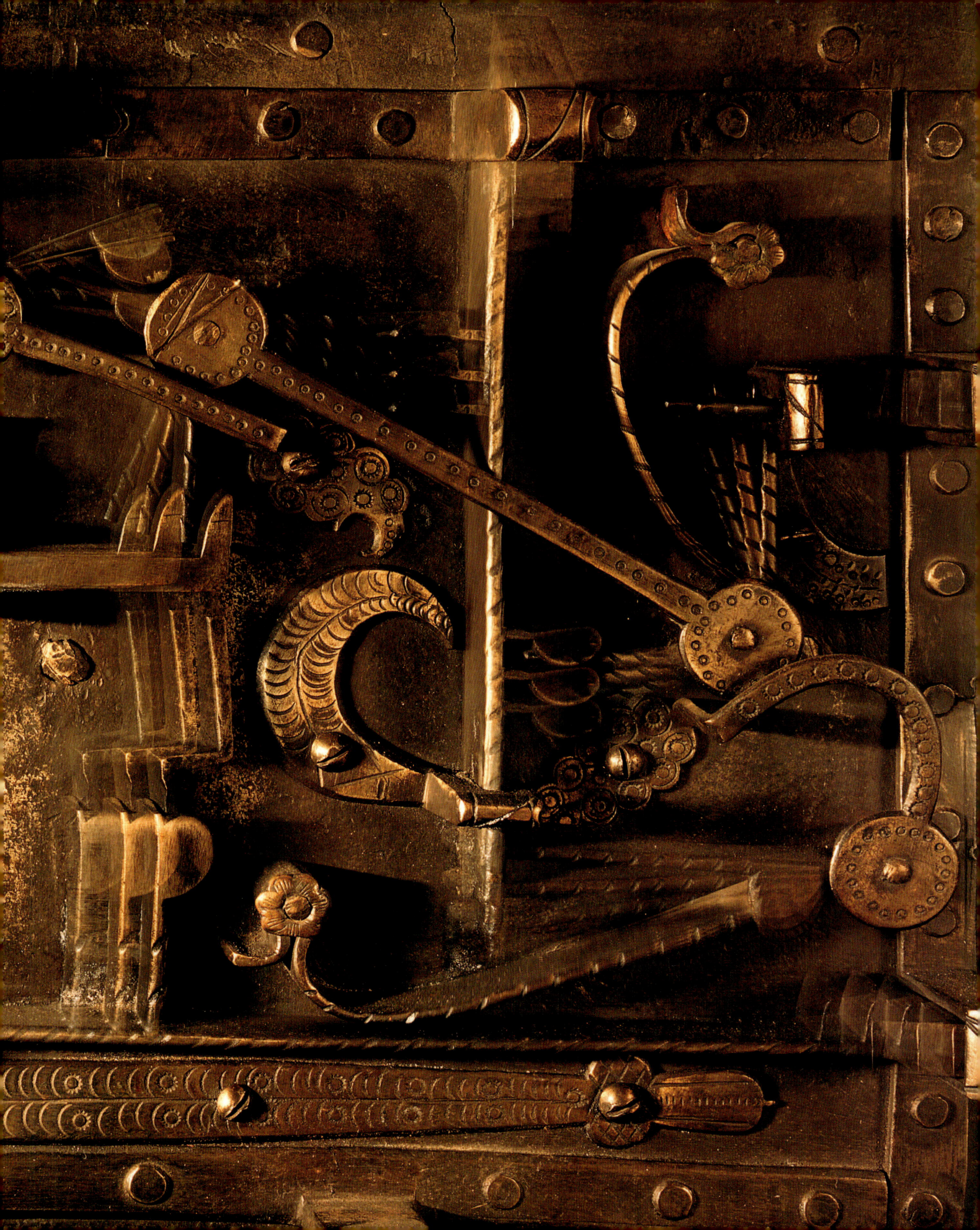

lifelong interest. He is also a very good pianist and the Bösendorfer in the Kanaal Gallery used to belong to him, until he got arthritis and couldn't play it anymore, so I bought it.

To this day, I continue my studies in Zen. Whenever I am in the Far East, I make time to visit monasteries to talk to the monks. I have wonderful contacts with monks in Thailand and Cambodia in particular. They may ask me to drink tea with them, or I might just take a walk through the cloisters talking to the monks I meet as I go. Sometimes I am asked to visit the head monk, who may or may not speak a little bit of English. Often, I am asked questions about Europe, but mostly I engage in a wonderful, almost wordless communication. These expeditions have inspired me greatly in my thinking, and the philosophy embodied in the lives these monks lead has been a very important influence on my life, too.

Another important influence in my life has been that of music, and I value my many musician friends such

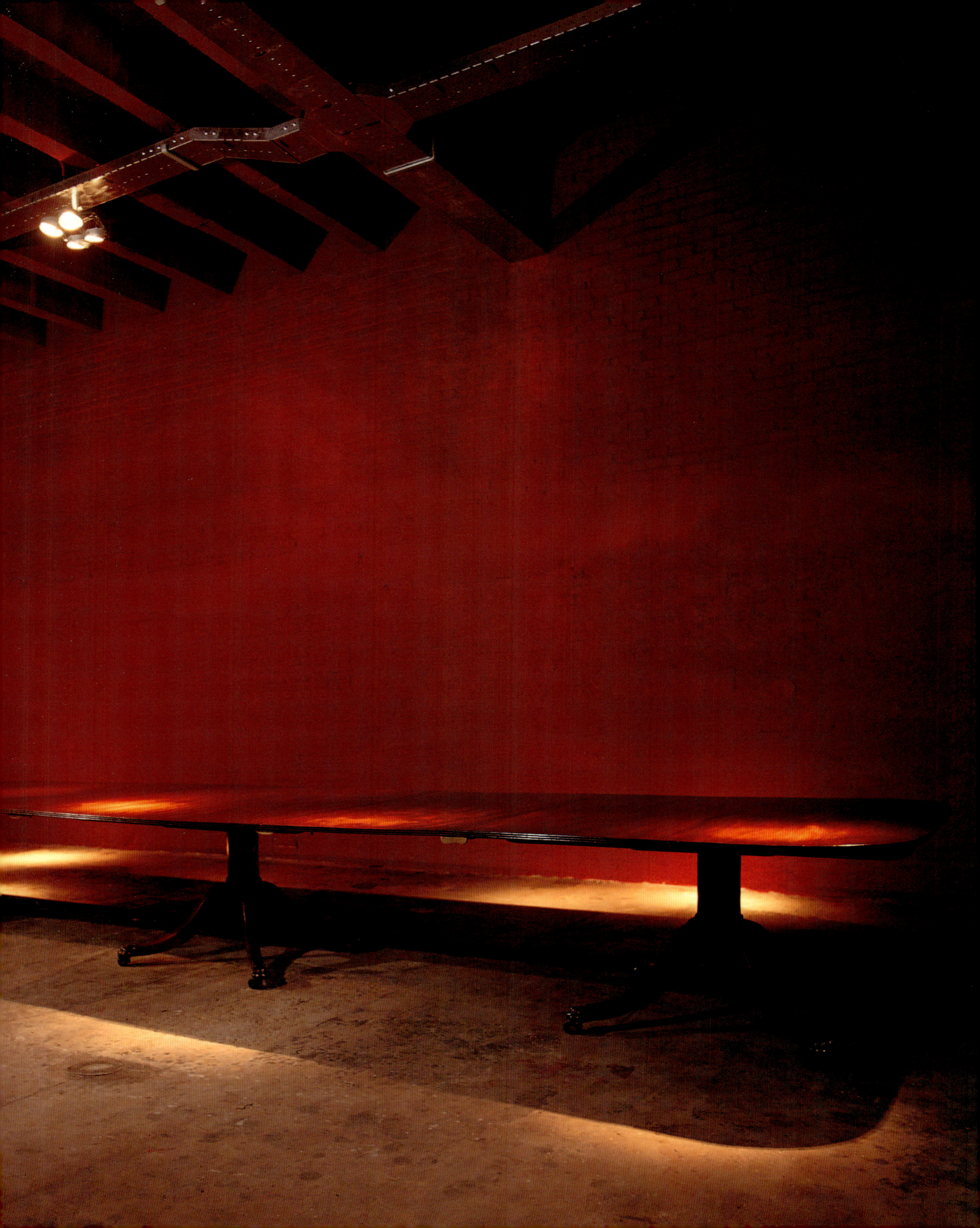

as Semyon Bychkov, John MacLaughlin, Katia and Marielle Labeque, Koen Kessels, and many others. They buy recordings for me and we talk about music together very deeply.

But, of all those who have been my mentors and who have influenced me, my wife, May, is the most important. She has a very strong graphic vision and intuition and she's the opposite of snobbish. She always brings me back to reality. She's very artistic and has a wonderful eye; she has helped me look at things and perceive their value and beauty without being influenced by whether or not they are worth a lot of money.

I remember, for instance, how important her eye and her judgement were when we moved to the castle. By this time we owned Vlaeykensgang, an entire street of houses leading off the cathedral square in Antwerp, which we had bought and restored. We had filled virtually every house with our belongings, but before we moved we had not decided where we were going to put everything we owned. Van after van arrived from our houses and warehouses in Antwerp. May directed where some things should go, and I decided on others. When we had finished, I couldn't believe it. In that sea of paintings, furniture, works of art, silver, and curiosities, there was not one piece or one picture we disagreed on. She felt just as I did—and that, I may tell you, was a wonderful experience. I will never forget it.

55

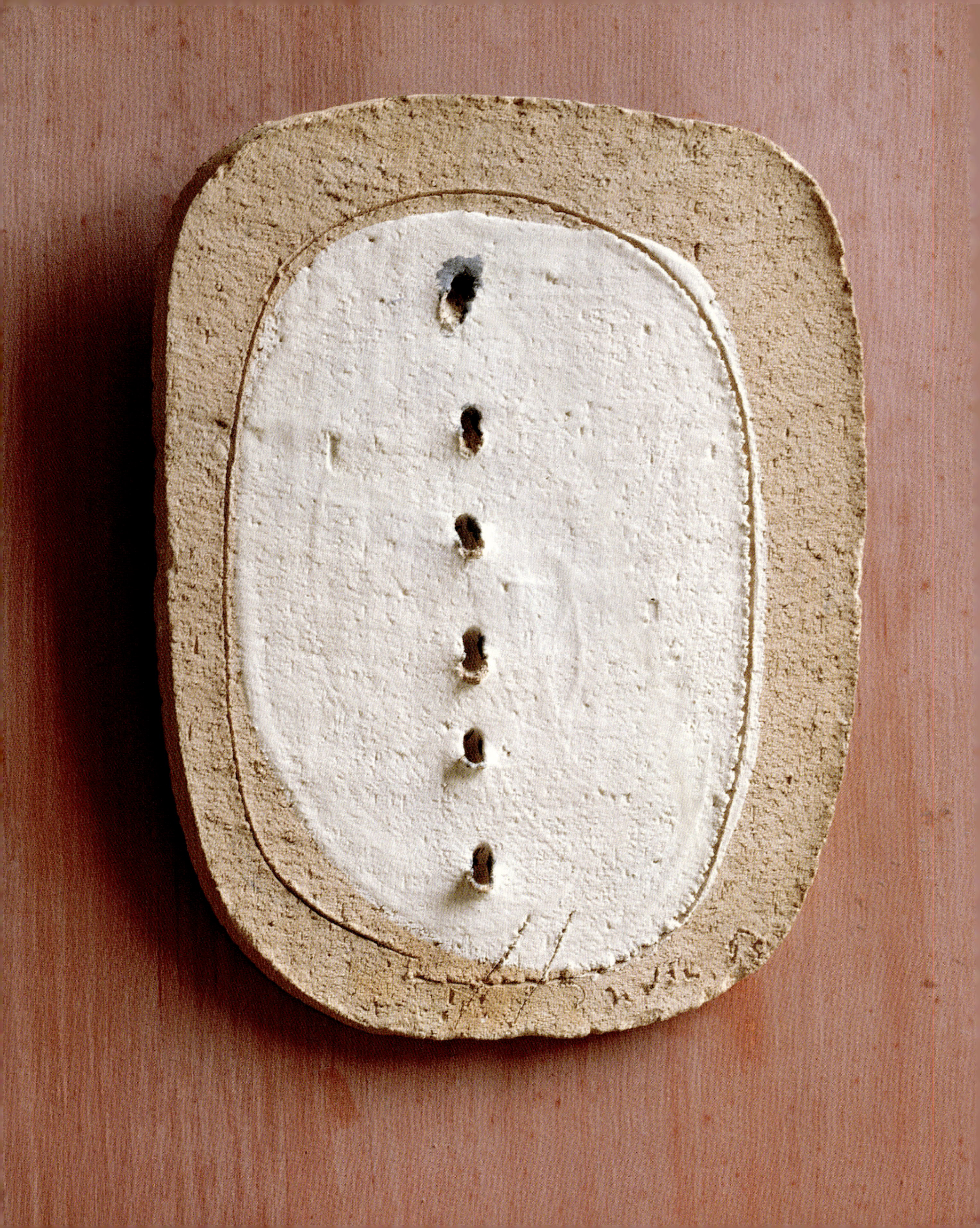

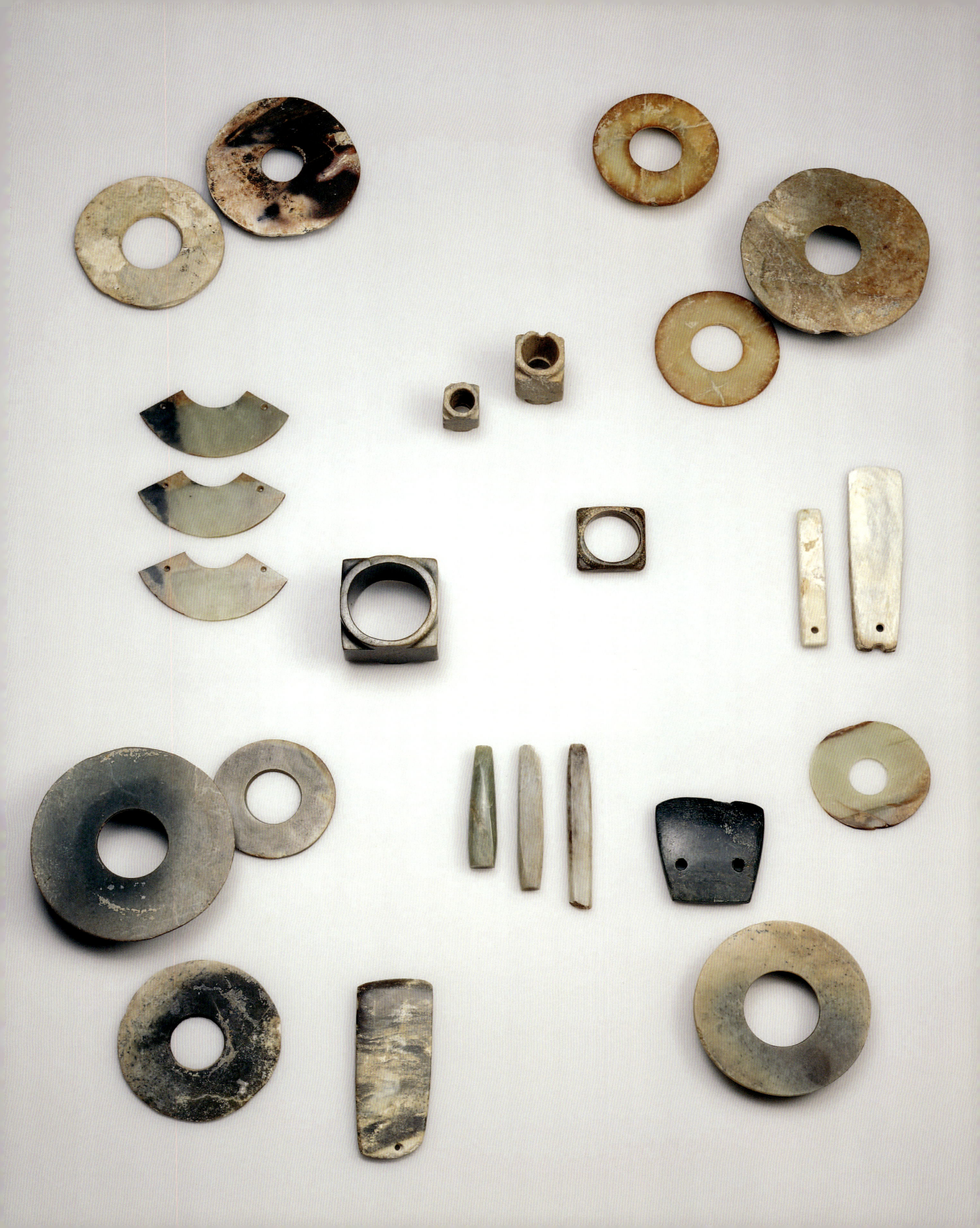

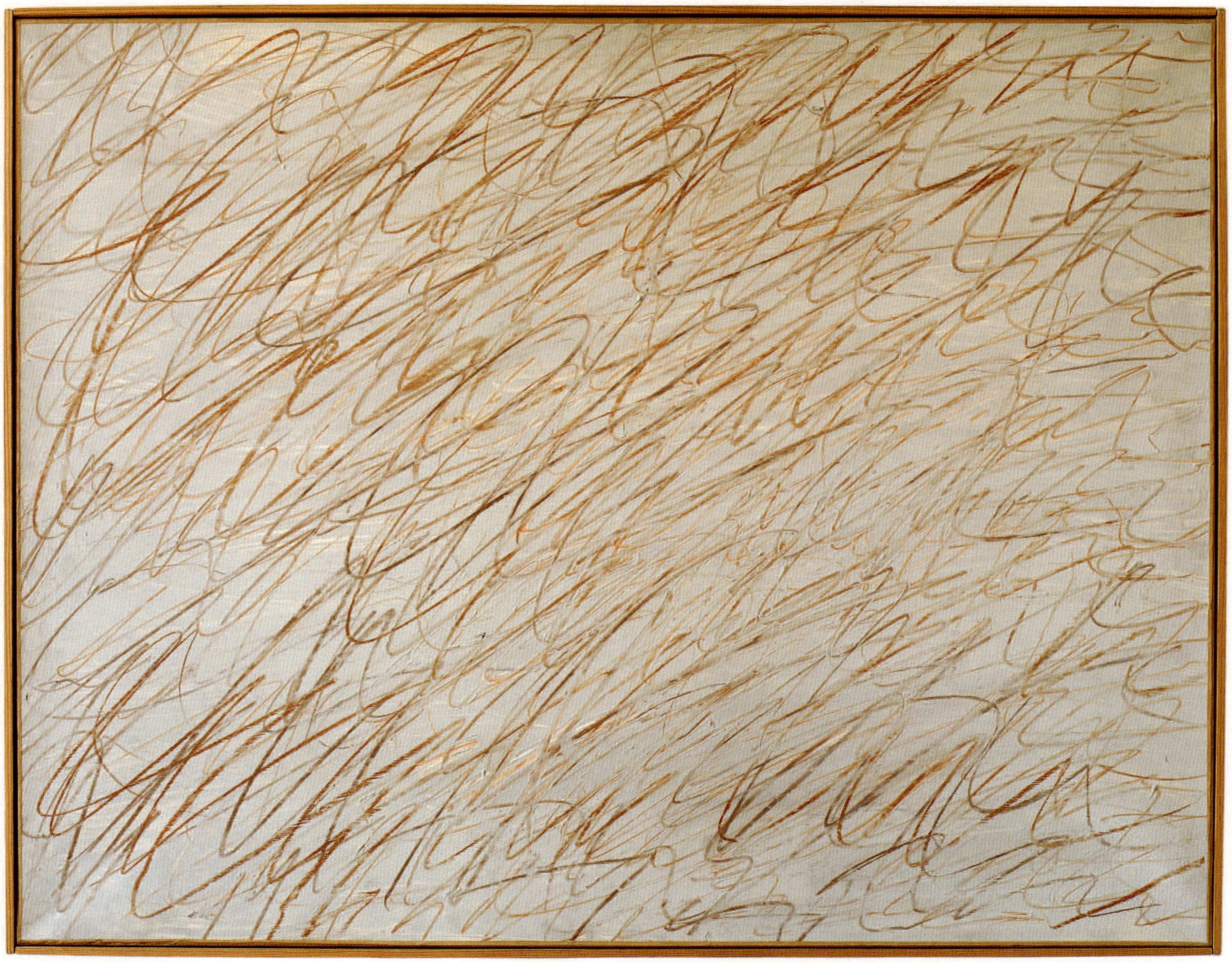

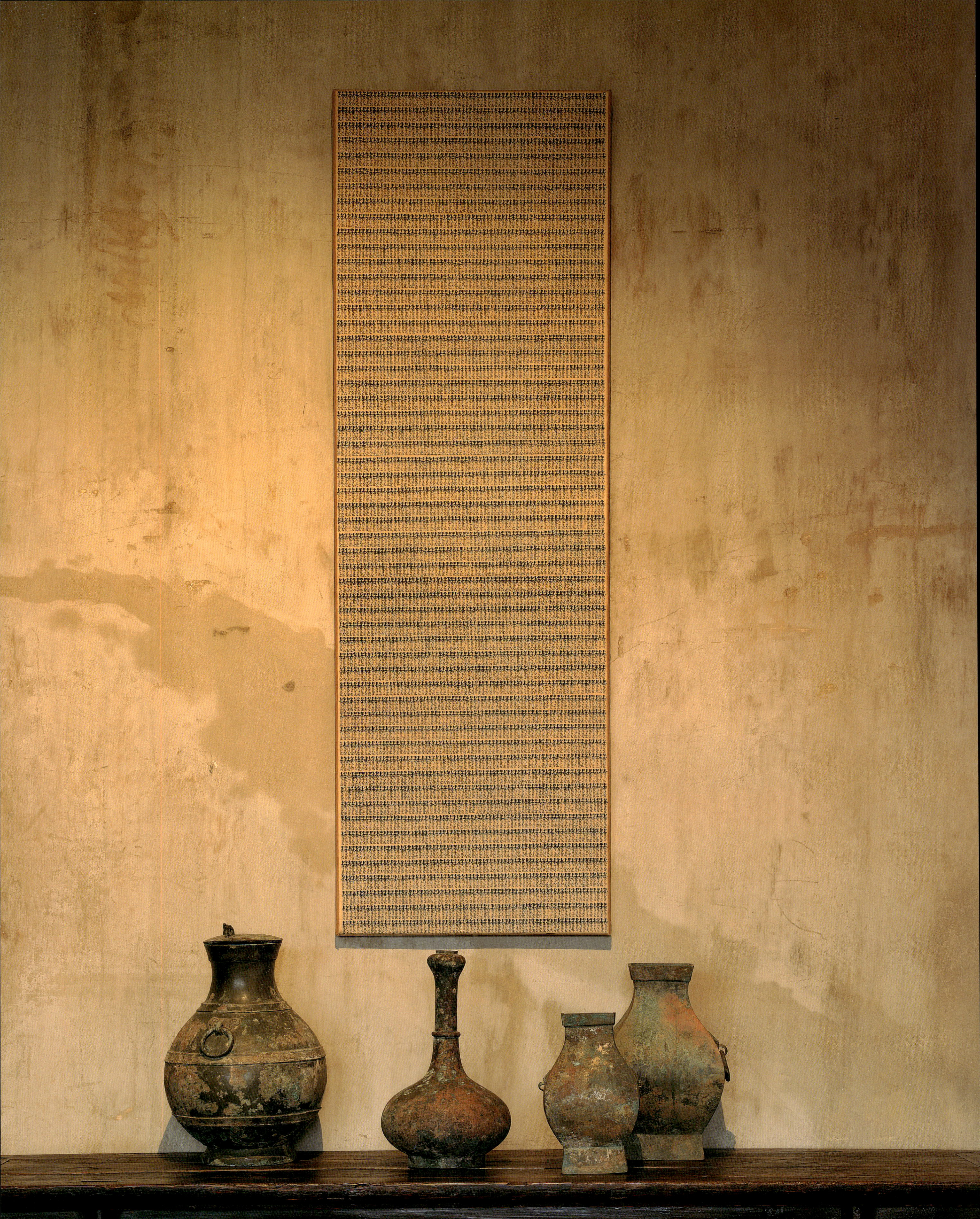

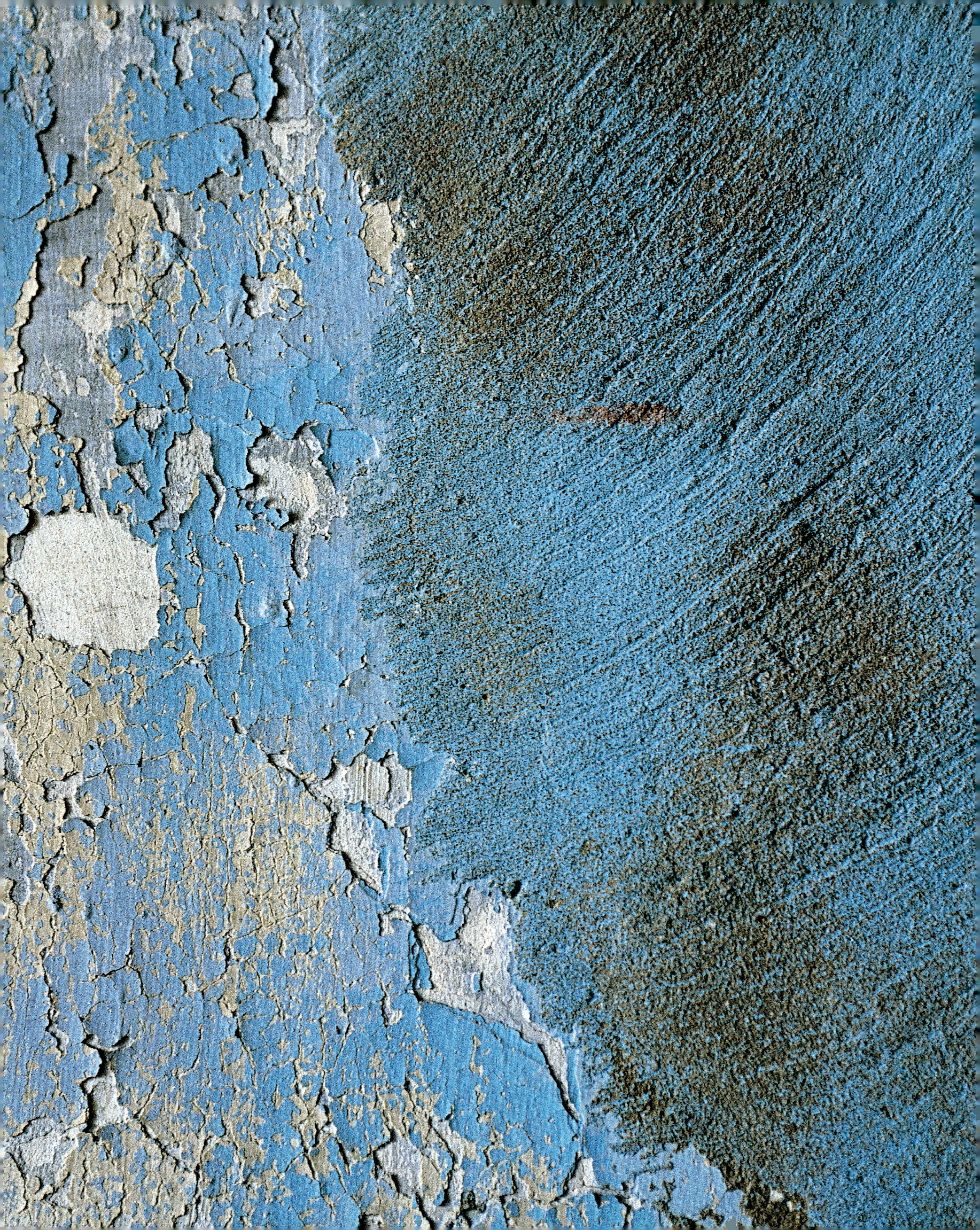

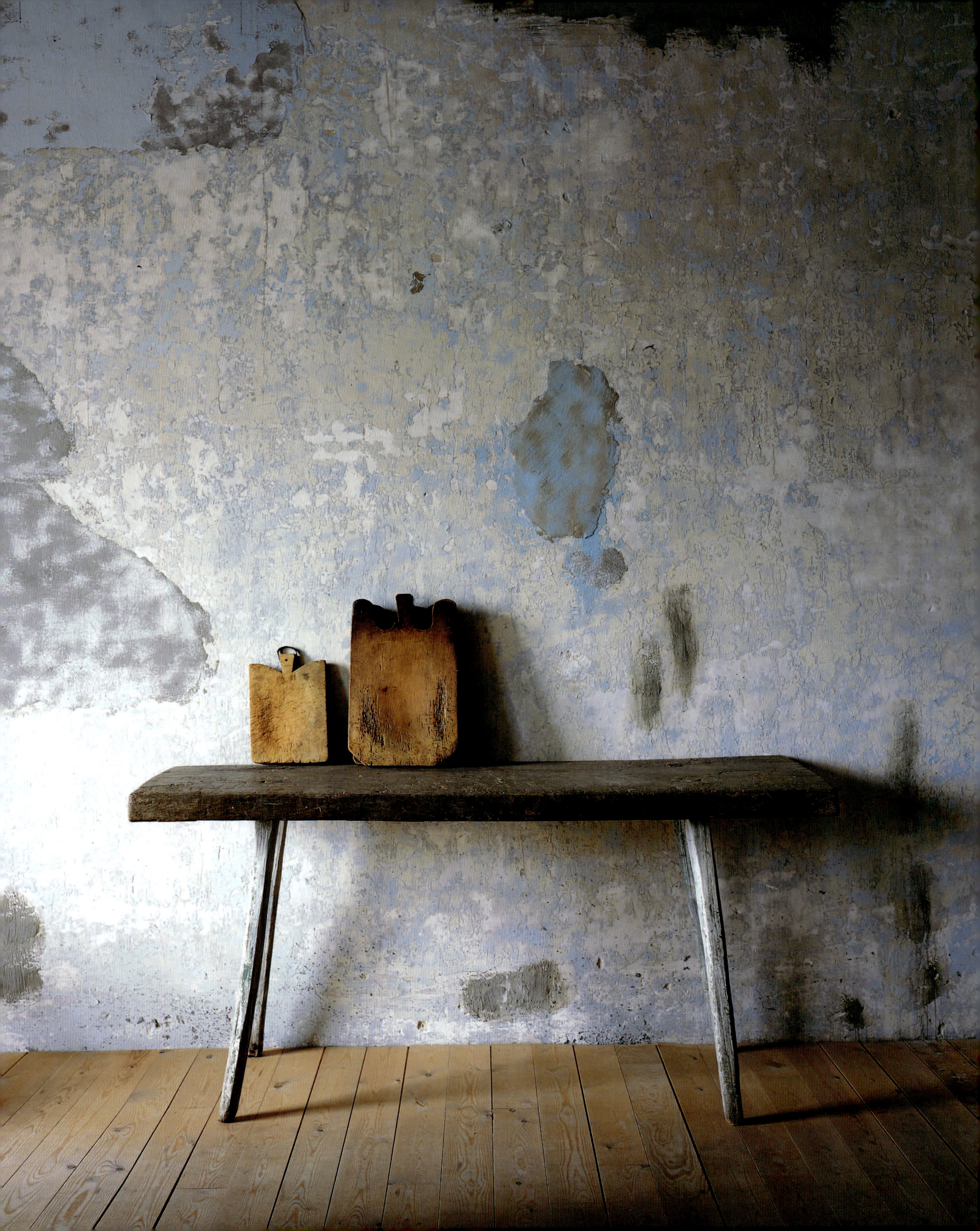

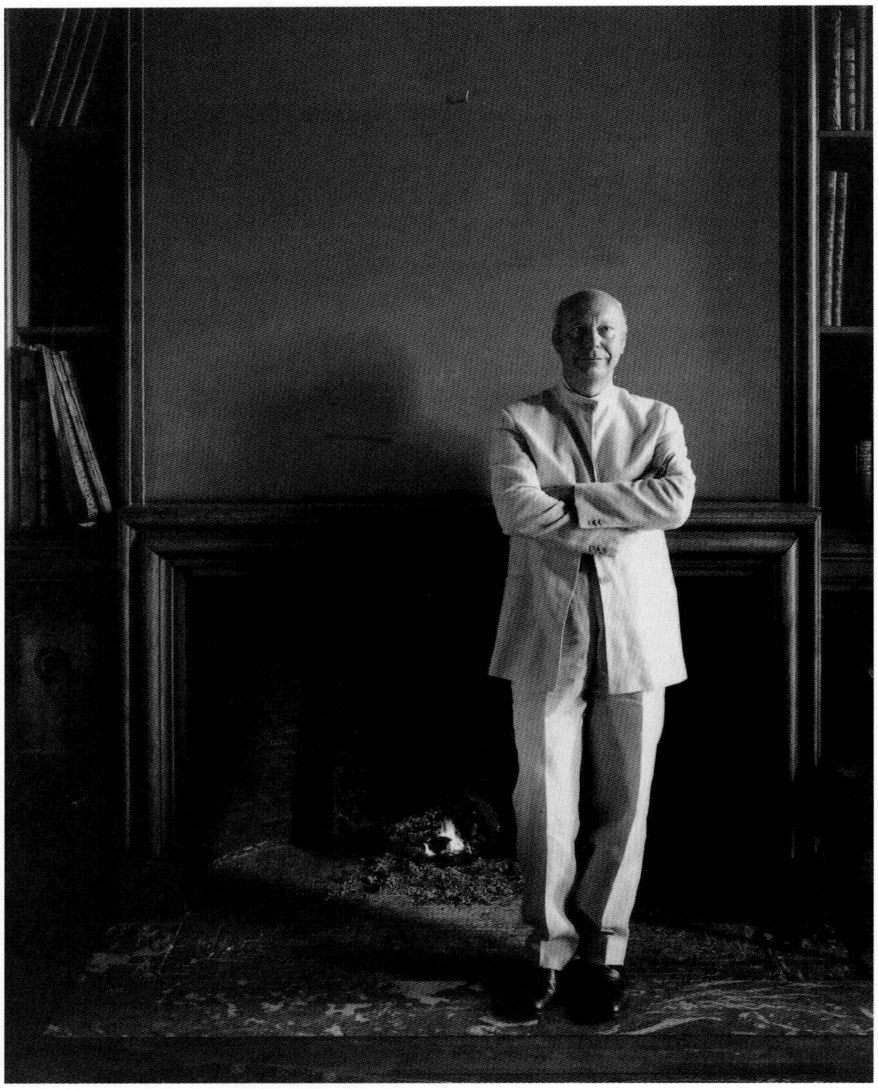
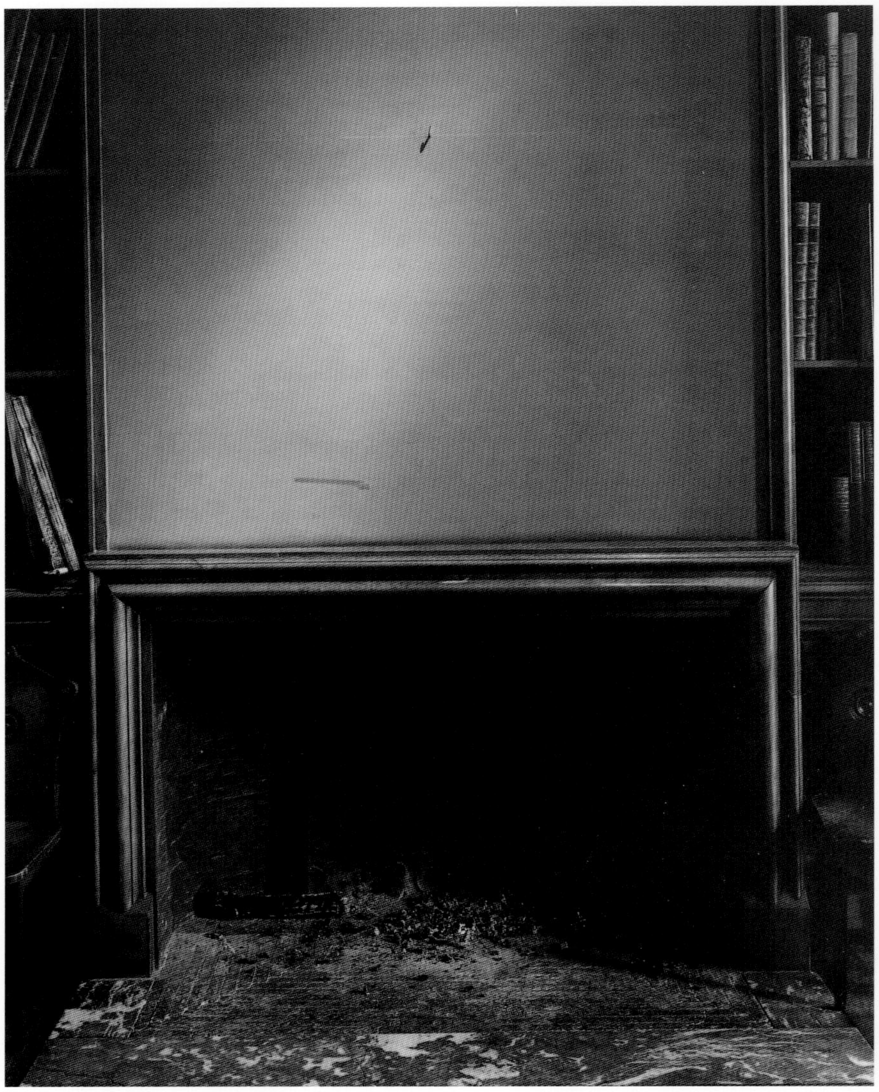
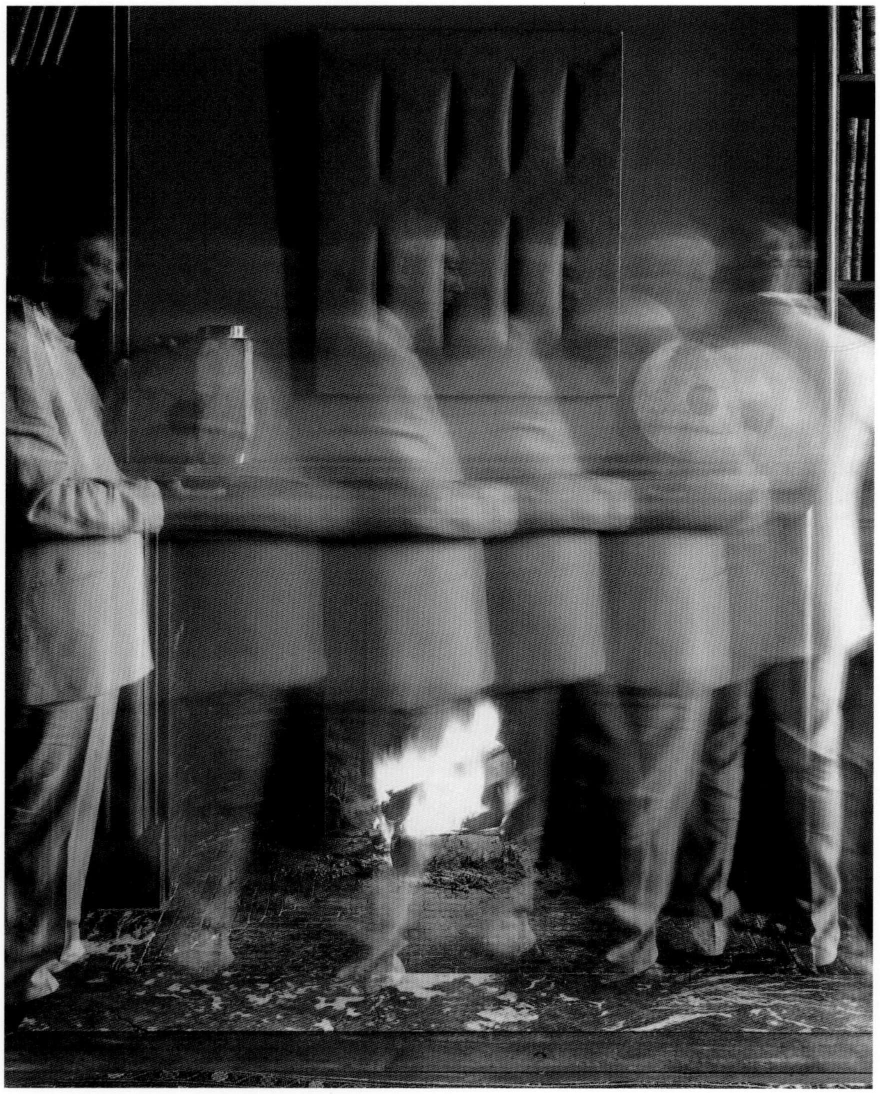
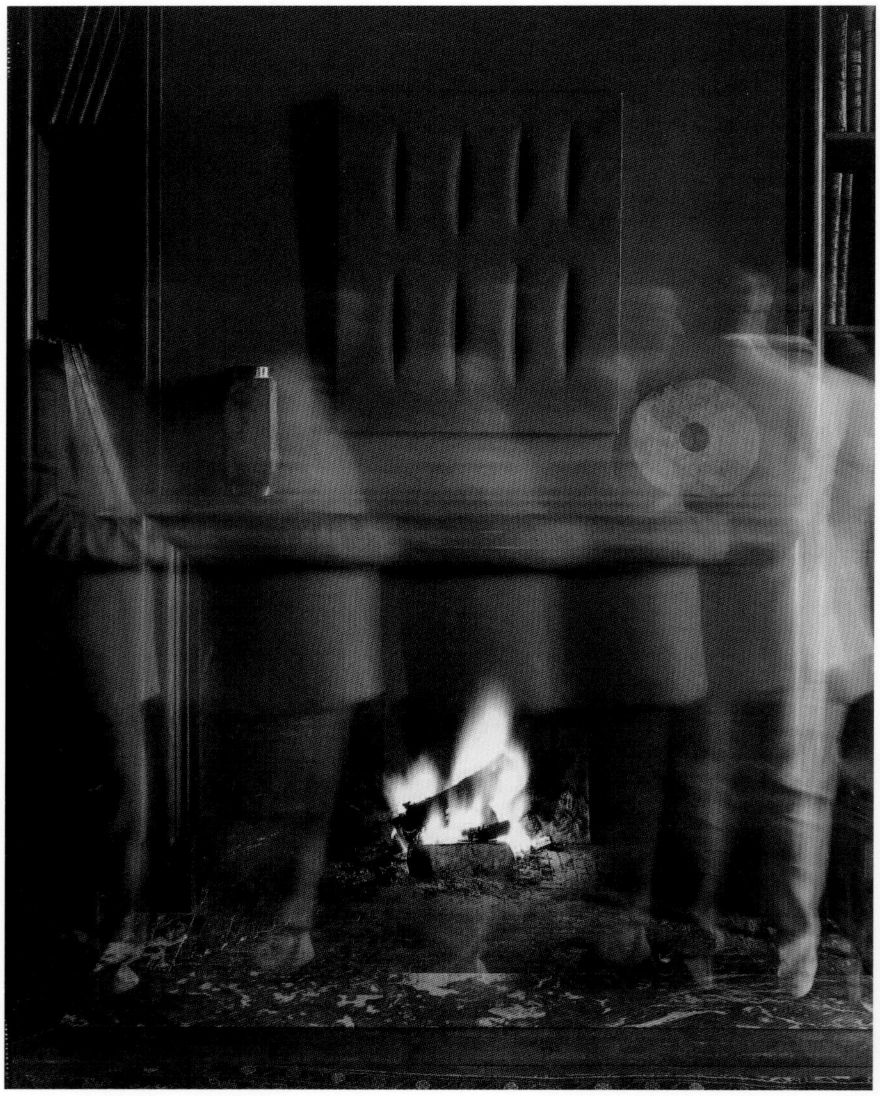

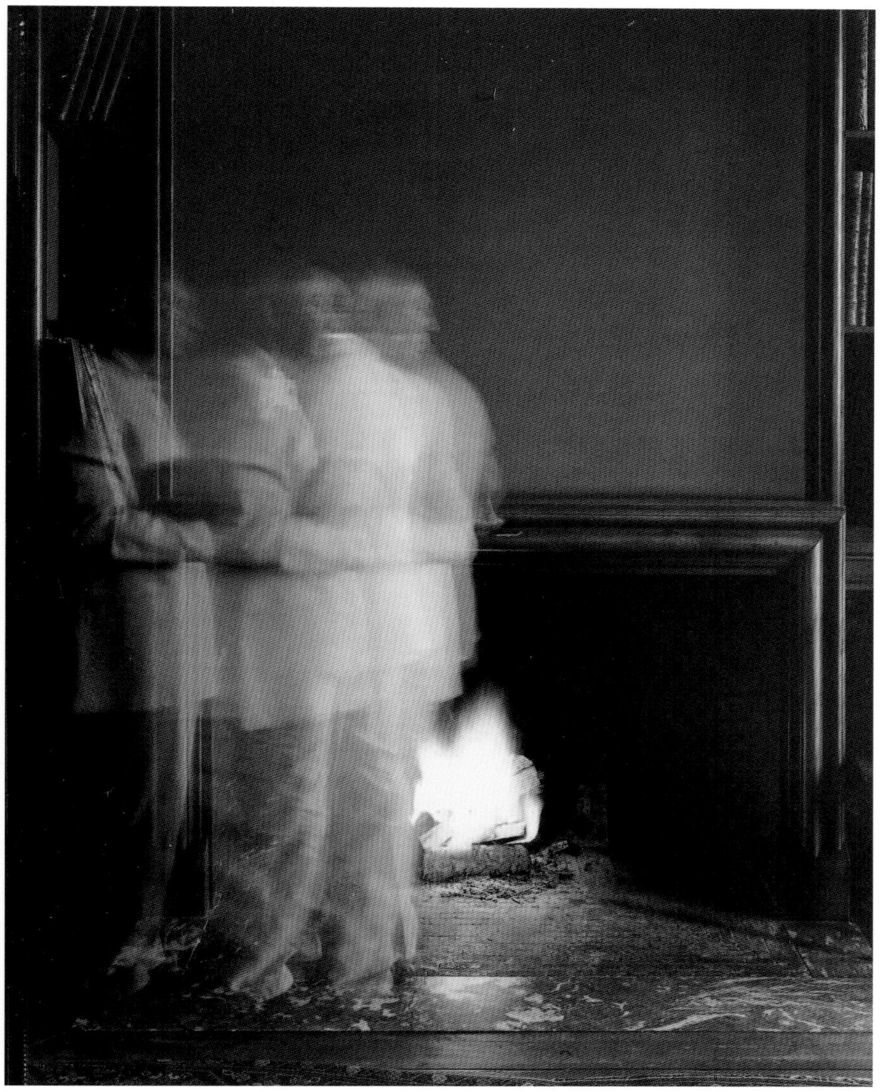
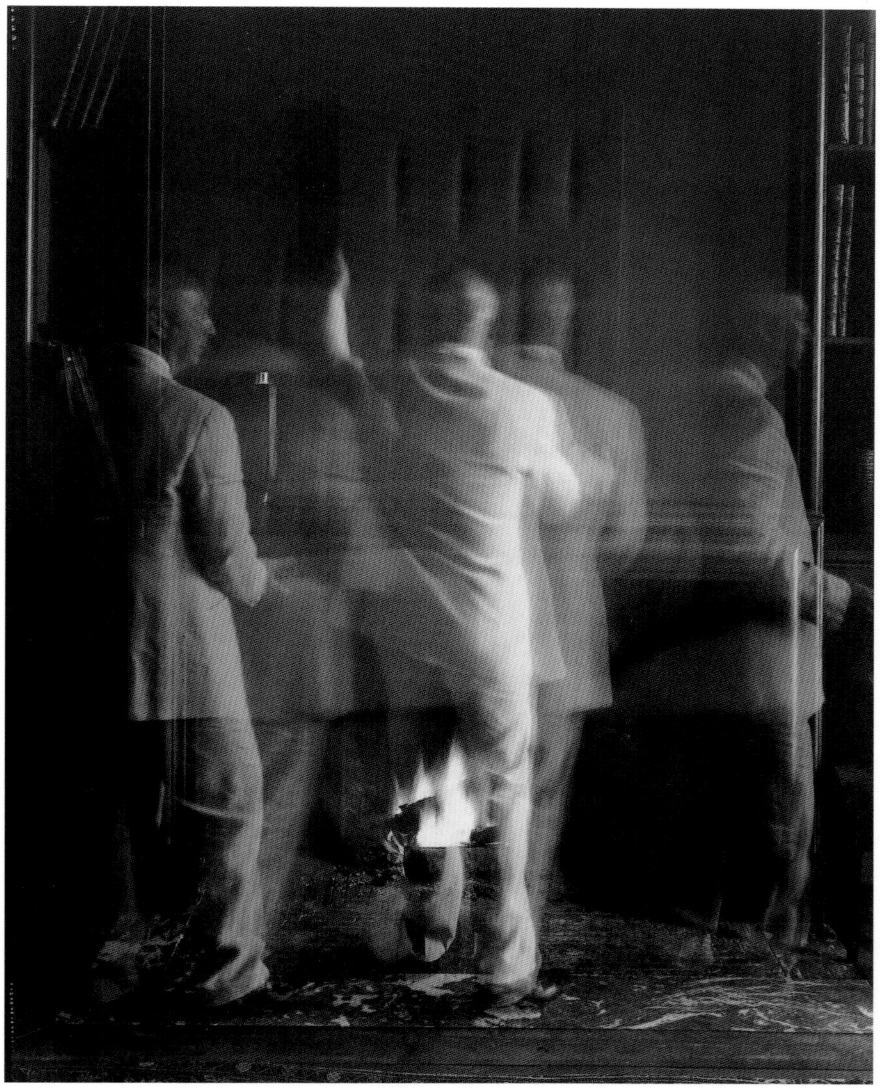
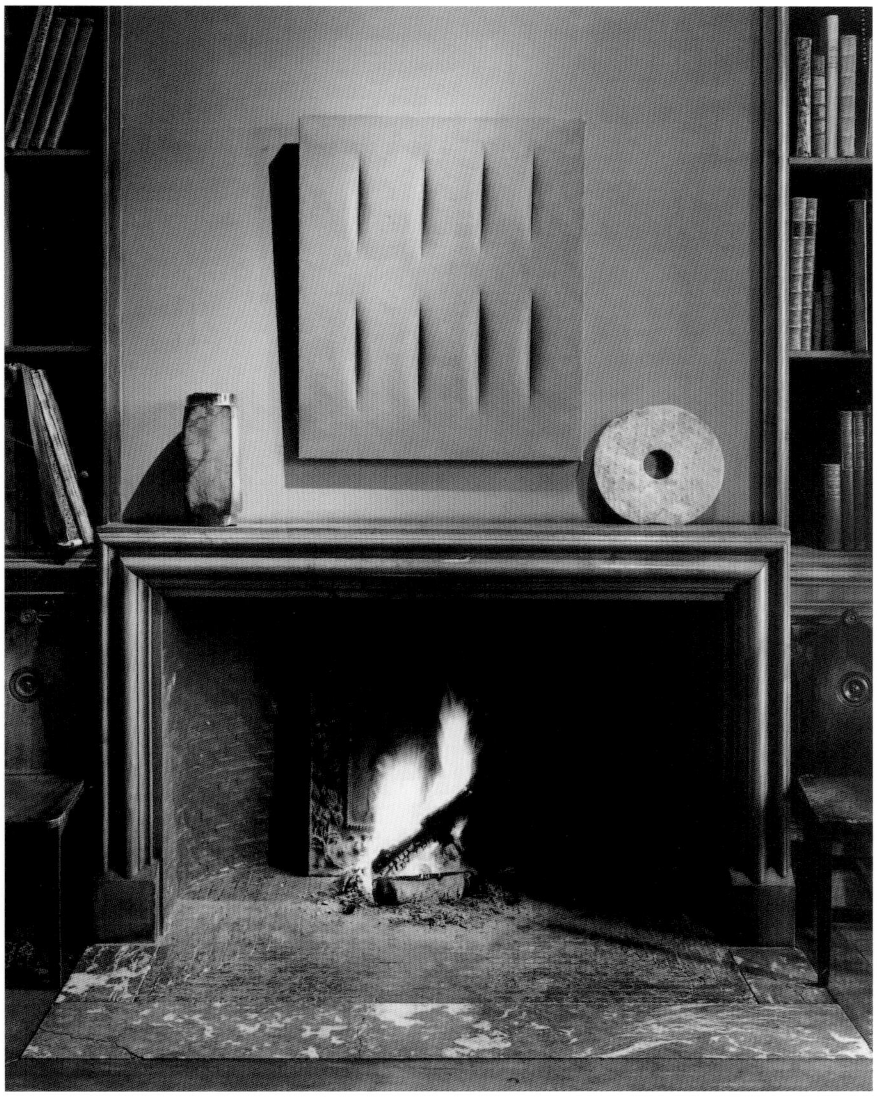
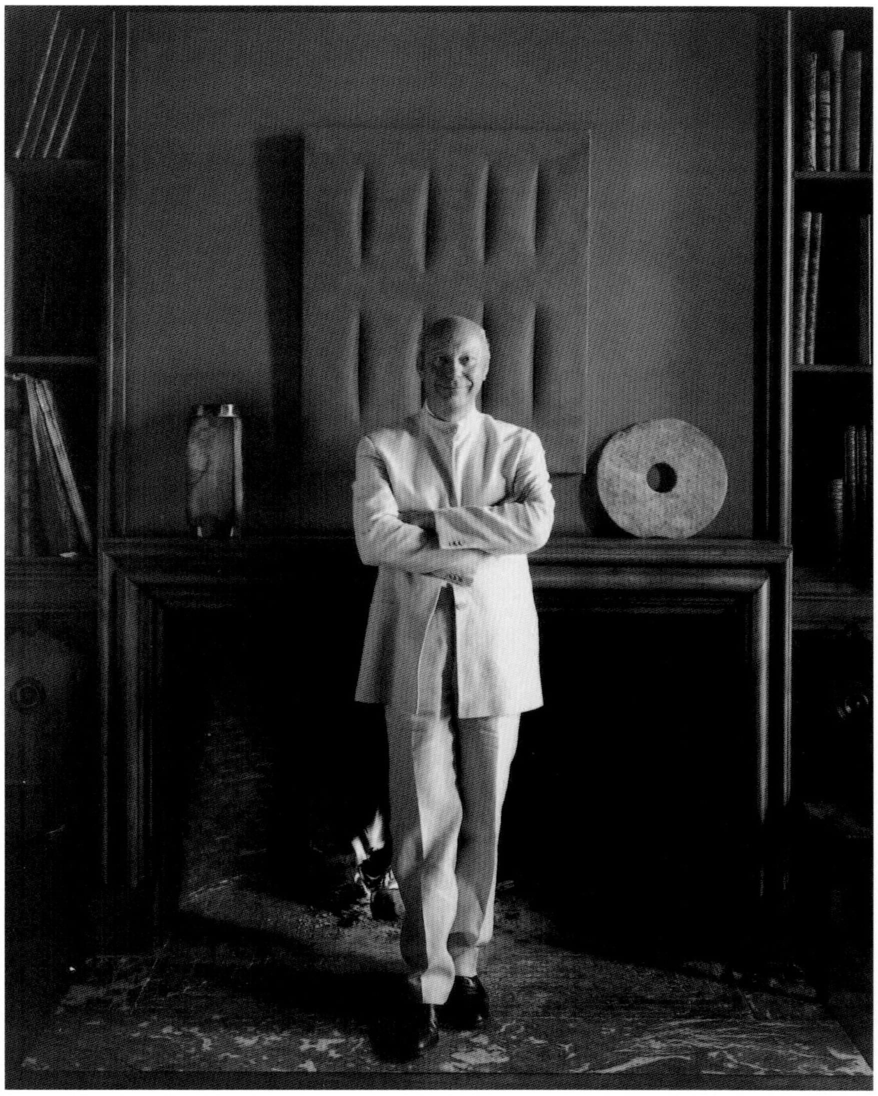

"It is not that one should look for purely utilitarian effects or aesthetic delights but rather a way of discovering the mind-set... what is found in the mind must be in tune with the subconscious."

Professor D. T. Suzuki

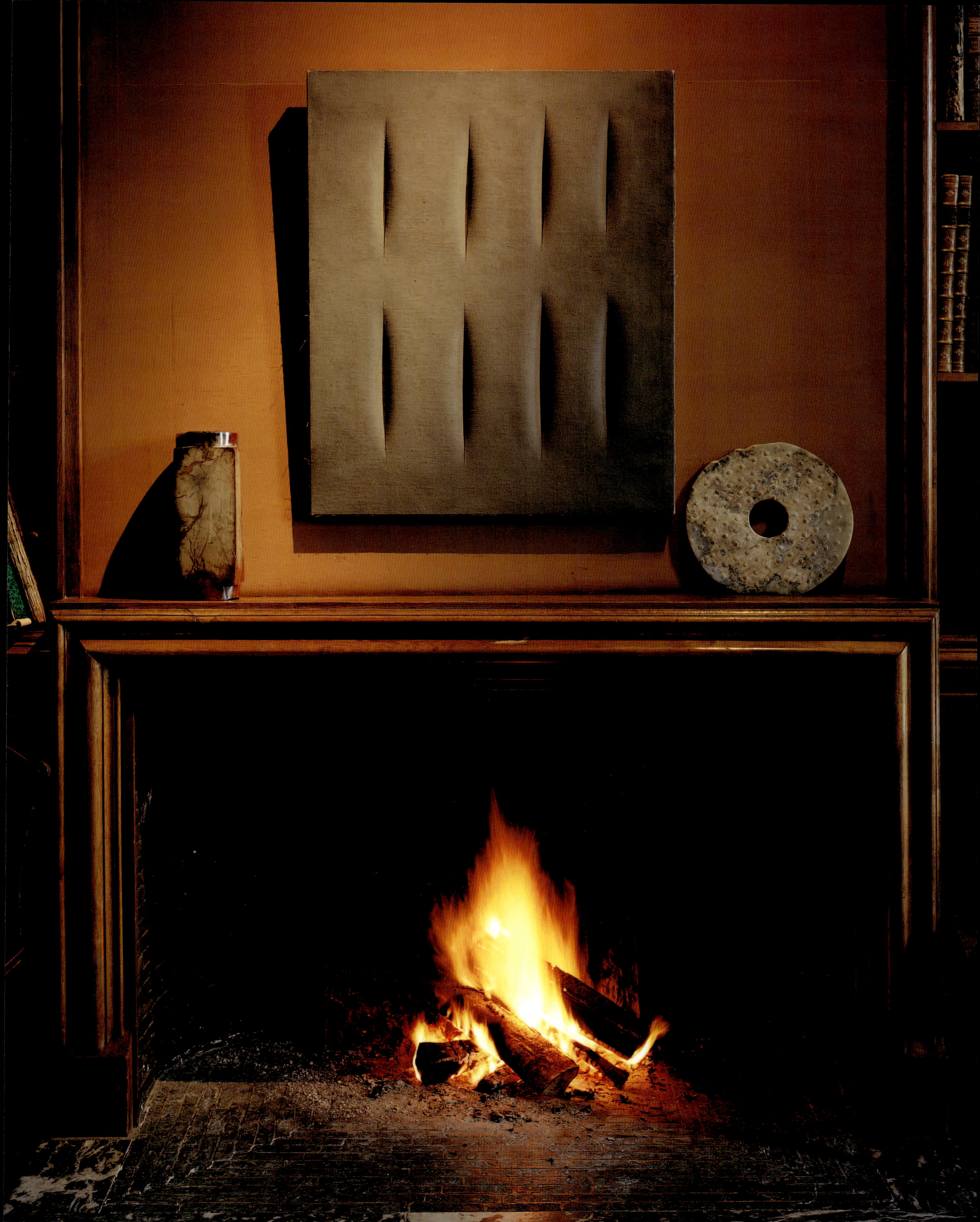

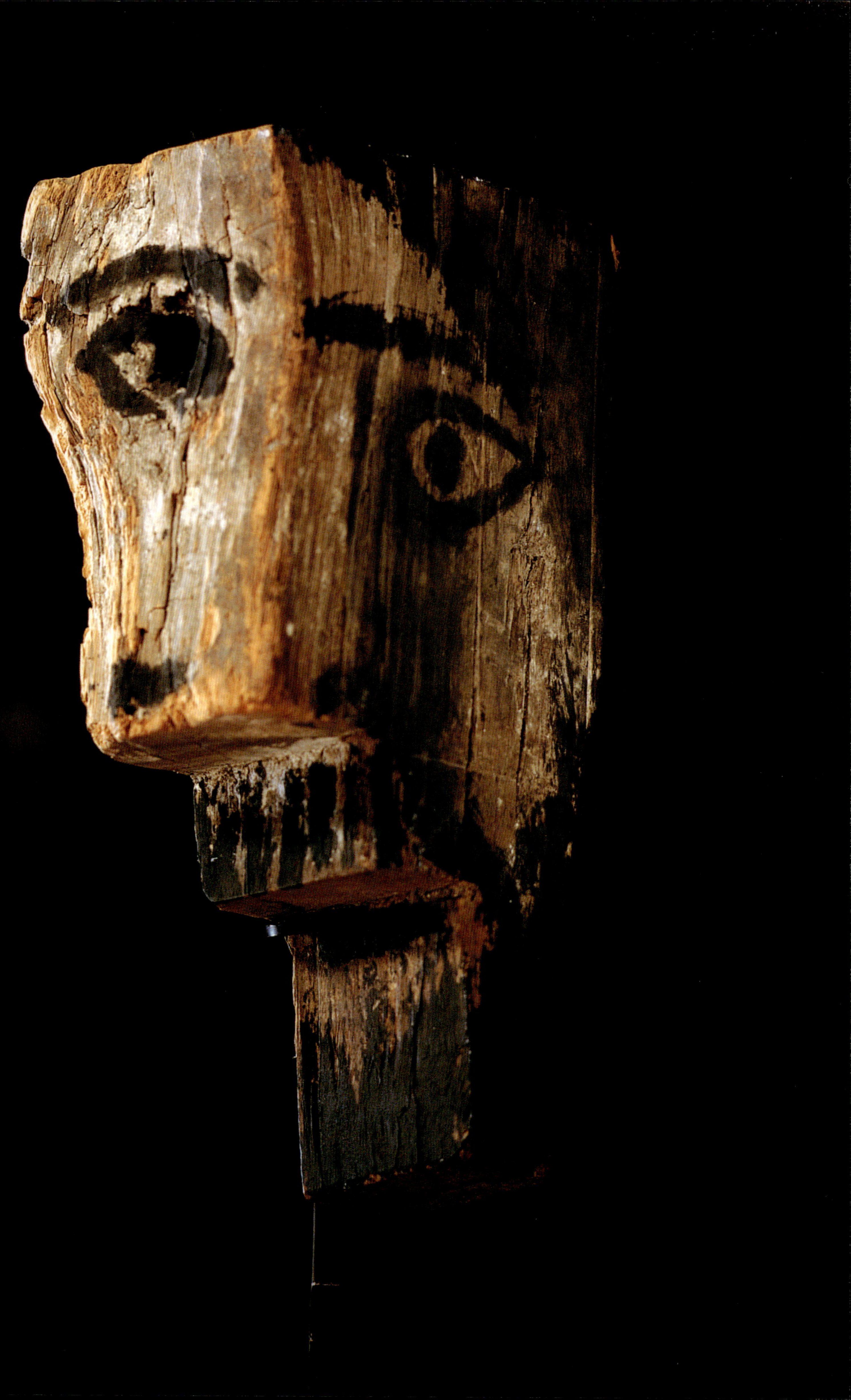

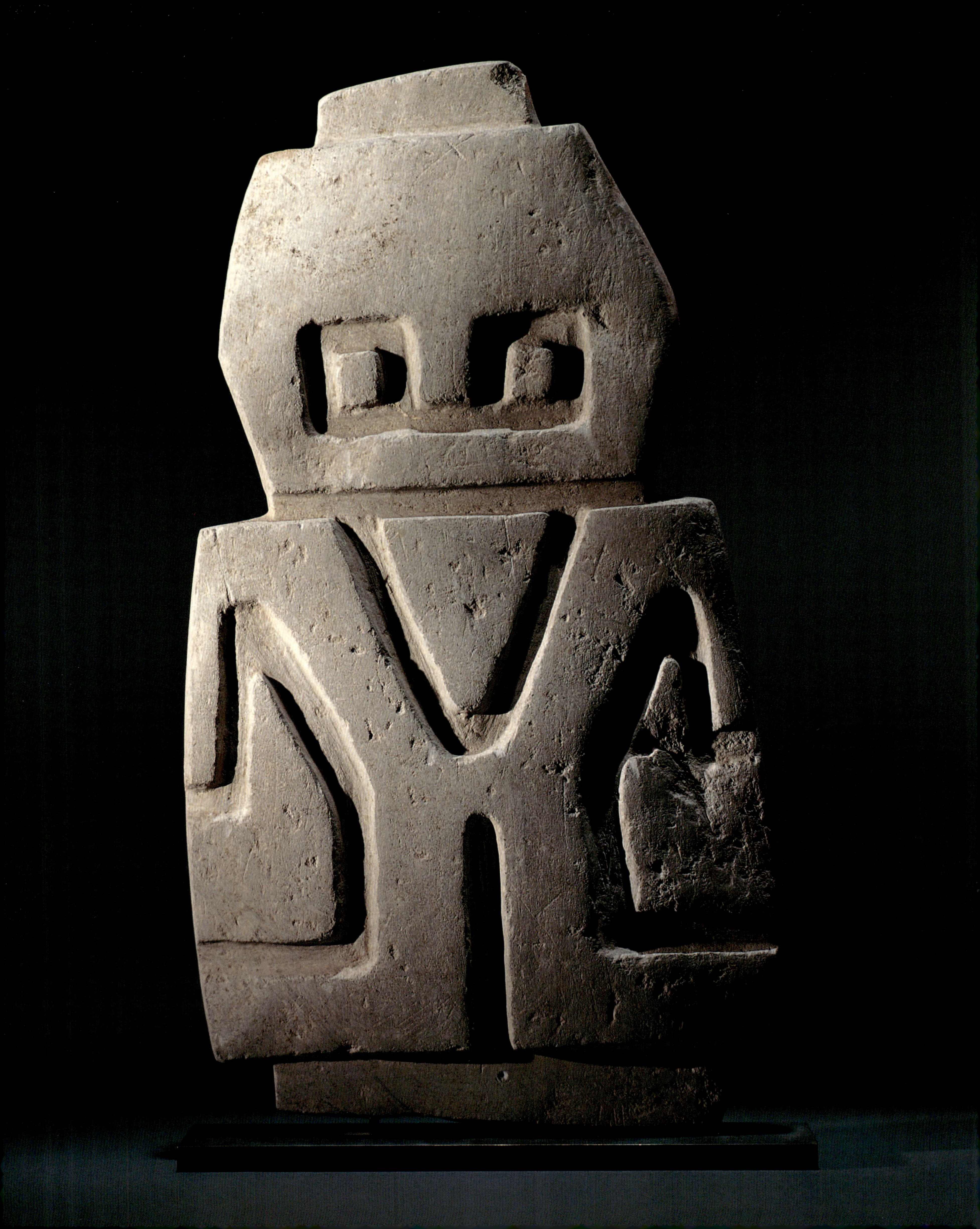

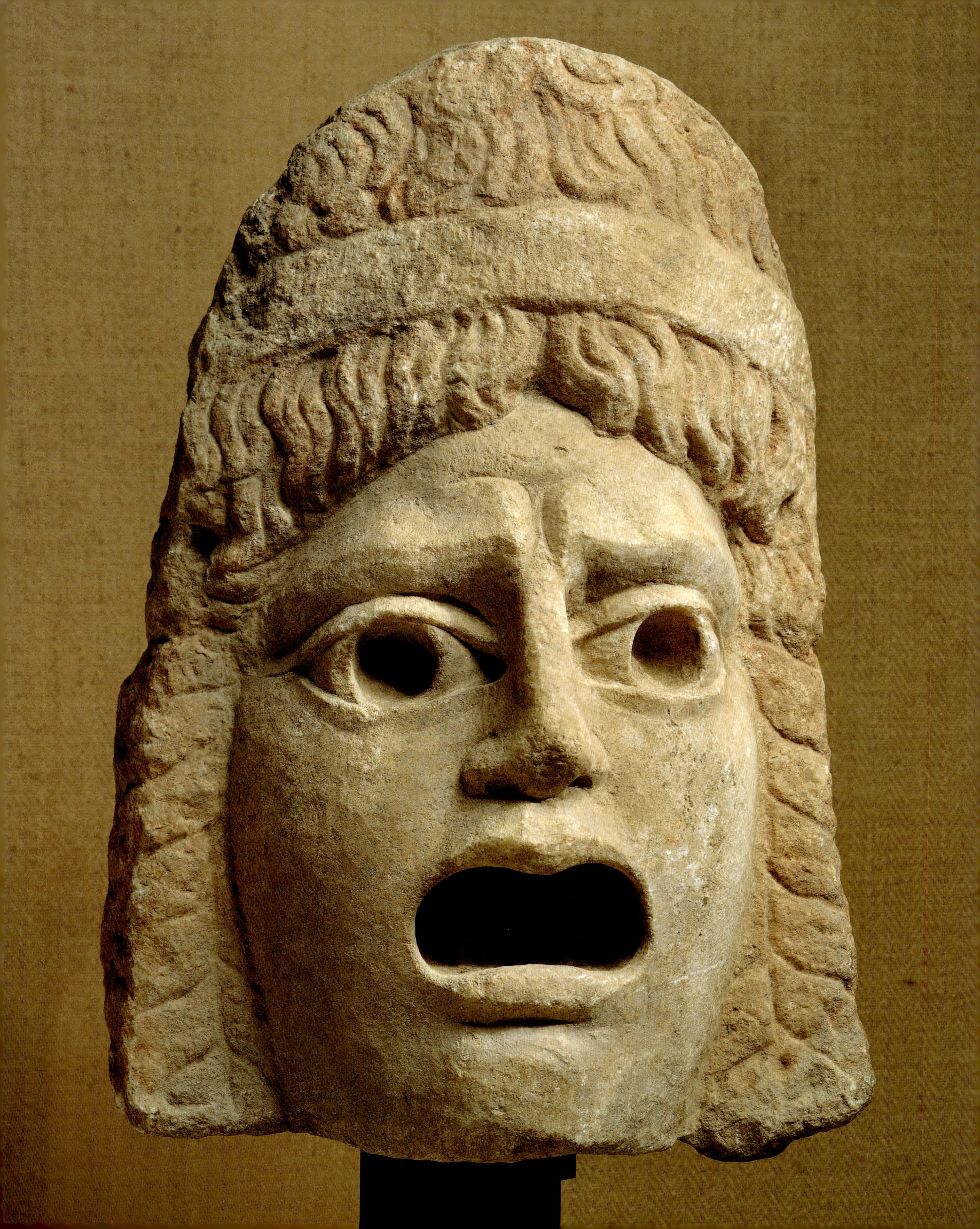

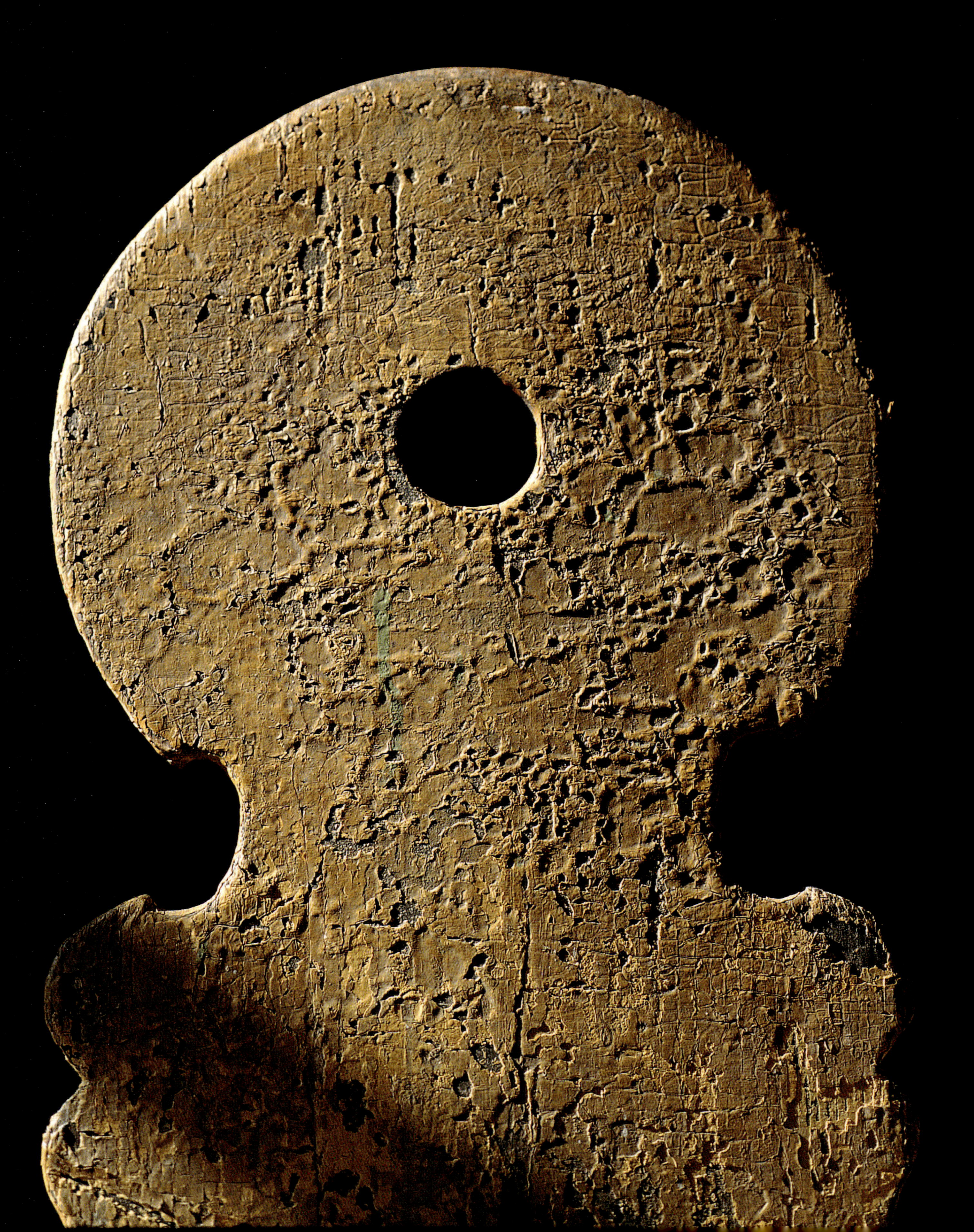

"Simplicity is
the mean between
ostentation
and rusticity."

Alexander Pope

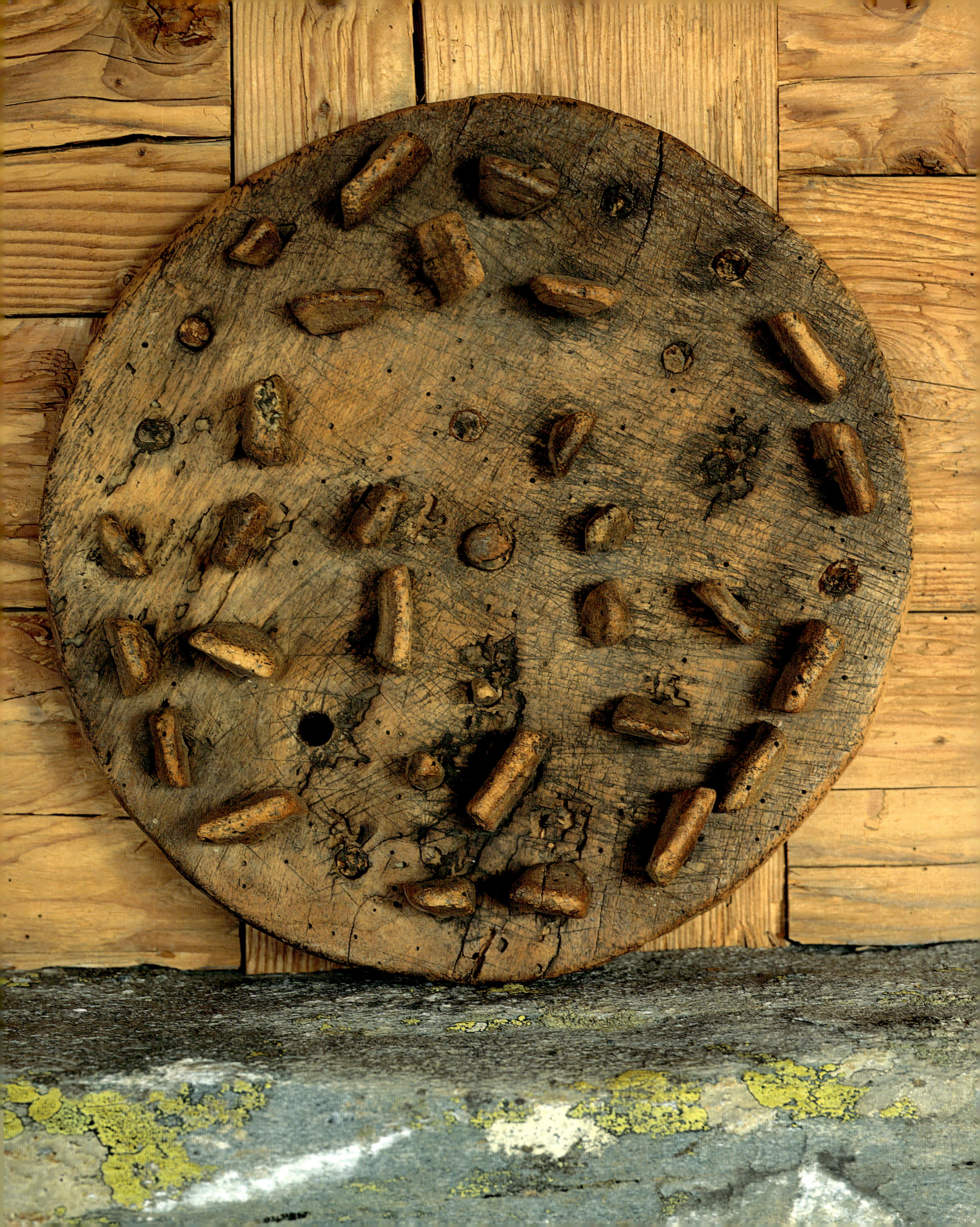

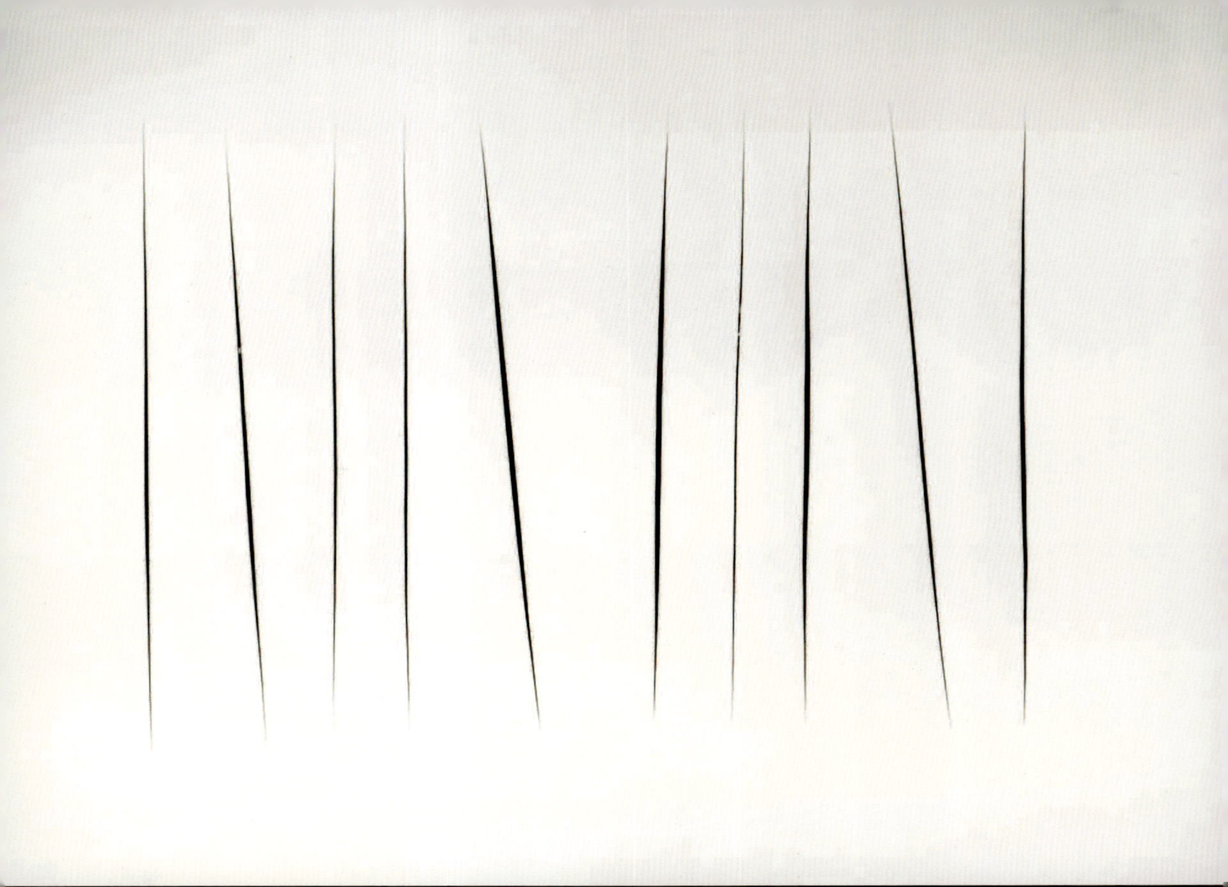

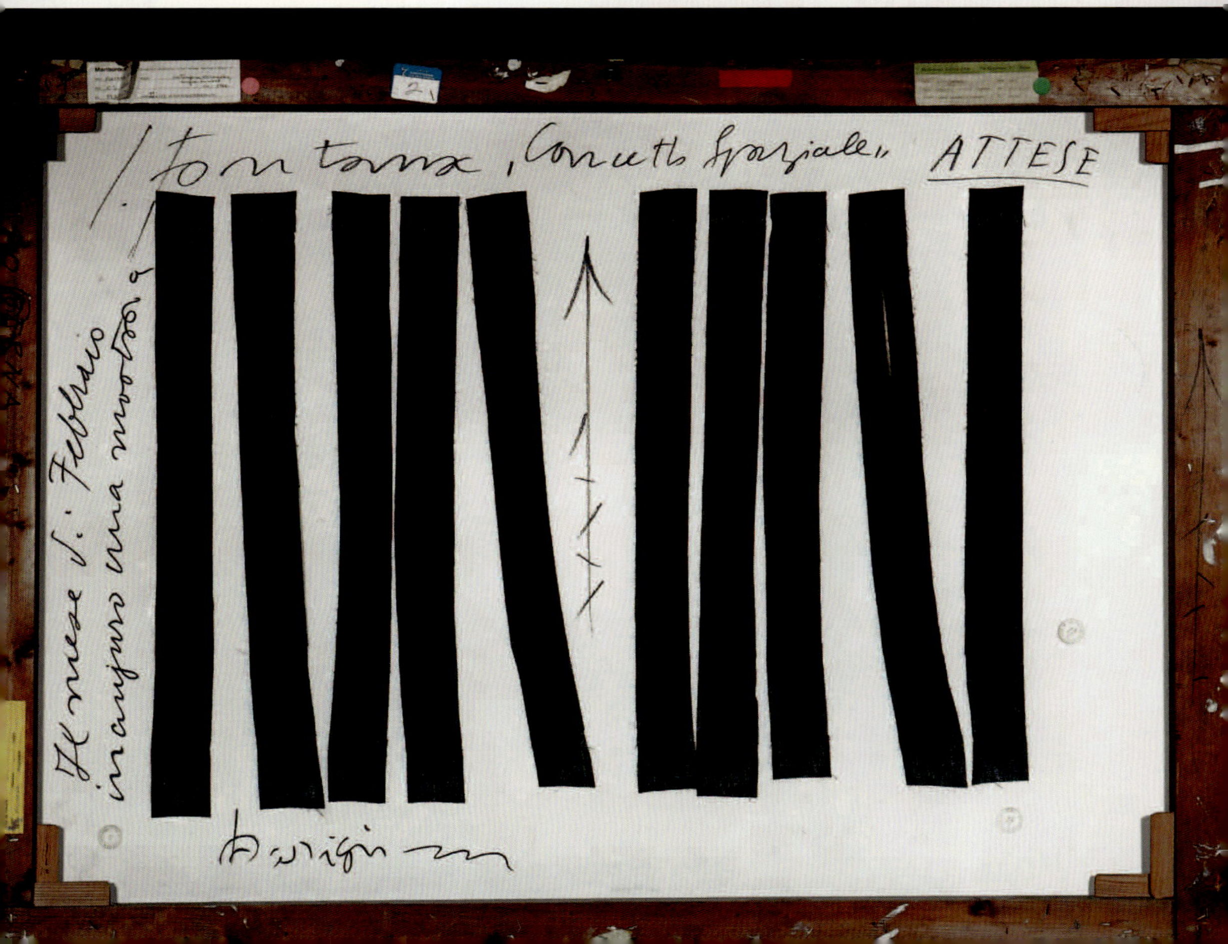
Fontana, Concetto Spaziale, ATTESE

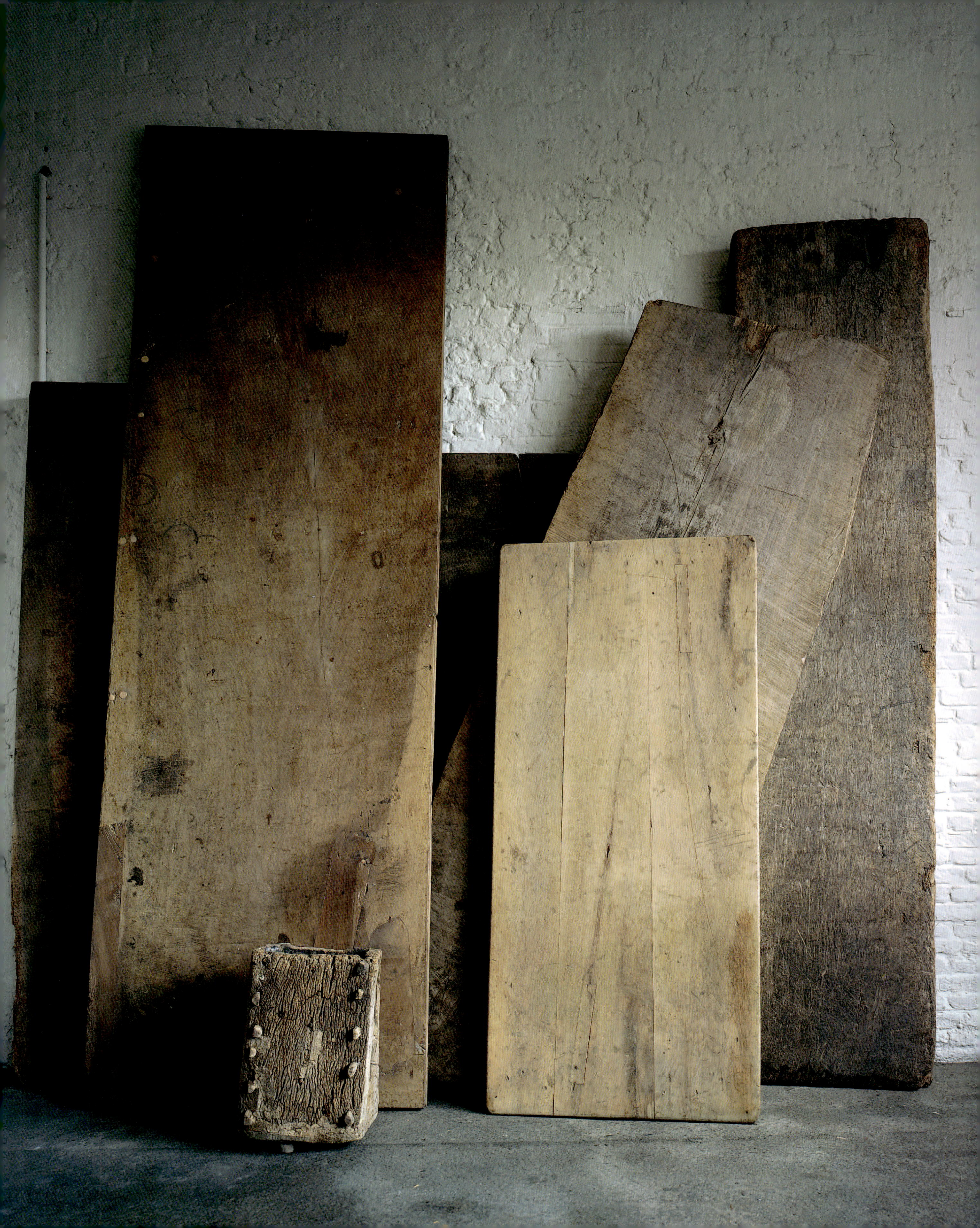

métier

I was lucky that my aesthetic education and the discovery of my métier took place during the 1960s, the golden age of finding and buying the finest English and European furniture and decorative arts of the sixteenth, seventeenth, and eighteenth centuries. It was an unhappy time in English social history, for due to crippling inheritance taxes, many large and important country houses were stripped of contents that had been assembled and exquisitely arranged by their owners over the centuries before the houses were pulled down.

A lot of the smaller treasures were not noticed by the experts in the sale rooms; there were such huge amounts of things to be sold they missed things which I then rediscovered. In those days, thirty years ago, taste was very classical, so the curiosities that I have always loved did not interest people, but later on, when tastes changed, they became more valuable. Whenever I visited England as a young student, I went to antique shops to find things that appealed to me and were cheap enough to buy with my pocket money. I also explored the attics of houses belonging to my father's English friends and would buy little treasures they no longer wanted. My circle of clients in Antwerp grew during this early period and began to include several antique shops.

The wholesale dispersal of important collections of furniture, pictures, works of art, and curiosities—the fruit of generations of aristocratic British patronage of the finest artists and craftsmen—was very sad. But it gave me wonderful opportunities to look, to learn, and sometimes to buy.

I must admit that at first I bought quite a few things about which I knew very little, but I would bring them back to Antwerp and study them, buy books on the subject, or talk to knowledgeable collectors, and in this way I not only started forming my library, but also began to educate myself in the three-dimensional arts.

During my student days I pursued ever more special finds for clients in Antwerp. I learned, for instance, from a casual meeting with the daughter of a family friend at a cocktail party that some of the contents of one wing of Woburn Abbey, the seat of the Dukes of Bedford, were for sale as they were clearing the rooms to be opened to the public. For the first time, I borrowed money from my father—my previous finds having all been purchased with my pocket money. My father made me pay interest promptly on the fifteenth of every month, which rather shocked my family at the time. However, it did teach me something very important about the value of money and how to conduct a well-run and successful business.

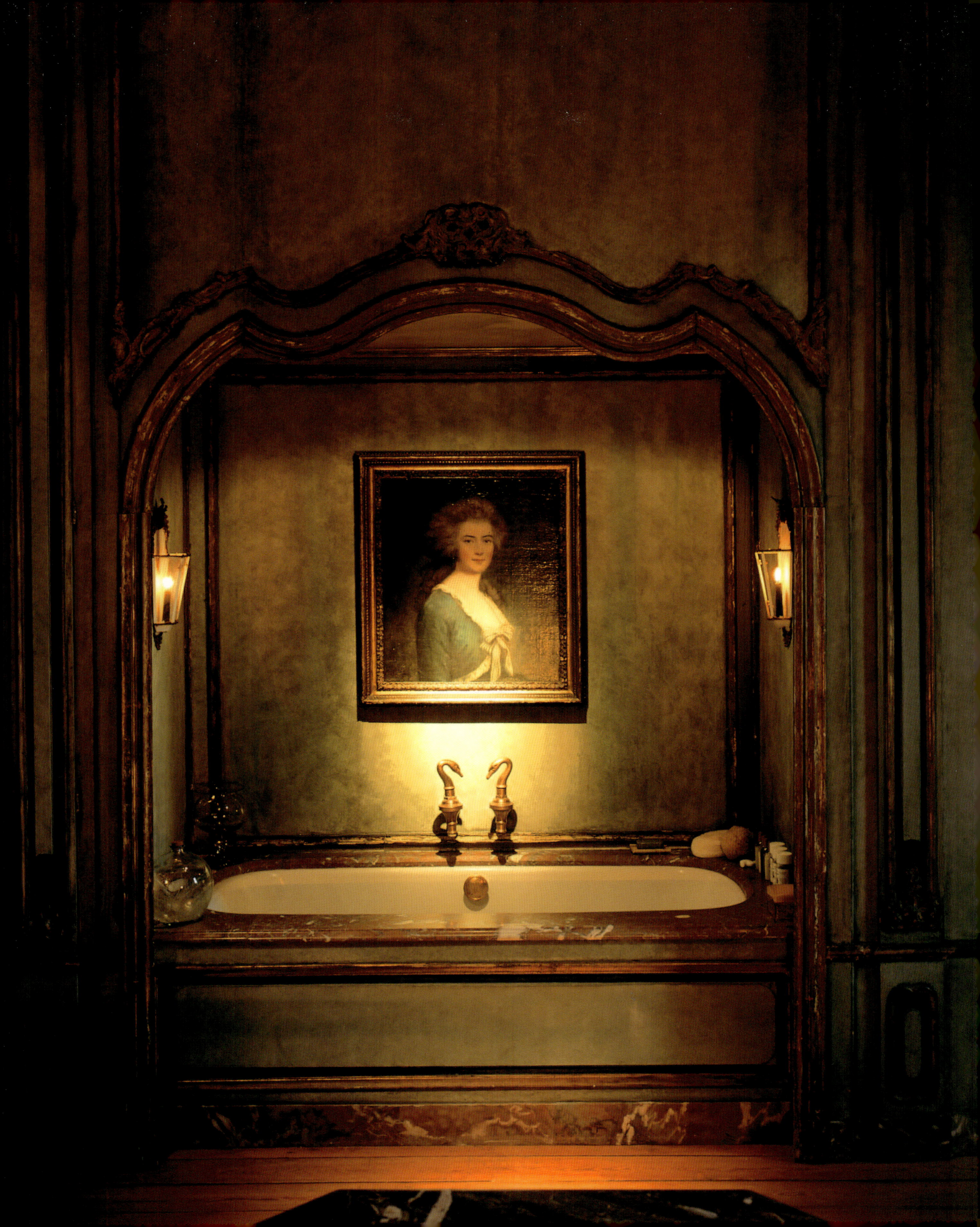

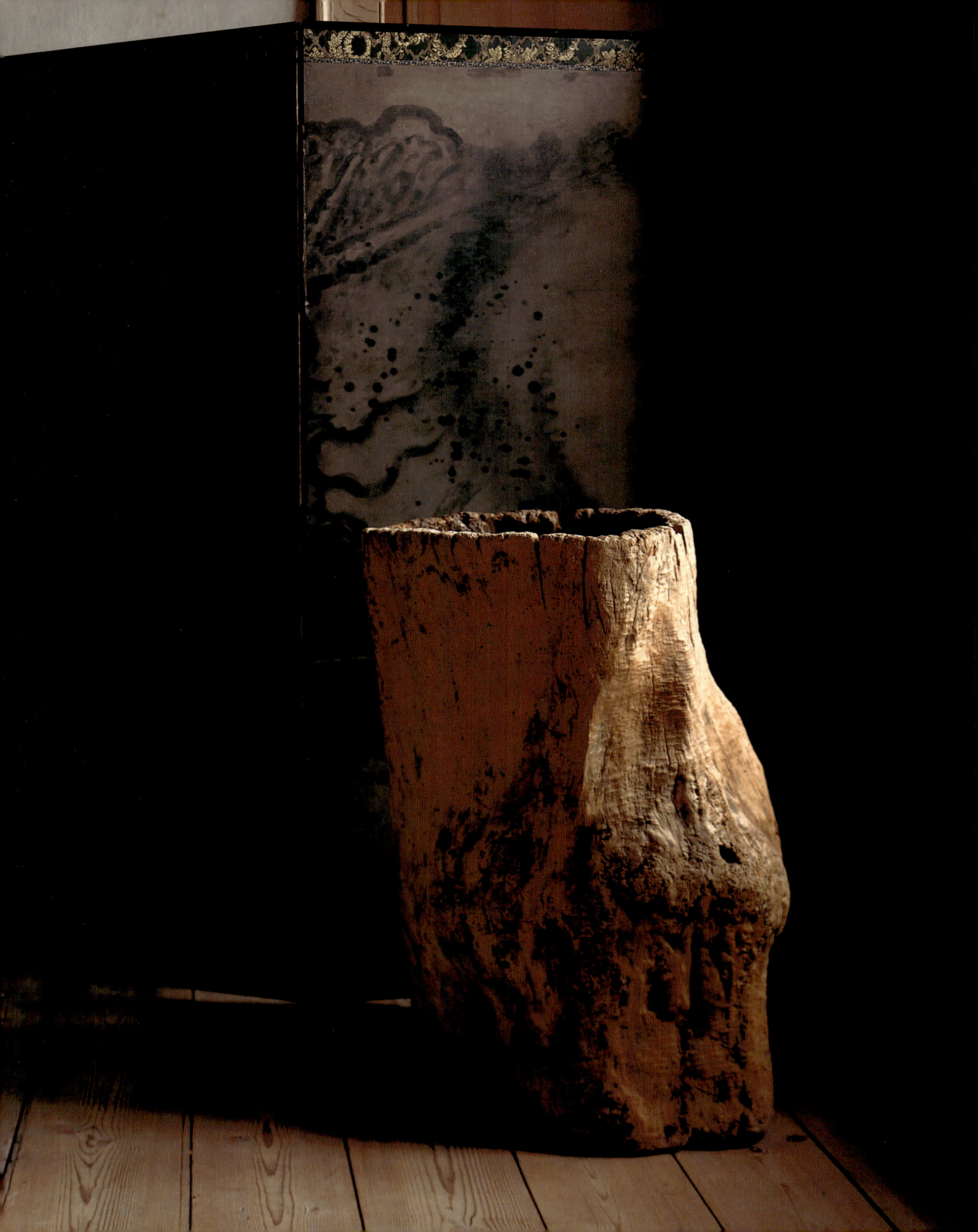

Using this borrowed money, I bought a great many interesting works of art from Woburn and sold them at a handsome profit. But I did not sell everything. I still possess a Gainsborough portrait of one of the many daughters of George III. It hangs in the castle where I can see it every day, a gentle reminder, if one were needed, of my first adult foray into dealing.

The success of his first investment led my father, who was very shrewd, to invest further in the acuity of my eye. I started buying fabulous silver in England. In particular, a great deal of beautiful Huguenot silver, which at that period nobody really liked in Belgium, preferring French silver. And I bought fabulous Dutch and Belgian silver in East Anglia from descendants of the Dutch who went to live there in the sixteenth and seventeenth centuries.

I have always preferred the plainness of Huguenot silver to the very fancy stuff, just as I have always preferred very strict, plain Chippendale to the more elaborate Chinoiserie pieces, and I have never liked Sheraton. I love architectural English furniture such as that of William Kent. I even like Gillow. And I'm very enthusiastic about earlier furniture of beautiful patinated walnut, the first period of luxurious English domestic furniture.

Soon, backed by my father in my increasingly large purchases of French, Italian, and Oriental works of art, and in particular of splendid silver, I persuaded some of my clients in Belgium to form collections, telling them that not only was this silver beautiful, it was a third of the price of French silver of the same date. Now it is much more expensive—the value of everything changes according to the taste of the time.

At eighteen, having finished my studies with the Jesuits, I decided I would go to university to study economics because at the time I believed that buying and selling works of art could only ever be a wonderful hobby and I would have to pursue a different career to make money. I had thought of taking over my father's business since I liked horses, but realized I would never be as good at judging them as he was. I had no clear idea what to do and studying economics bored me, so I left university and went into the army to do my national service.

My private clients also grew in number and in importance. For instance, I must have been only about nineteen when I met a very nice acquaintance of my parents, who had bought the most enormous house from a very grand family. It was a beautiful country house with a lot of empty showcases, but she had no objects to put in them and she asked me, a young boy, to find her beautiful objects. She gave me 200,000 francs a month, about $26,500, and said I could spend it on whatever I liked. I bought a collection of china. I bought silver. I bought bronzes. I bought her beautiful wooden and ivory objects. Then I arranged everything for her in groups in the showcases. This was the first time I not only discovered works of art, but also arranged them for a client.

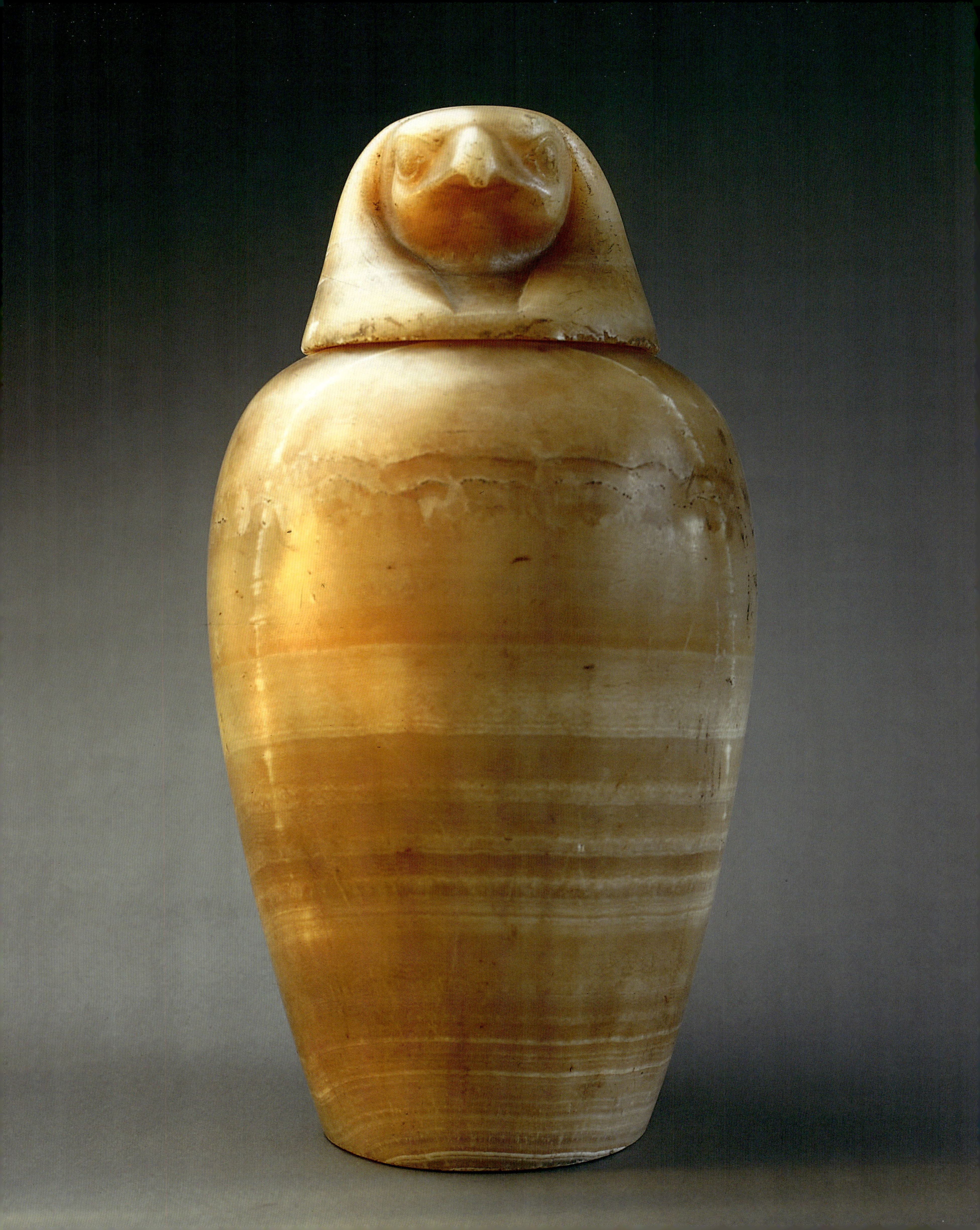

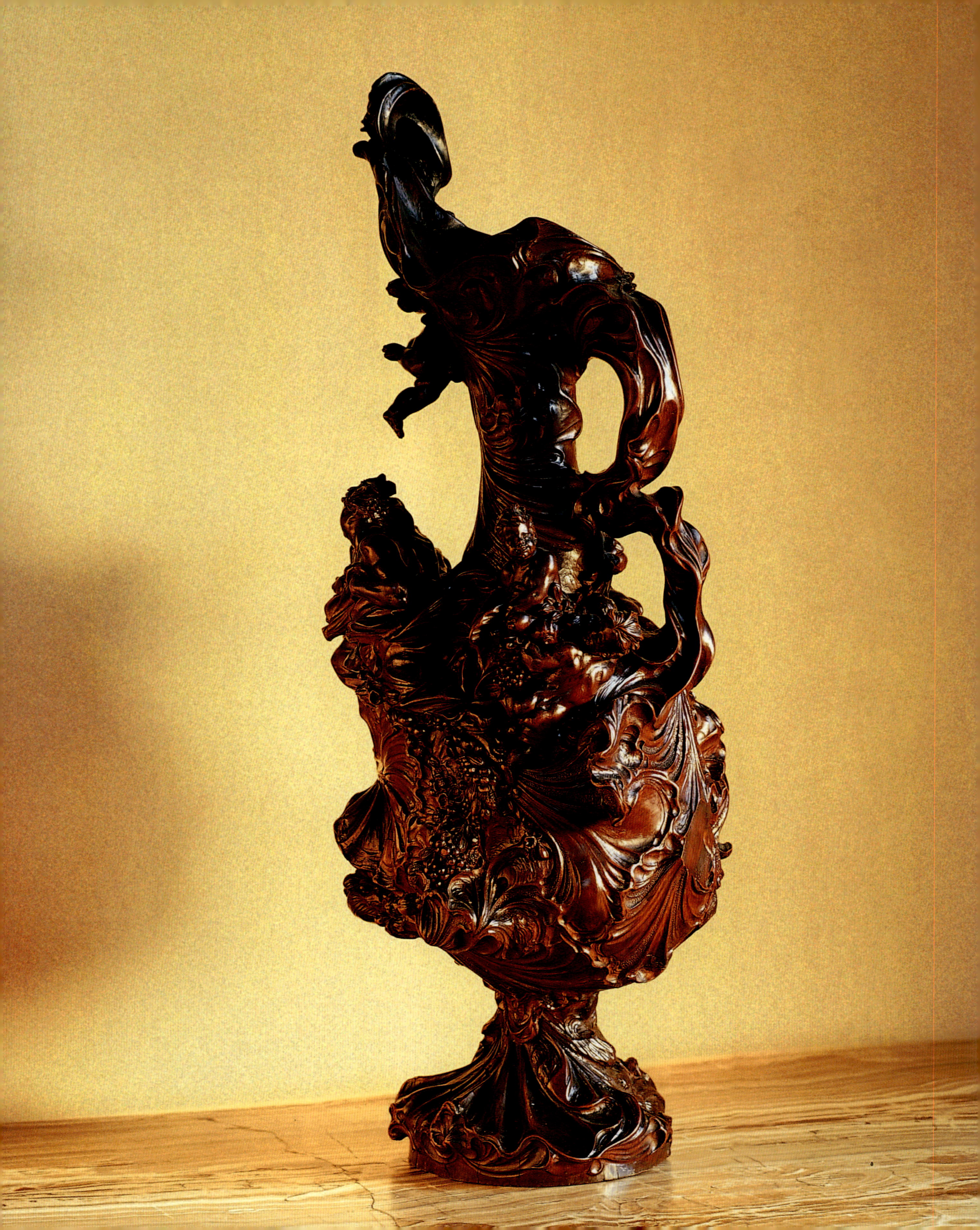

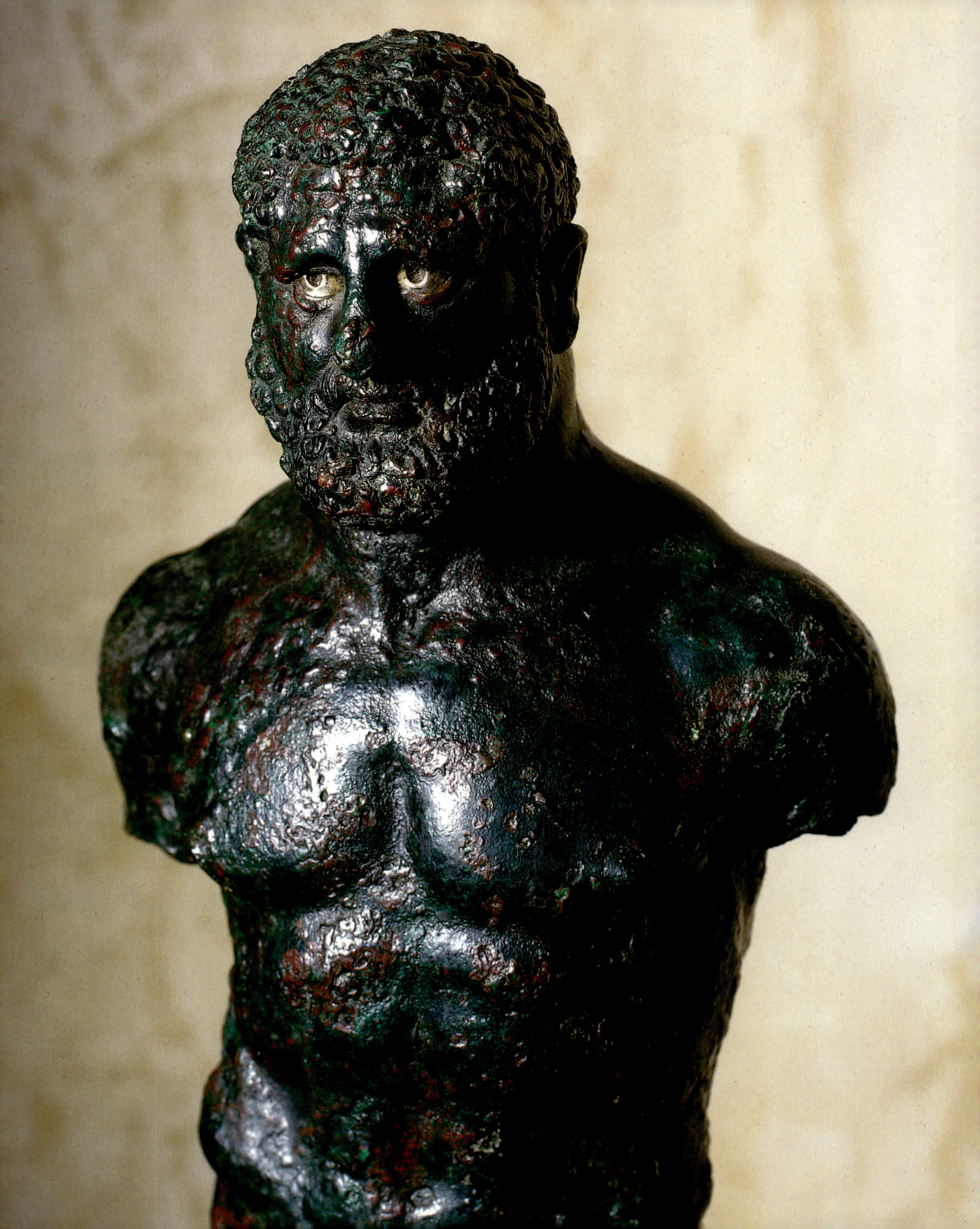

All my life I have sold beautiful things with the understanding that I will always buy an object back at the same price for which I sold it. If someone doesn't like a work of art anymore, they can always swap it for something else. So when I decide what price to put on a piece, I ask myself whether I would take it back for the same price. The answer must always be "yes."

Everything I bought was simply because I liked it. If I had little knowledge of the piece, I kept it for a while and studied it, often asking the opinions and advice of collectors and curators I had come to know. First I loved an object with my heart, took the risk and bought it, then I did the research—and that is the way I still work today. It is the best way of discovering extraordinary objects in odd and out-of-the-way places; one must always expect to find something very special around every corner.

I have always tried to be quite open-minded when I look at a work of art. Something about an object must strike me like a *coup de foudre* that I can experience physically. This is always the most exciting moment. If the object is for sale, I will do everything I can to acquire it and I always want to keep it forever. Usually, though, I am so excited by these special pieces I can't keep quiet about them when clients come to see me; they are always the first things to be sold.

My new client was really delighted with the contents of her showcases, especially when she had her collection valued and realized how much more it was worth than she'd paid for it. So she believed in my eye and told all her friends. In a way, it was Madame Cleiren who pushed me further toward pursuing my métier.

Even while I was in the army I was constantly being asked whether I had anything interesting for sale—and I did. In 1967, for instance, I bought a magnificent Magritte canvas *La Mémoire* for $2,400. It had been estimated at between $1,600 and $3,000 by two salerooms, one in Antwerp and one in Brussels. My father hated the picture and was horrified by the amount I had paid for it. Eventually, I had studied the picture so much I laid it flat on the floor in my room because I couldn't look at it anymore.

Then some friends of my father's visited him while I was away in England and offered him 375,000 francs, about $50,000 for it. My father couldn't believe it. He phoned me in England and said, "I've got some really mad people here who want to give that much money for such an ugly thing." And I said, "Fine. I'll sell it." I wish I hadn't now because today it must be worth about $3 million.

After that, even my father acknowledged that I had discovered my true métier. So when I left the army I had no trouble in deciding that henceforth my passion and my hobby would become my life's work. I have never regretted this decision.

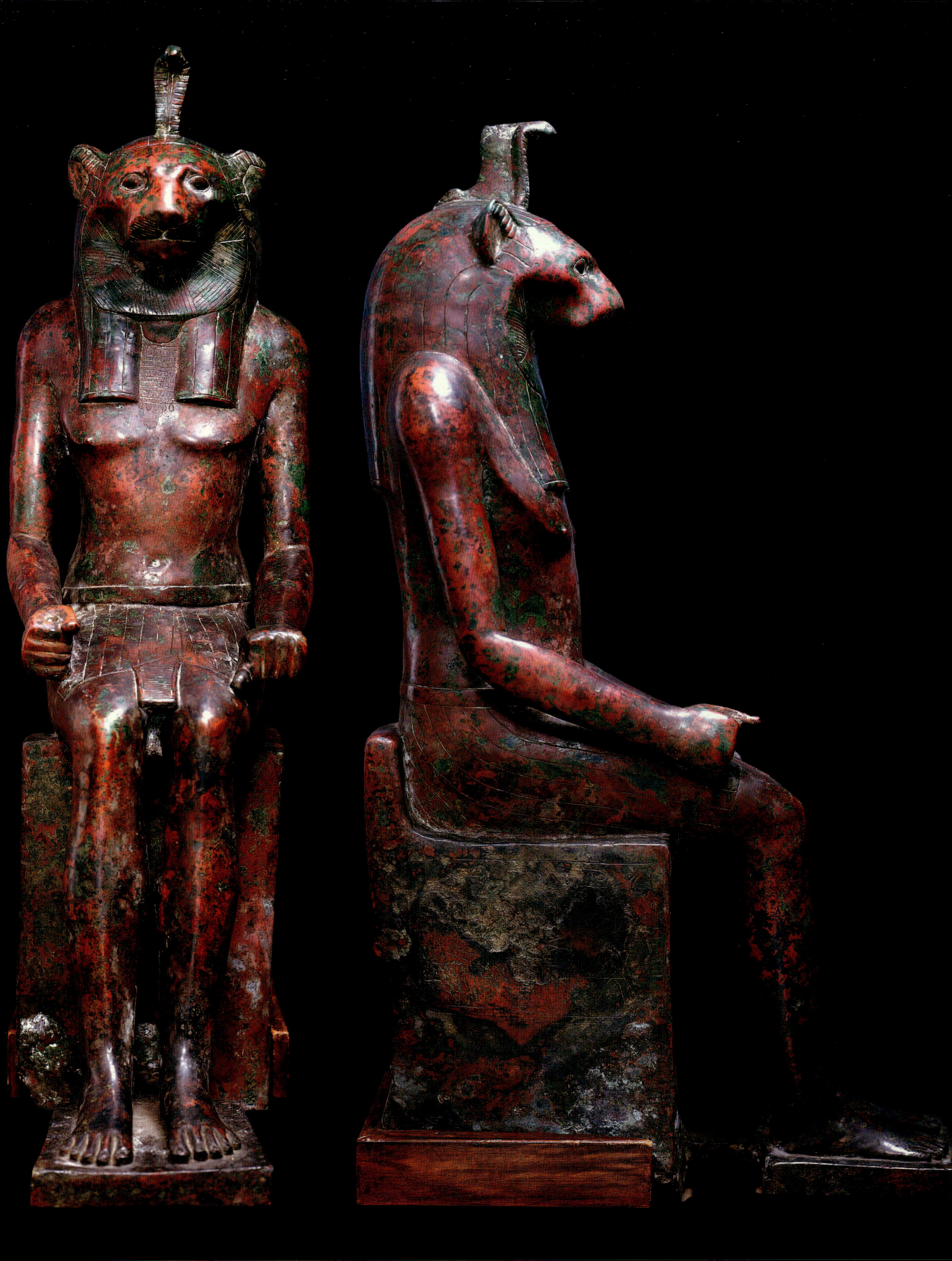

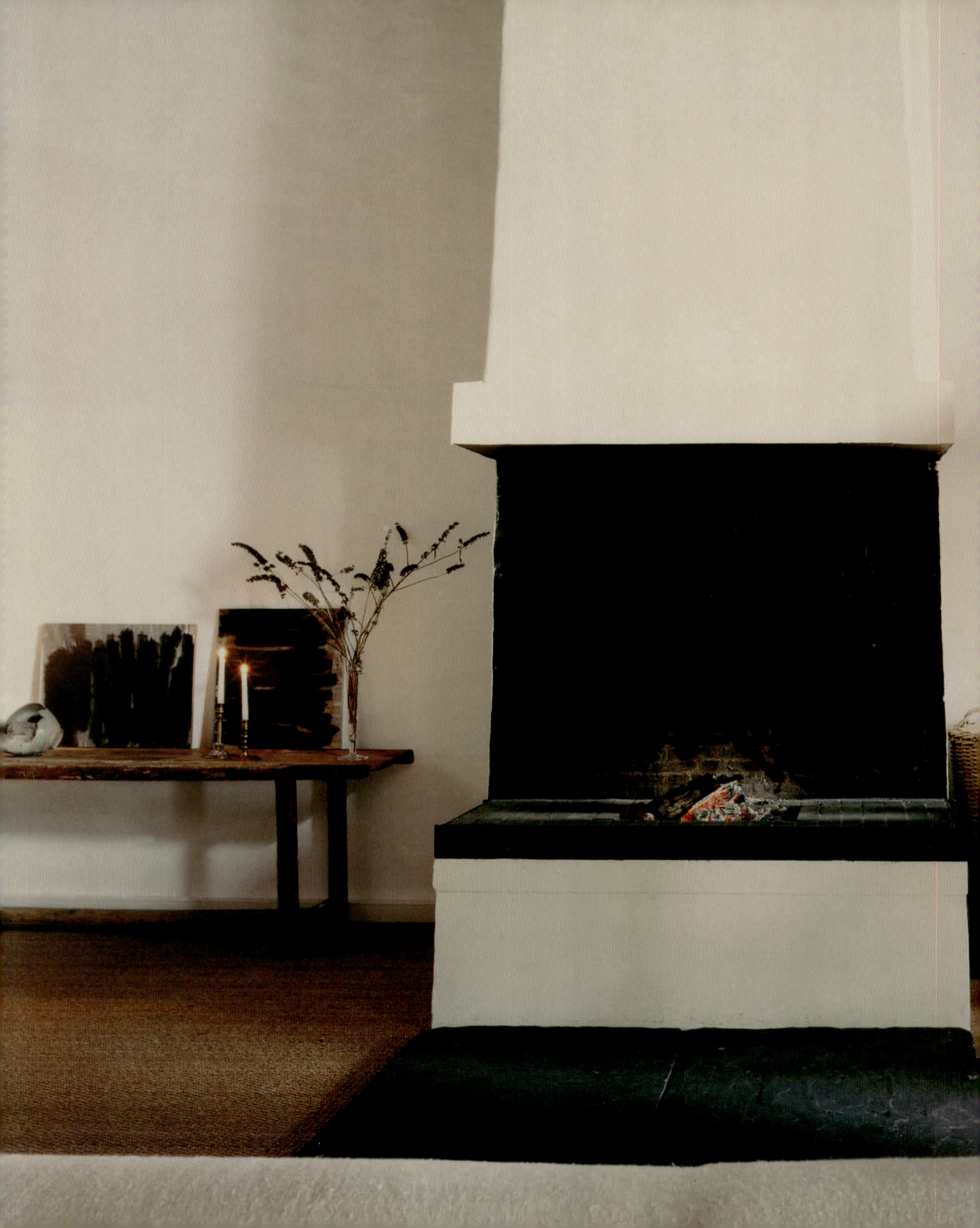

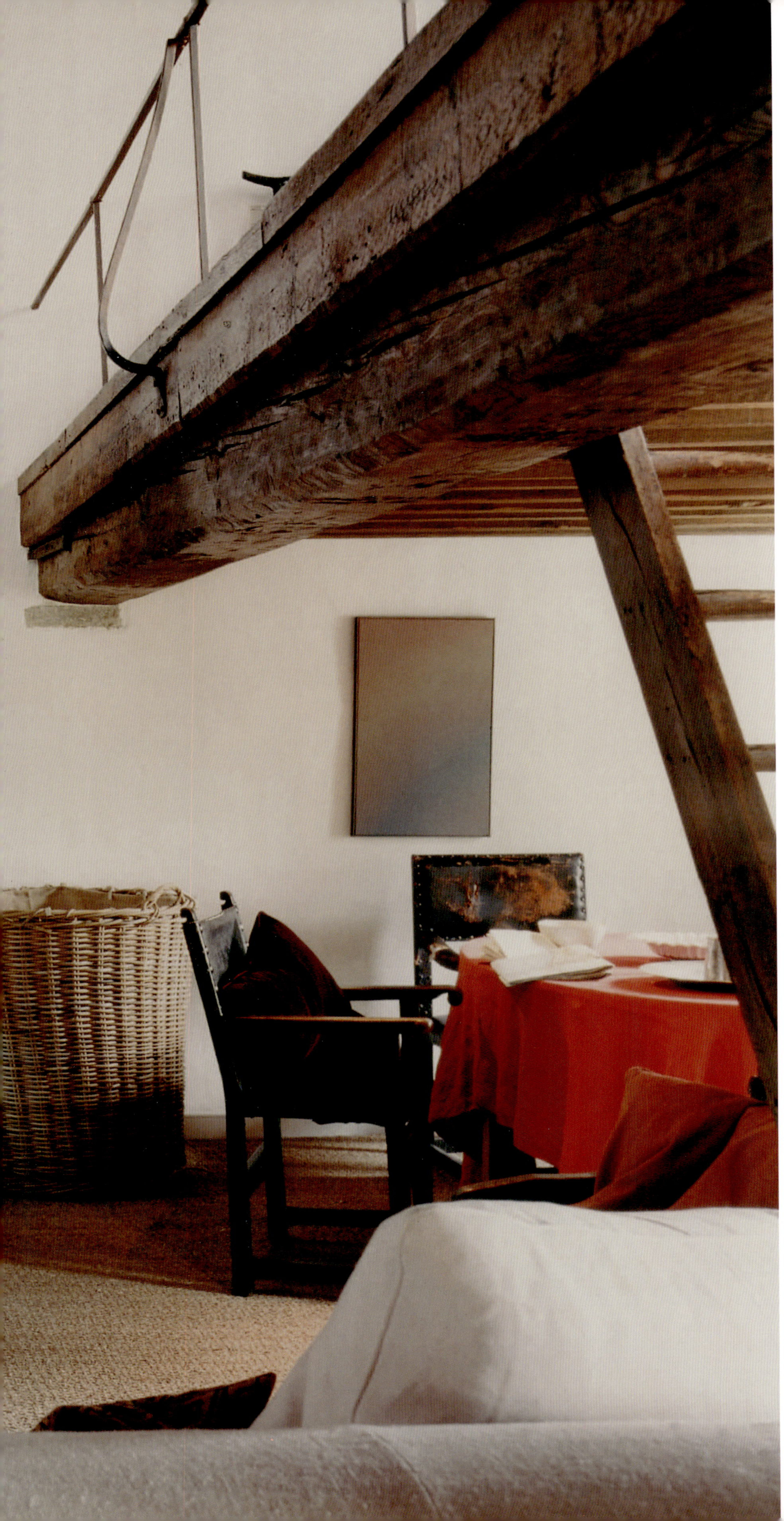

restoration

After I finally determined that my métier lay in buying and selling beautiful things, I decided I wanted to buy more than just furniture and works of art. I also wanted to buy and restore the neglected and unloved sixteenth-century houses in the center of Antwerp, just as my mother had done.

My mother never lived in any of the houses she brought back to life. She always rented them to artists, encouraging them to bring back a better, more useful life to the quarter around the cathedral. But I wanted to live in such a house myself and use it as both my home and my business, so when clients came to find antiques or works of art, they could see exactly how I perceived the essential qualities of the objects and works of art I'd discovered, and how I thought they should be arranged in rooms with other objects. In other words, I wanted to show my clients how they could live with such things themselves.

The neglected area of the Vlaeykensgang was very beautiful, consisting of houses built by rich merchants and aristocrats when Antwerp was at its mercantile peak. And, thanks in part to my mother's efforts, it sheltered the Antwerp avant-garde, which made it interesting to me. I love the area, because it's a wonderful, secret part of the city, all hidden in very tiny corners. In those days, it was extremely jazzy and very interesting and I found it very exciting.

At the beginning, I lived with my parents off and on while I restored the houses one by one. I spent half my time camping out in one or other of the houses I was in the process of restoring. I finally moved out of my parents' house altogether when I was around 23 and met and married May when I was 27.

When I first saw Vlaeykensgang, I fell so much in love with it that I immediately decided I must buy it. First I had to borrow quite a considerable amount of money from my father to buy the entire tiny cobbled street. To restore the houses I had to borrow more from my father—and make enough money letting them and satisfying the growing demands of my increasing circle of clients to pay my father the interest. It was, to say the least, a challenge for a twenty-one-year-old just starting his own business.

Before we were married, May and I restored and decorated a really beautiful house for ourselves. It was a sixteenth-century building, originally used for roasting and grinding coffee, like a little factory. The cellars and the first floor dated to 1557, and it had original beams and chimneys. Opposite, in the Vlaeykensgang, was a large nineteenth-century factory which we turned into a large loft for our own flat. But we spent far too much money on it and a month before it was finished we decided we couldn't afford to live in it, so we used it for selling contemporary Scandinavian and Italian furniture which

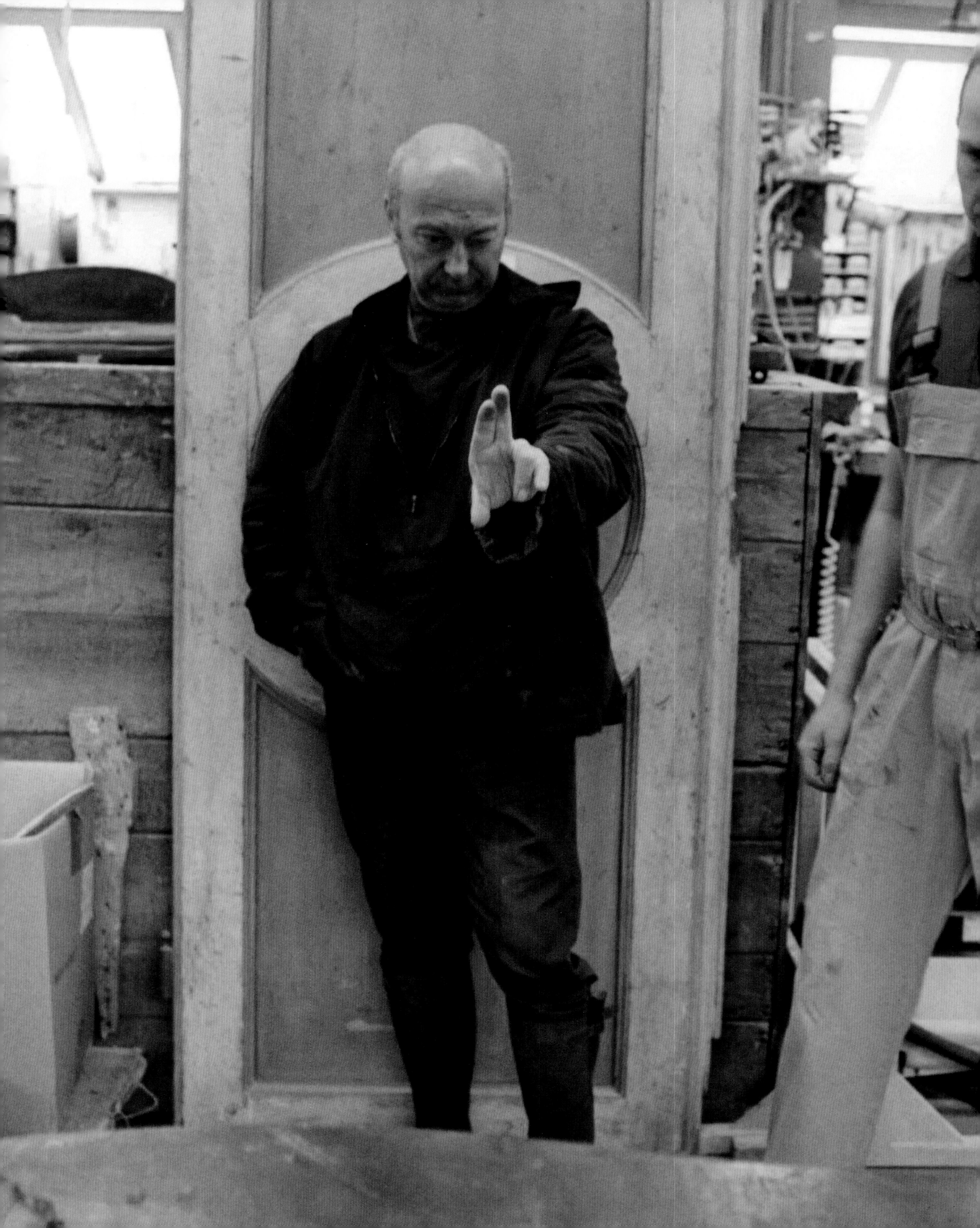

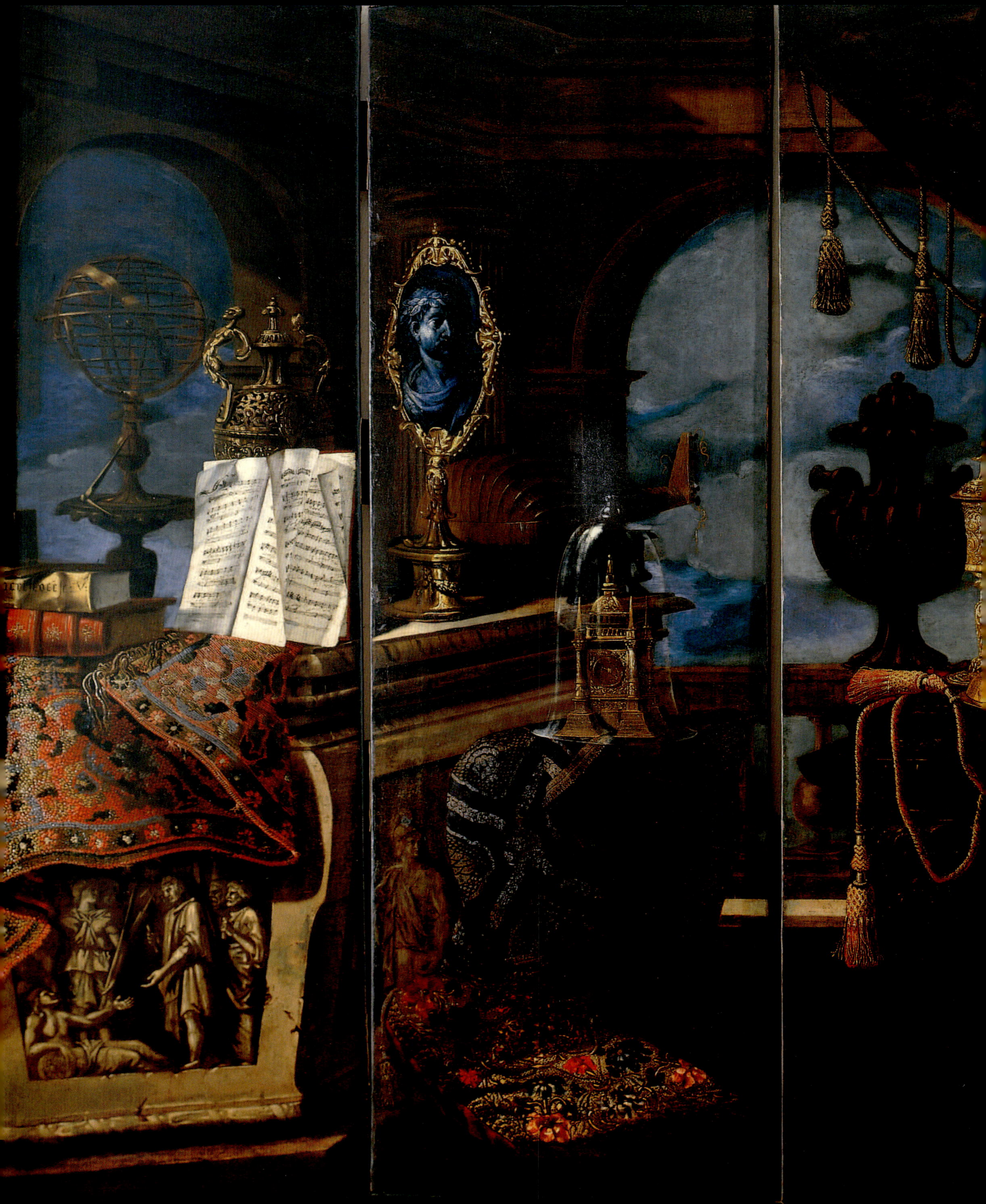

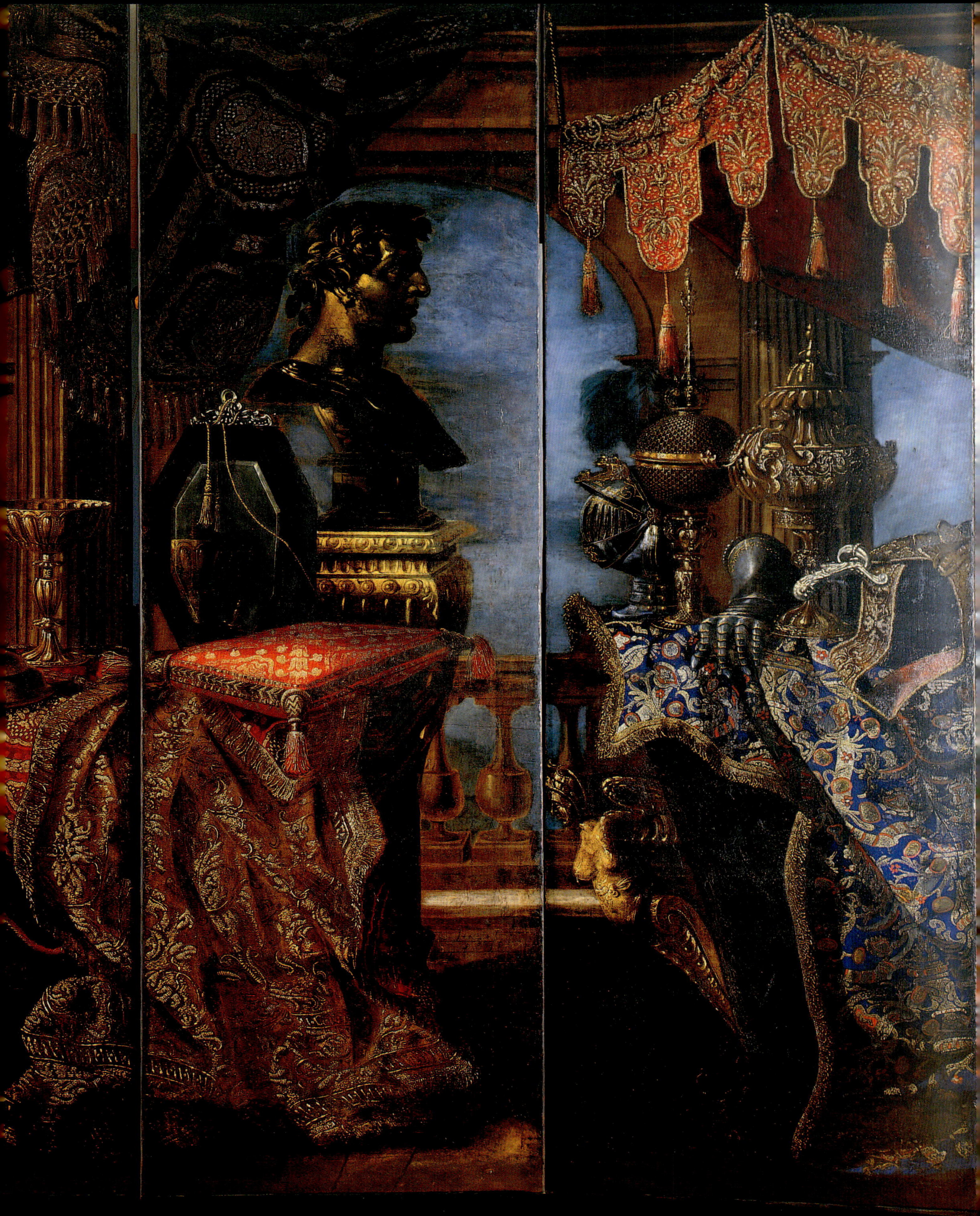

we mixed with antiques. It looked, even then, like a modern loft of today—my son, Boris, lives in it now. We moved into another house on the street, built in 1608 for the Mayor of Antwerp, Nicolas Rockox. It was like a little palace. The year 1608 was an important year in the history of Antwerp for it was when Rubens returned from his sojourn at the court of the Gonzagas. It was really beautiful, with columns and a courtyard, and we lived there for seven years until it became too small for us.

Because the little street was so near the cathedral we could clearly hear the carillons of the famous bells. When we were first married, May and I started to organize bell concert evenings on Monday nights. All the houses were lit only by candlelight and firelight, just as they would have been centuries before. Every Monday more and more people came from all over Belgium, and then Holland, to hear the bells and be transported back for a moment to an older Antwerp. In the end, these bell nights became a victim of their own success. Too many people crowded into the little street and the main square.

These days, the street is very different from the slum my mother discovered. You approach its entrance from the great central square in front of the cathedral. A tiny opening leads into a very narrow cobbled alleyway, with houses in a perfect state of repair, looking much as they would have 500 years ago, leaning over toward each other and almost obscuring the sky. Through tiny gateways can be glimpsed even smaller courtyards full of potted plants. You are walking through the world that Vermeer and de Hooch painted. A narrow, private, enclosed world of prosperous merchants and their richly dressed wives, playing their musical instruments in rooms painted in pale washed colors, furnished with plain, beautifully carved furniture standing on black and white tiled floors, the walls hung with textiles or covered in gilded and stamped leather, the ceilings of heavy oak beams, the whole place shining with cleanliness. So the street was gradually reborn and a new generation of Antwerp citizens moved in, becoming an important factor in the continuing regeneration of the city center.

As my business as a dealer in rare objects and in engineering their new spaces became more and more successful, it spilled out beyond my own house into the neighboring houses. I used some of them to display and store furniture, pictures, and objects; others as workshops. Because the narrow little street had become famous through the bell nights, more and more people wanted to live there and the houses became potentially very valuable—far too valuable to use as storerooms.

When clients came to buy from me at home in Vlaeykensgang and saw how I had restored and furnished my house and the way May and I lived in it, they began to ask me to do the same for them. That's how I started not only selling my clients their furniture, pictures, and works of art, but also designing the environment in which they would both be seen to their best advantage and lived with most comfortably. It's what we call *gezelligheid* in Flemish, which translated means "warm and charming."

Almost by accident, I became an advisor on every aspect of the interior world, from architecture and color, to the minutest domestic detail. "Please come to my house," my clients would say, "and tell me where should I put this piece of furniture, or this picture," and this led them to ask me how they should decorate their rooms.

The idea of "decoration" I developed in those early days—which I still passionately believe in now—is

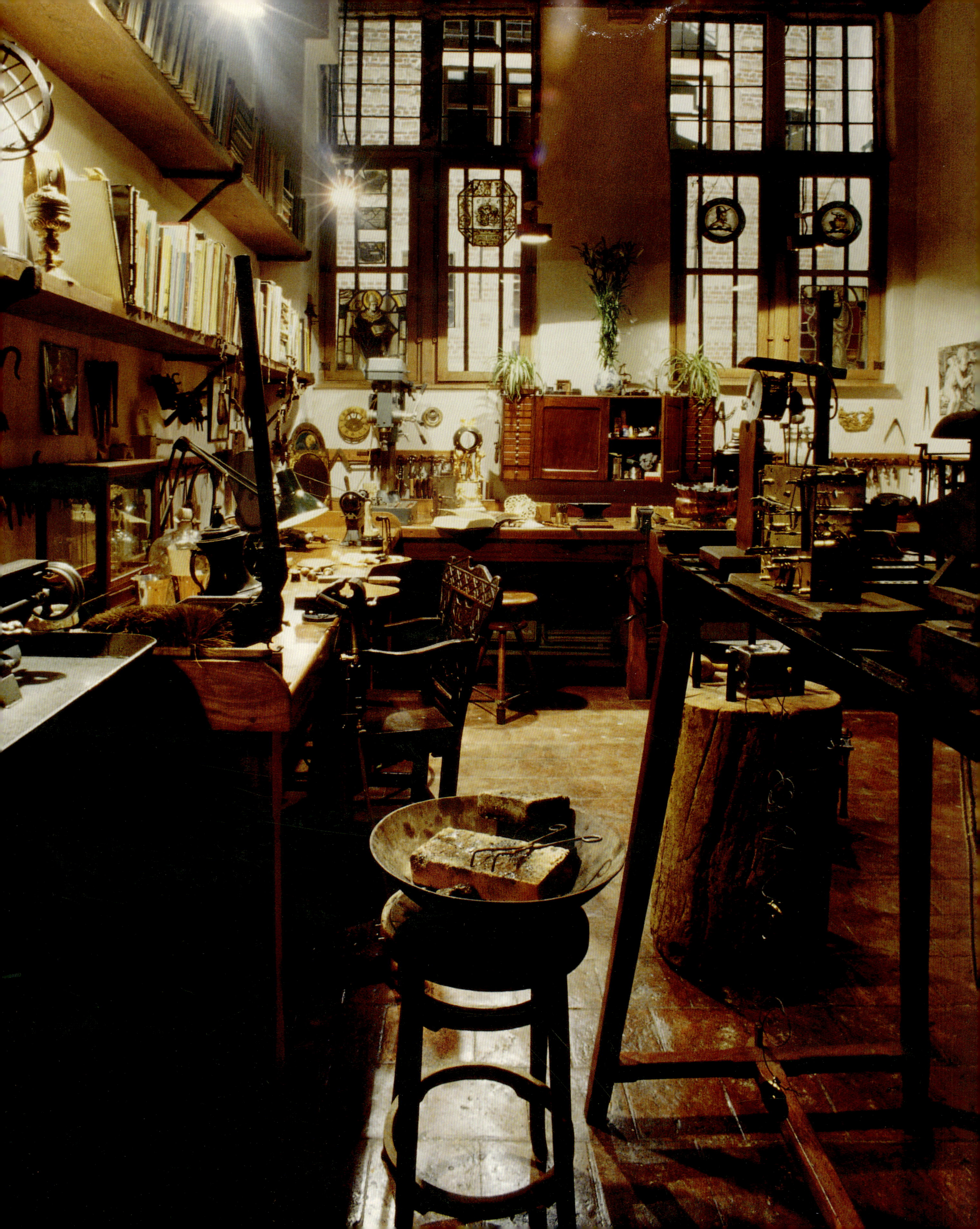

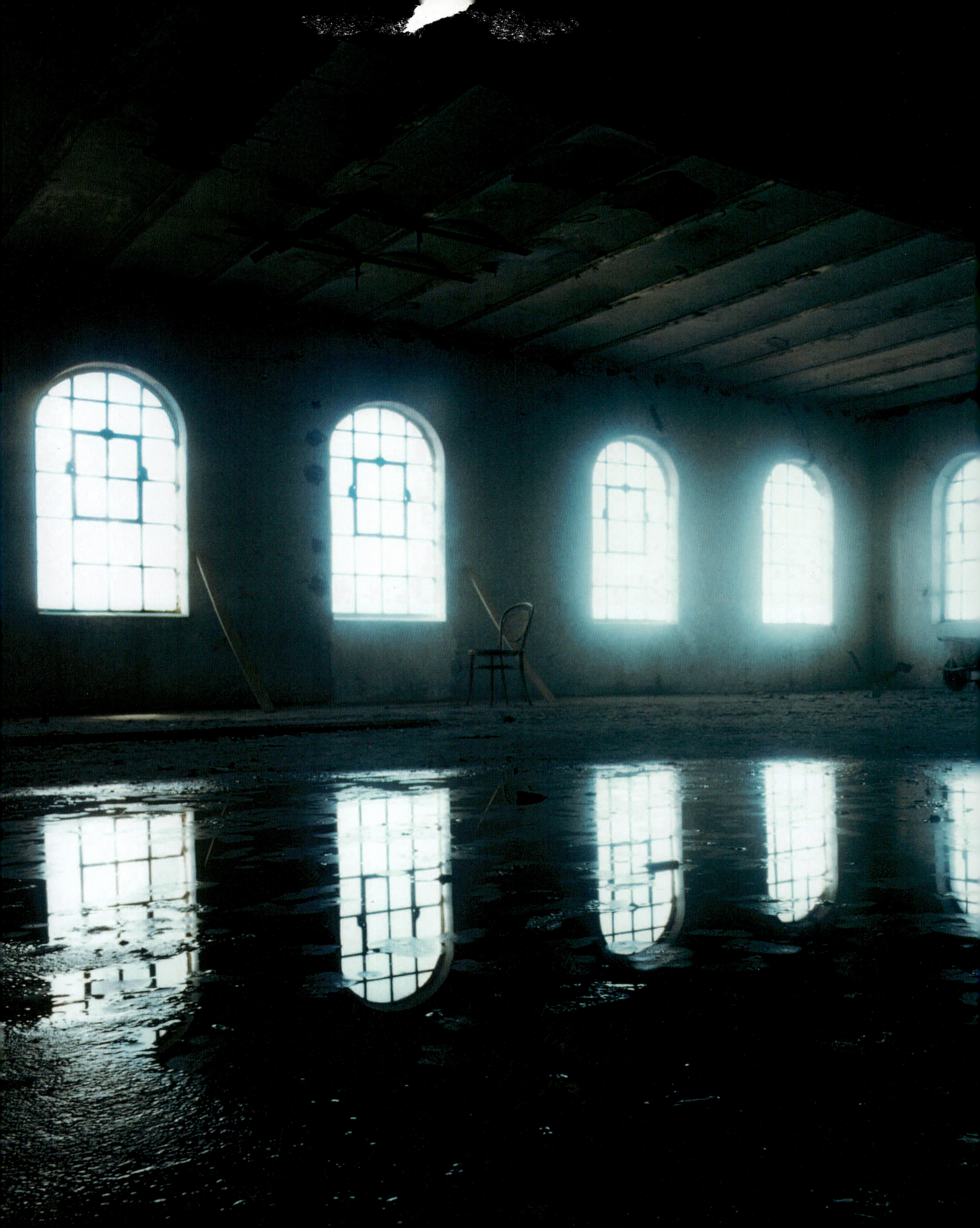

"non-decoration." I love architecture and I love works of art of all periods, everything that is real and of real worth. As far as possible I try to avoid anything that looks "decorated." I try to find a harmony between people, furniture, architecture, and works of art, which leads to a comfortable, intelligent, and inspirational lifestyle. This, in a sense, becomes a portrait of the owners. When their house is finished my clients should feel not as if it had been decorated recently, but as if they had always lived that way.

Nowadays, I personally supervise between twelve and twenty major decorative and furnishing commissions a year. About thirty smaller projects are undertaken by the business, which employs about 100 people, including six architects. I am always very discreet about the identity of my clients, but they range from royalty to pop stars, museums, industrialists, bankers, artists, musicians, and collectors. I have rearranged palaces, castles, country houses, and even contemporary apartments.

I have also designed furniture and accessories that I cannot find in the forays I make into the past. My company makes very comfortable chairs and sofas, sofa tables, lamps, and silver beakers. The spare, elegant forms of this furniture are always inspired by Egypt, China, Ancient Greece, even primitive *arte povera* made by shepherds or monks living their lonely lives in the mountains, who made the purest, most minimal items, to last for hundreds of years. Over the years I have collected a considerable amount of this primitive work for myself because I find the respect its makers had for simple materials and the fact that these artifacts have survived for hundreds of years harmonious with my aesthetics.

exhibitions

During the 1970s, as my circle of clients widened through Belgium and into Northern Europe, I made more and more buying trips to England where great discoveries could still be made. From Brighton to Scotland, I was buying great treasures all the time. It was a very exciting period.

I bought a beautiful twelfth-century Lohan Japanese head, for instance, which is now in my library. I look upon this portrait head as though the man it depicts were my spiritual master. I was also excited about a seventeenth-century iron chest, and a beautiful sixteenth-century Venetian *terra ferma cassone* with a painted interior, which was in the first gothic room I lived in, built circa 1500. The room had a big fireplace, and a beautiful original floor and ceiling—I kept my mattress in the chest during the day. That chest! It was like my bedroom.

Sadly there are far fewer discoveries to be made these days. Twenty years ago, when I bought a whole collection there was always one great piece that paid for everything else. But all that is finished now and it's rare to be able to show a whole roomful of unique, historical, and exceptional pieces as I used to do when I first started to move toward becoming international via exhibiting at antique fairs.

As the 1970s and '80s continued, international antique fairs like the Paris Biennale and Maastricht—now the most important—provided a valuable international shop window for antique dealers. When I started exhibiting I didn't follow the accepted practice of arranging furniture as if it was in a shop. I was the first to arrange it in room sets. I wanted to lead the visitor to appreciate each individual work of art afresh, through visual relationships and, in some cases, clashes. For instance, making the absolute simplicity of an archaic Chinese bronze seem even more perfect by juxtaposing it with an elaborate eighteenth-century rock-crystal chandelier from the ballroom of a European palace.

Our first fair was in Antwerp, quite early in my career. I remember showing a fabulous marine picture by Beerstraeten. It was really beautiful. In those days (the end of the 1970s) I sold it for $110,000. It would be worth millions today. Soon after, we exhibited at the first Maastricht Fair. We had a huge stand, over twenty meters wide, and I painted it all in black. I had really wonderful things, including a baroque screen, signed and dated 1650. We sold a wonderful Daniel Marot table to the Museum Het Loo. I had unbelievable silver, too.

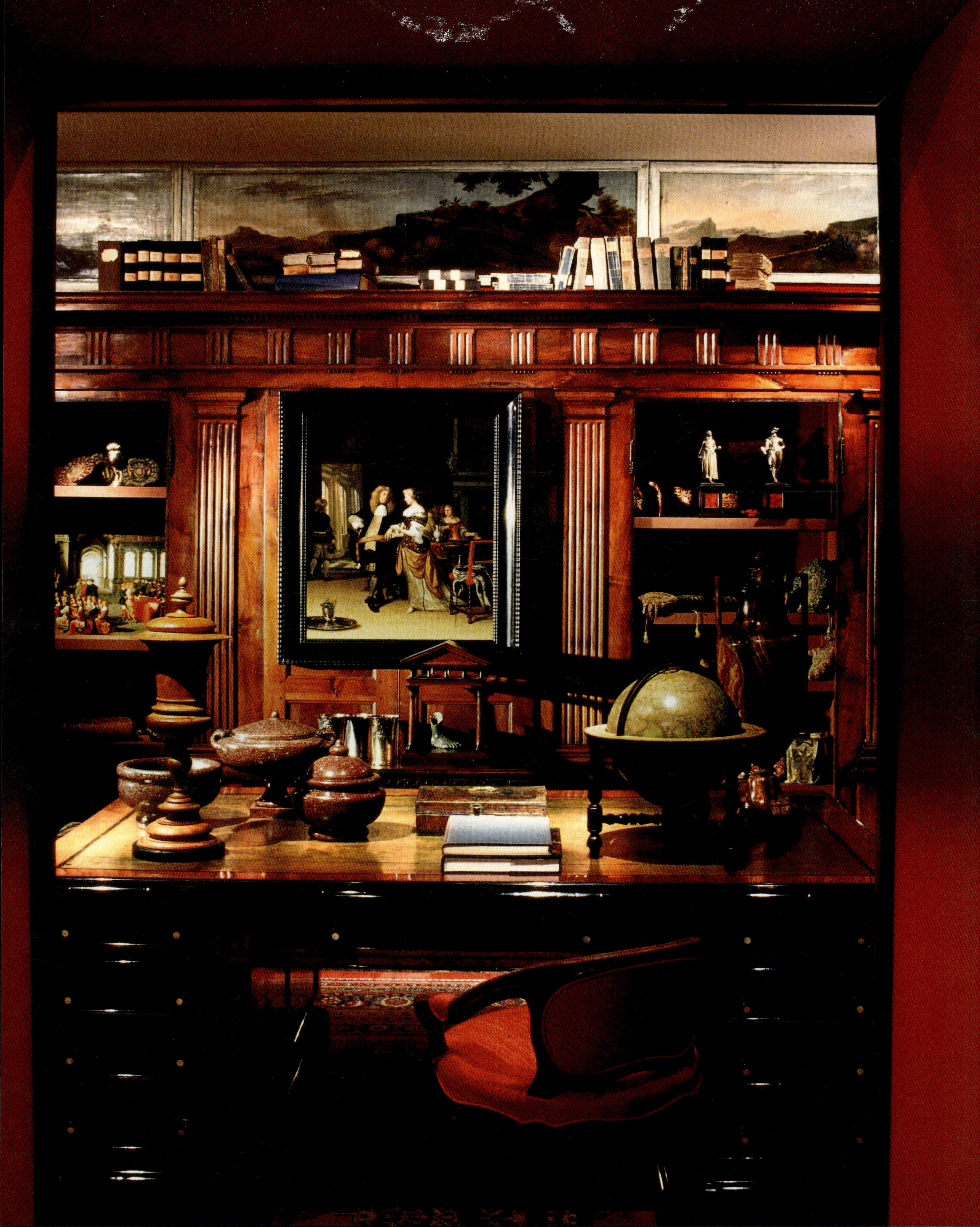

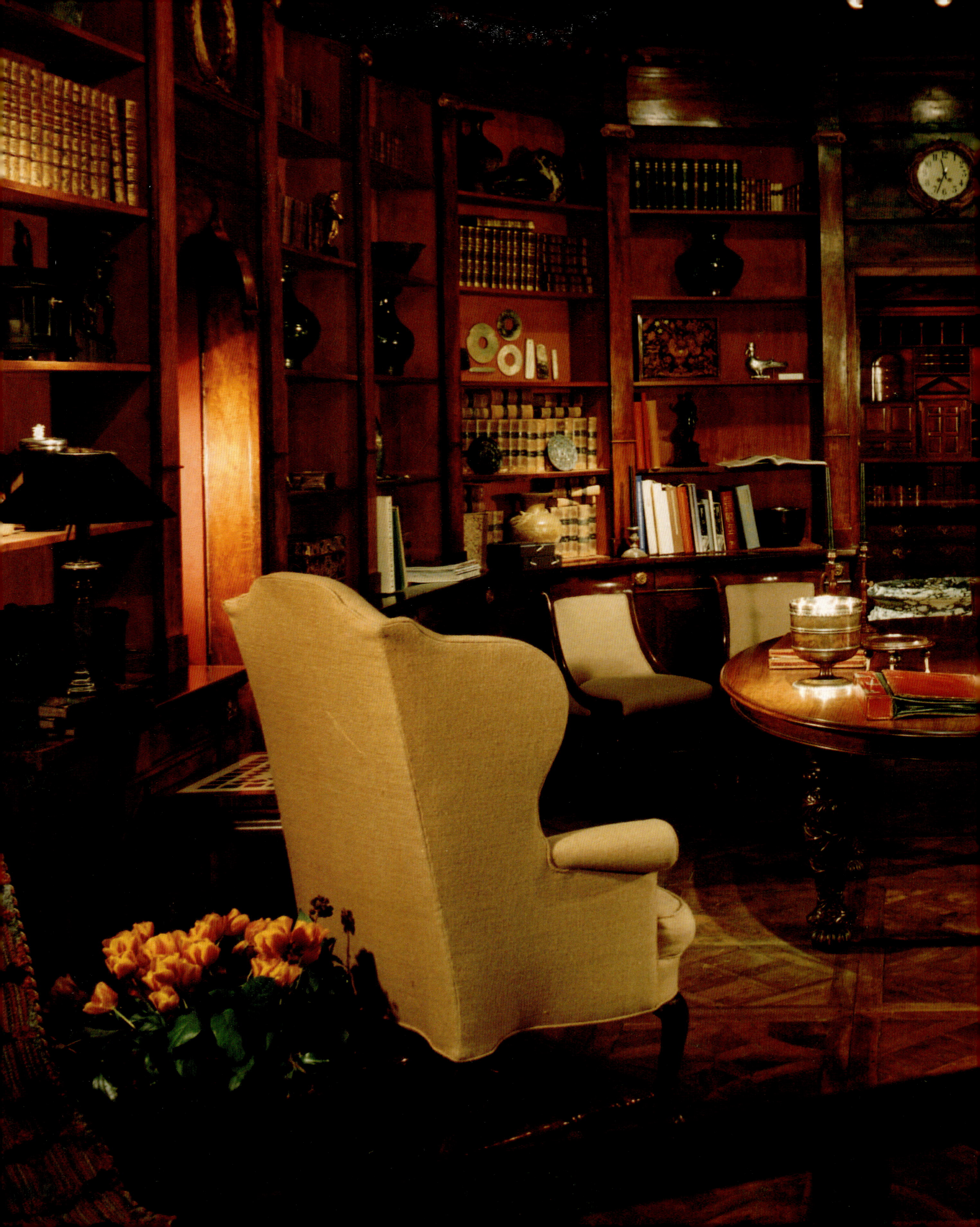

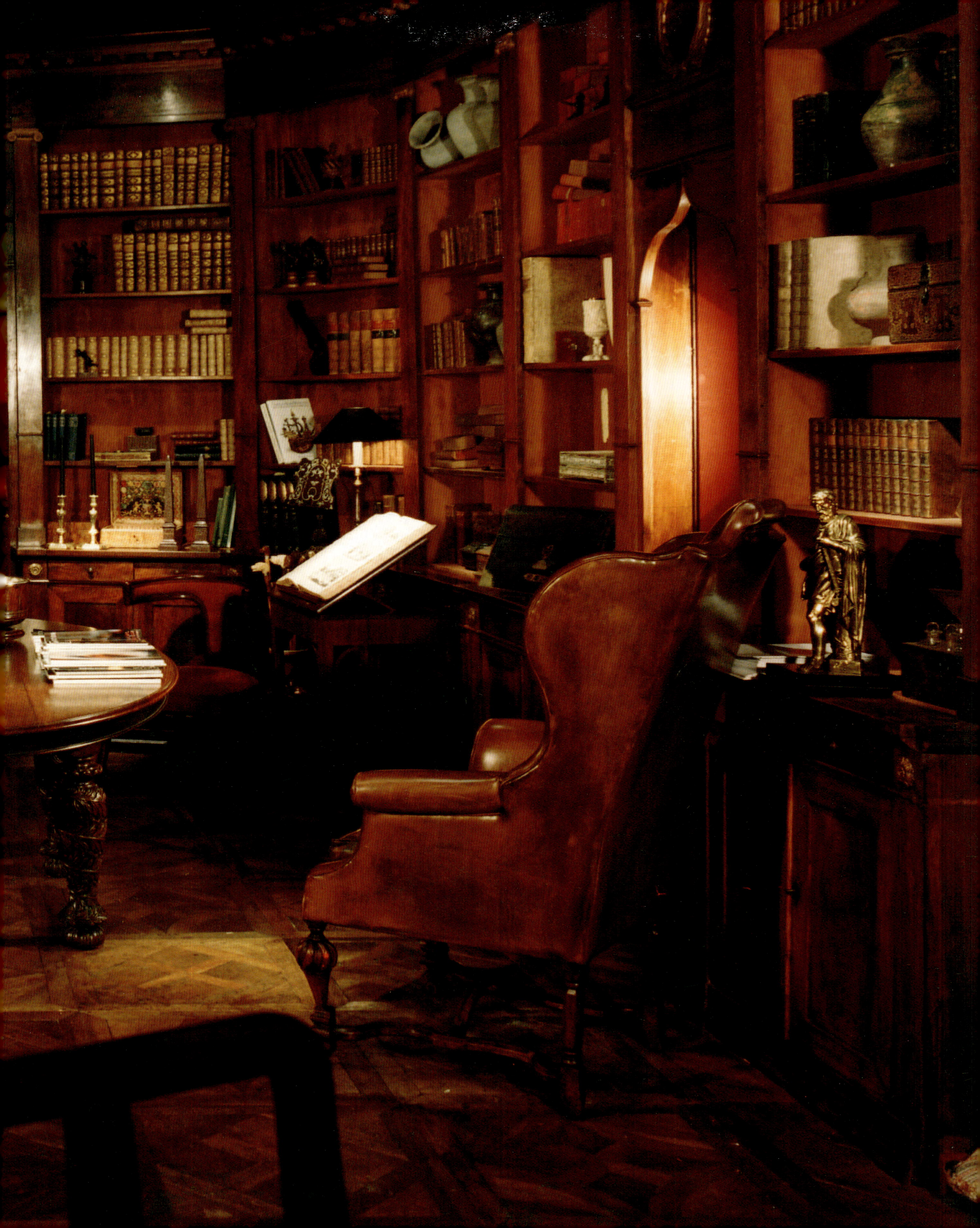

I designed the booth as three distinct rooms. The first was a dining room with a table set with a rare Delft dinner service, the walls were hung with six eighteenth-century mirrors and a beautiful eighteenth-century chandelier hung from the ceiling. Next was a large baroque room, with the 1650 baroque screen mixed with modern pieces in the way I like. I love the baroque and baroque music, especially by Bach. The third room was very meditative and calm, with a very simple table, one Tang vase and a sixteenth-century Japanese Zen screen.

These three rooms were emblematic of the continuing themes in my life. I love good food and therefore dining rooms. I love the baroque, because it is part of the fabric and history of my own life. And I love the spiritual life of great purity. These three themes make of me one whole person.

I was first asked to take part in the Biennale in Paris when I was thirty-four, in 1982. It could well have been a disaster. We were given a huge amount of space at the Grand Palais, including the staircase, and I worked extremely hard for months to gather the most beautiful things I could find. The idea was to recreate a seventeenth-century *cabinet de curiosités*.

When we arrived at the Grand Palais to set up, all the French dealers were building the most beautiful architectural booths. I saw all the skeletons of big arcades and huge rooms being constructed, and it all looked really fantastic—so pure. But one dealer was only doing Empire, another eighteenth-century furniture, and I felt terrified that no one in Paris would understand my taste. I felt so provincial—a little boy from Antwerp. I was so tired of trying so hard, I was almost sick of the whole thing. I went outside and just dropped down onto the first lawn I came to and slept for two hours.

Refreshed, I returned to the exhibition hall and found that the pure architecture of the other stands had, in my absence, been obscured by elaborate silk damask hangings and fussy wallpapers. The floors were being laid with faux marble and the pure proportions of the original constructions were being spoilt. I thought that hiding all this purity and the beautiful proportions with decorative details was a shame—and it really didn't work.

To their astonishment, I told my staff to rip out even the small amount of décor we had planned. I said, "Take it all out, we are going to show the Grand Palais itself." So we made the booth as empty as a big industrial loft, even down to leaving the Grand Palais' concrete floor and iron beams exposed. I kept the staircase like a cabinet, very rich and opulent, but in the big loft we mixed everything together.

Visitors were amazed at this huge space and its extraordinary cornucopia of objects from every period and culture all mixed together. A huge eighteenth-century rock-crystal chandelier hanging down was almost touching a large table, which was covered with an almost unbelievable seventeenth-century *toile de Lucca* tablecloth completely covered with embroidery, and heaped with silver. A beautiful French console of great rarity—made originally for Versailles—had come into my possession from a great English family collection. A pair of extraordinary black Sung vases, and a set of sixteenth-century Venetian chairs stood on seventeenth-century silk carpets. A *pietra dura* chest with rock-crystal columns and paintings on the doors of Eleanora Gonzaga and the Emperor Ferdinand II of Austria that was made for their marriage was truly magnificent. A fabulous renaissance Antwerp cupboard went to the Getty Museum. There were huge silver-gilt jugs which had belonged to Charles II and tooled leather walls that were bought by Rudolf Nureyev, a very faithful client, for the music room of his apartment in New York.

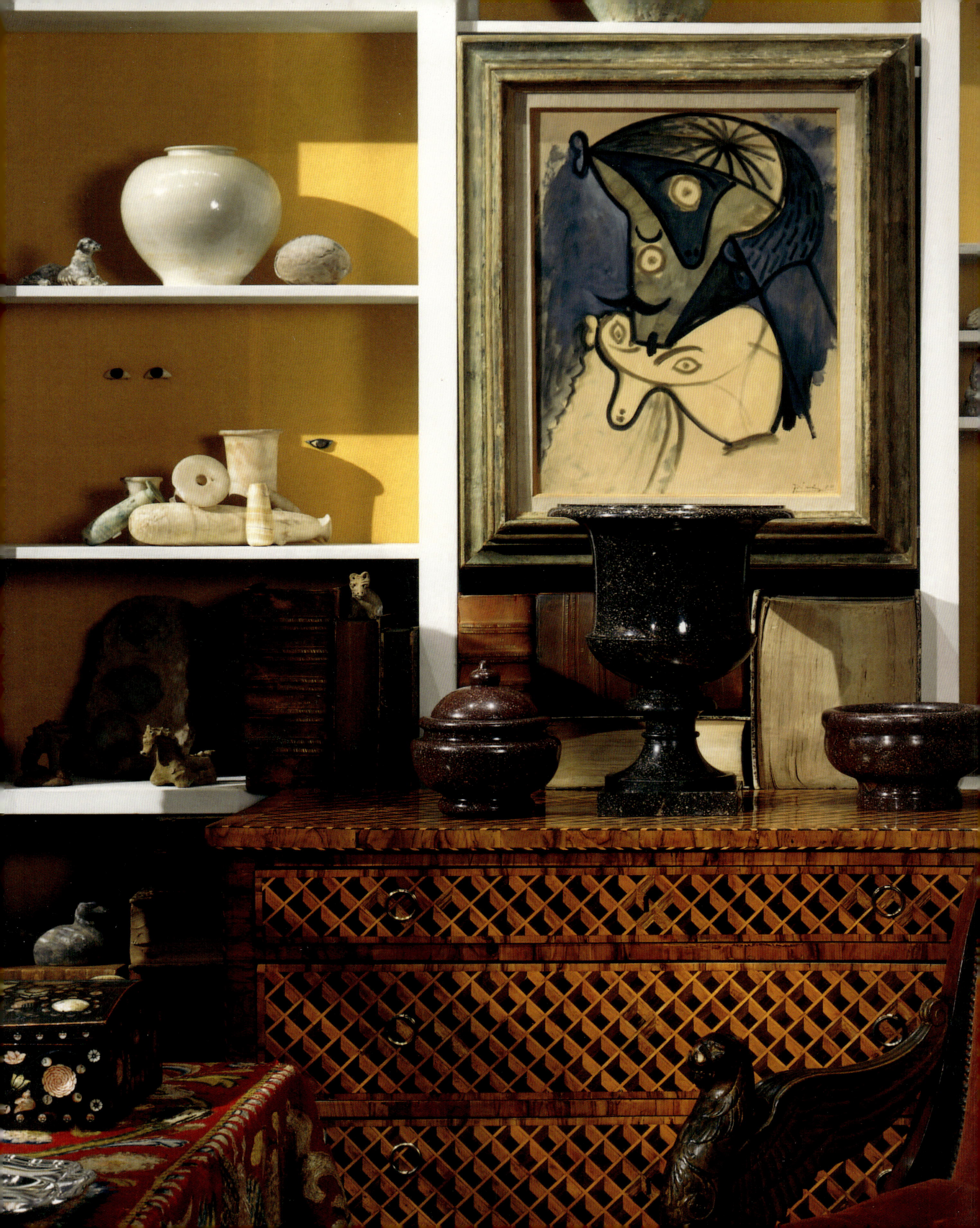

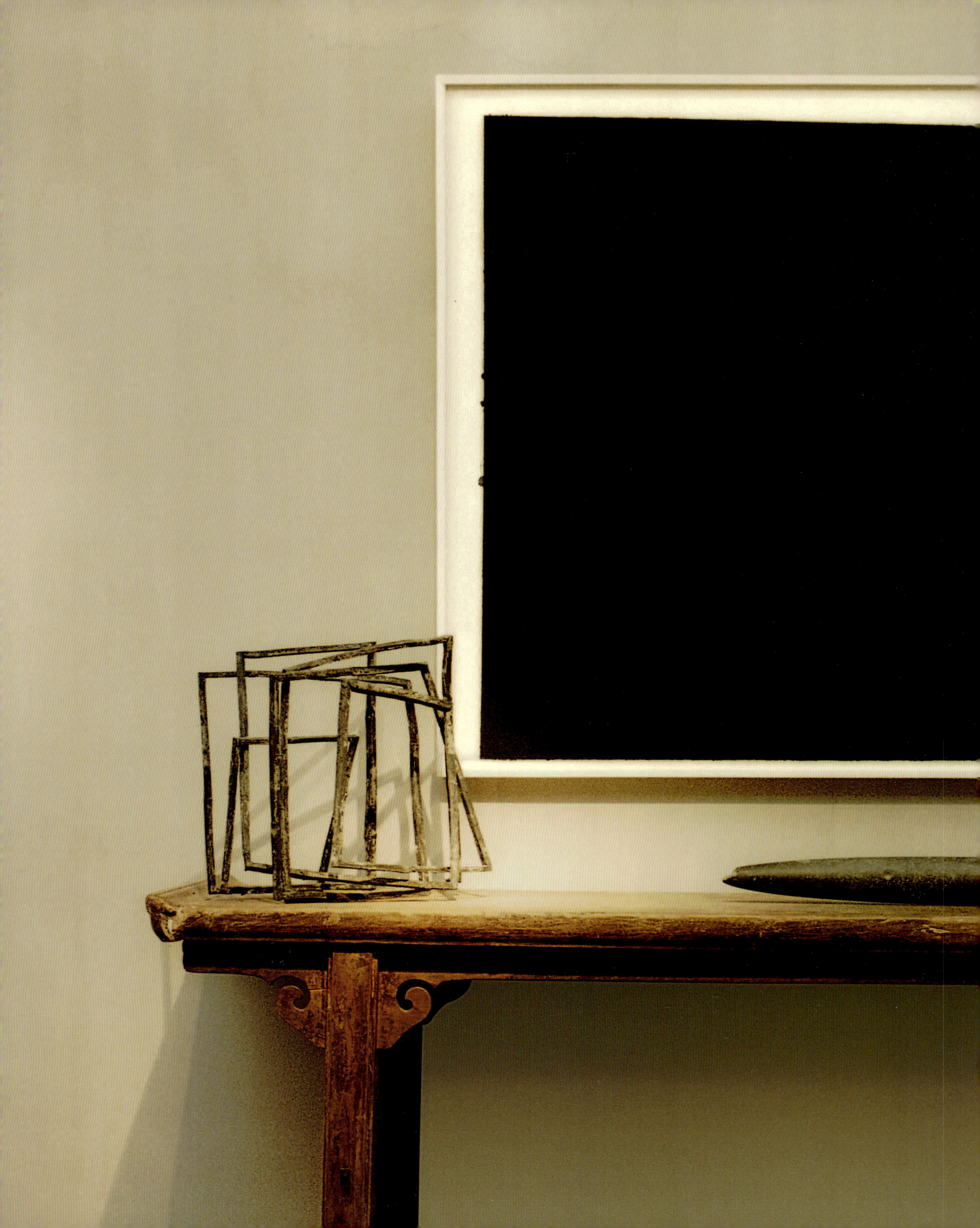

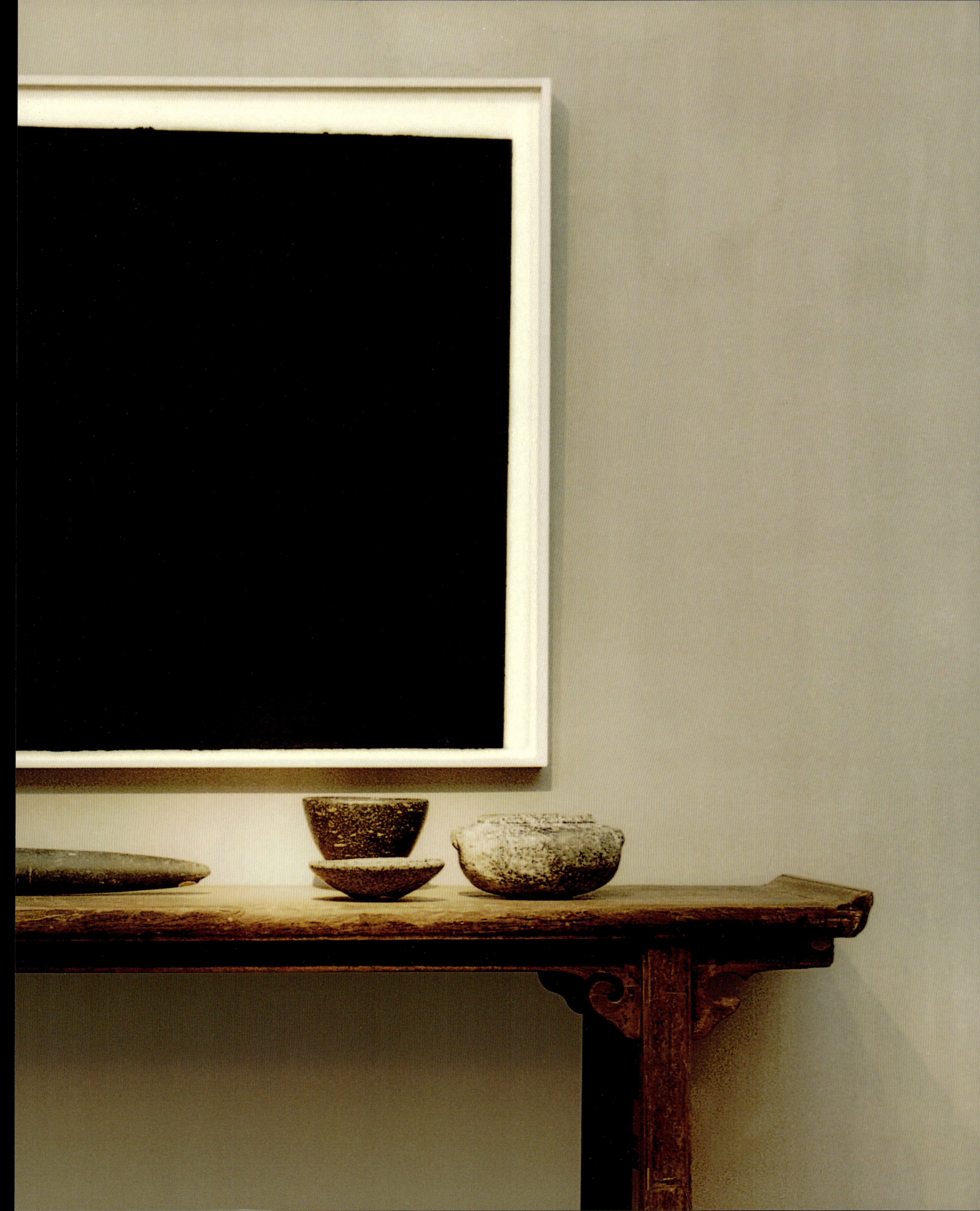

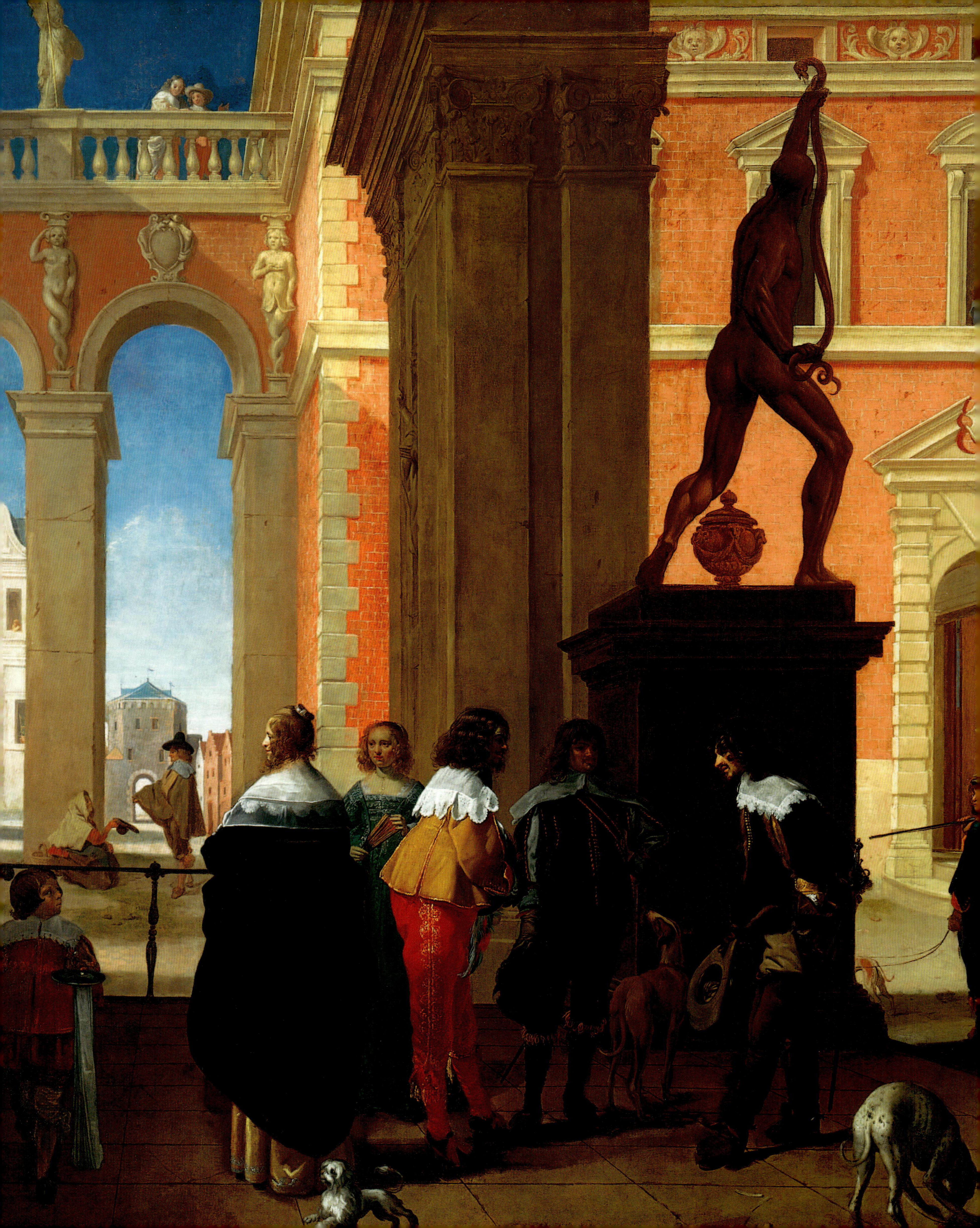

Hubert de Givenchy, the couturier and noted collector of eighteenth-century French furniture, became a client. Leading decorators from all over flocked to this revolutionary booth and its virtually unknown creator. My first Biennale exhibition made both my name and my minimalist antiquarian look internationally known.

We followed up this *succès d'estime* at the next Biennale two years later with something very different. The Hatcher Collection of Chinese porcelain had been salvaged from a shipwreck. It was all blue and white Ming, which I piled up in a huge booth. There were literally thousands of pieces of Ming. It was absolutely unbelievable—I have never seen such queues in my life. The very first piece Hatcher had brought to the surface was a porcelain garden seat which I had in my booth at the fair. When I heard that it was the first piece to surface, I decided to keep it for my own collection.

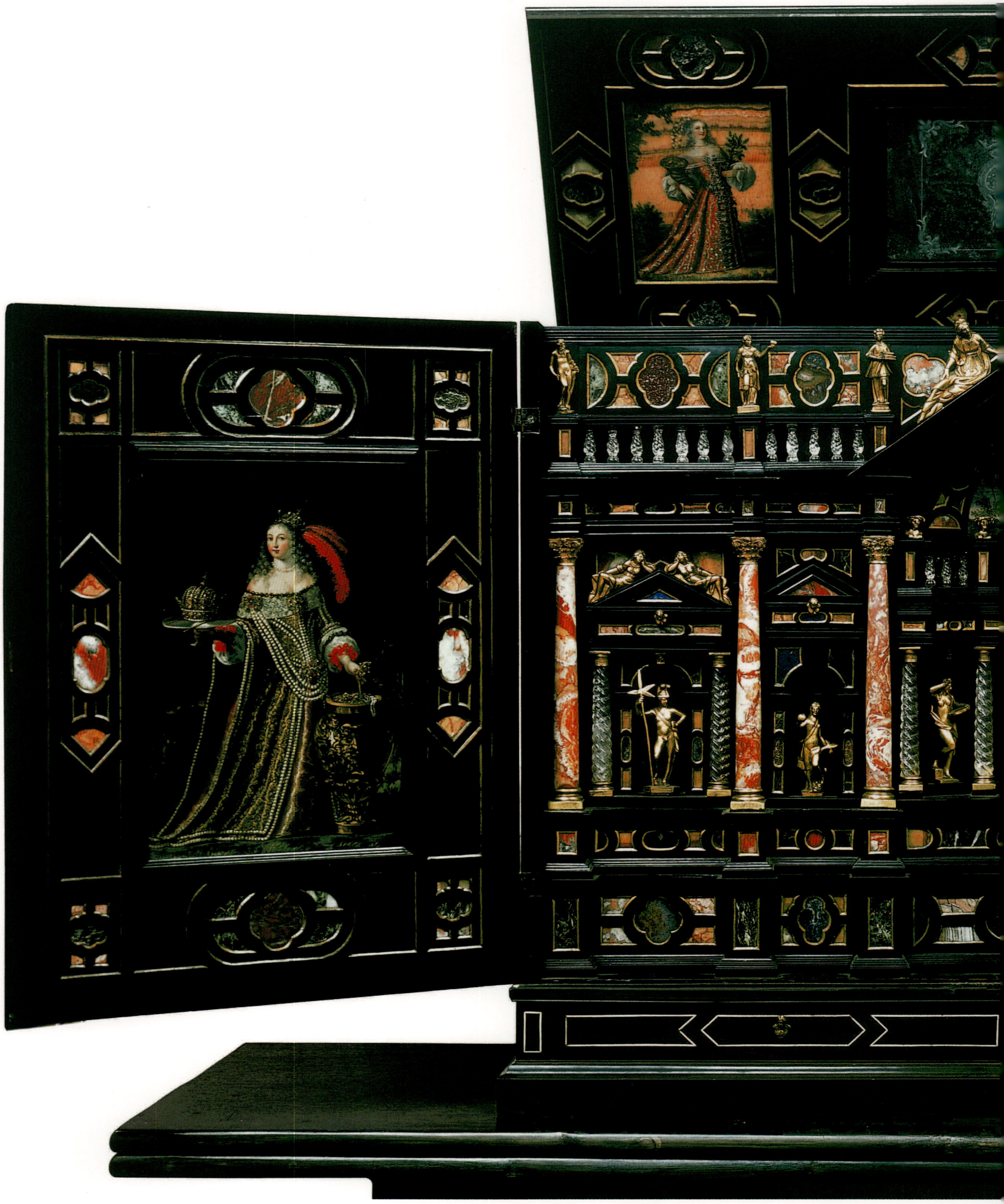

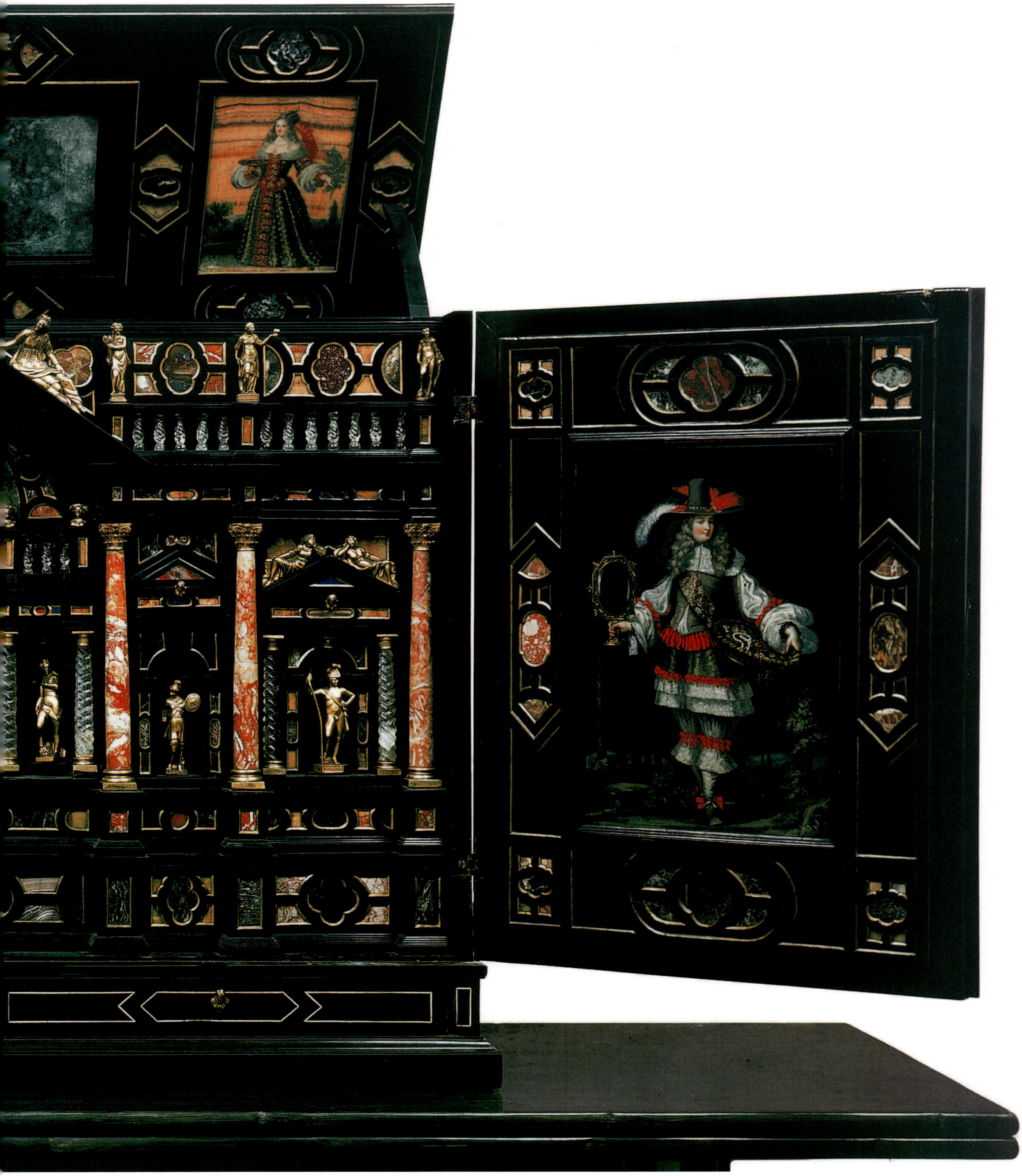

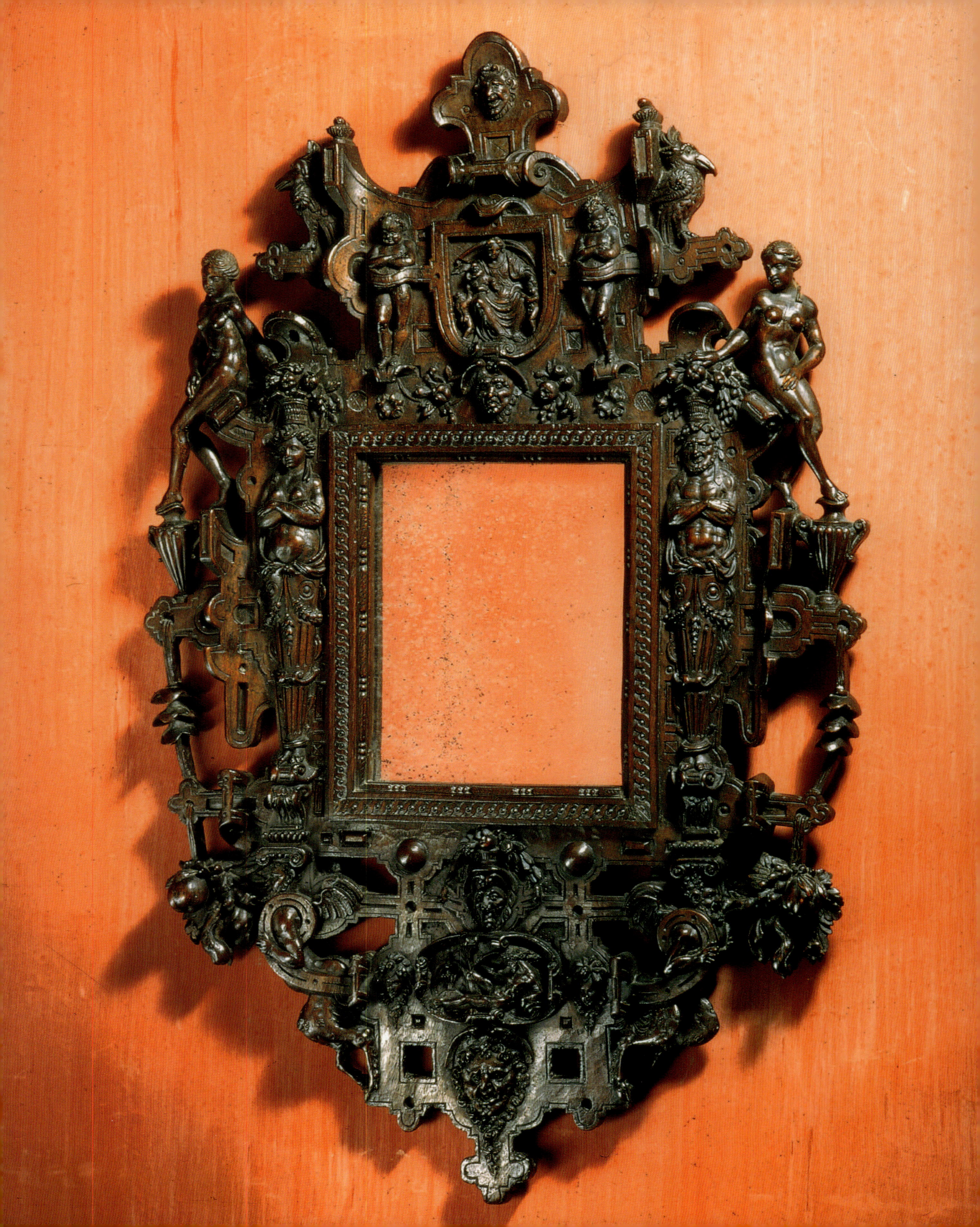

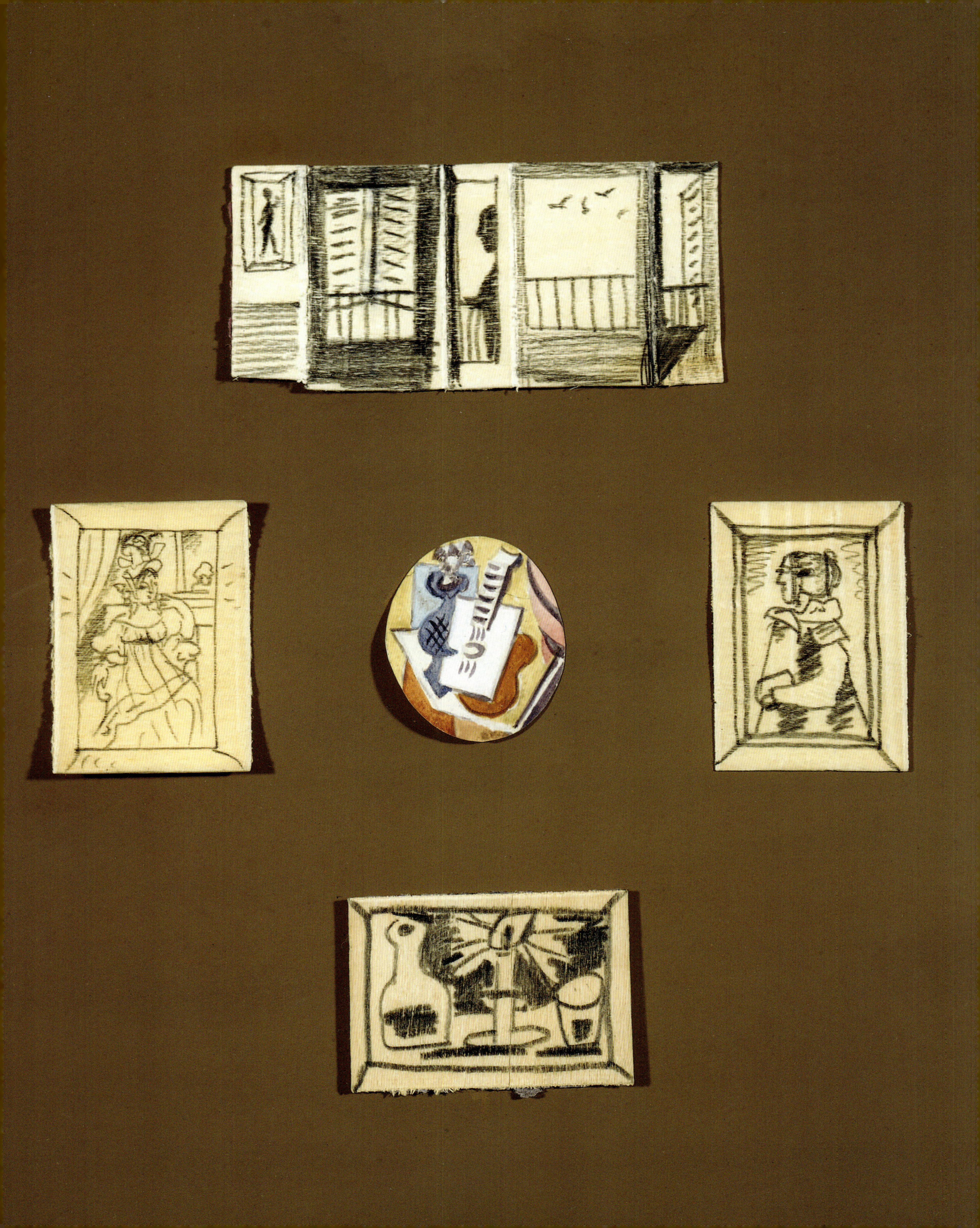

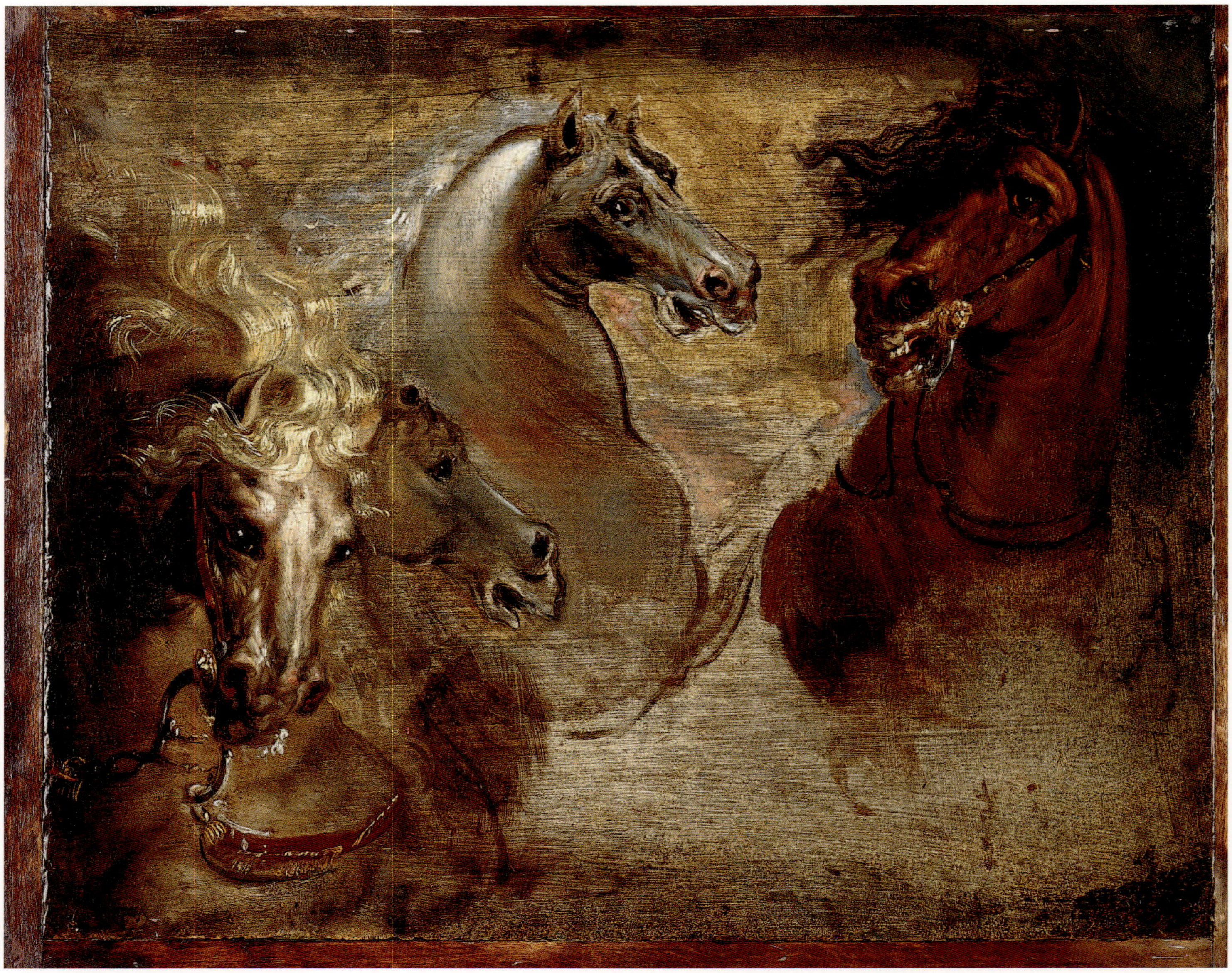

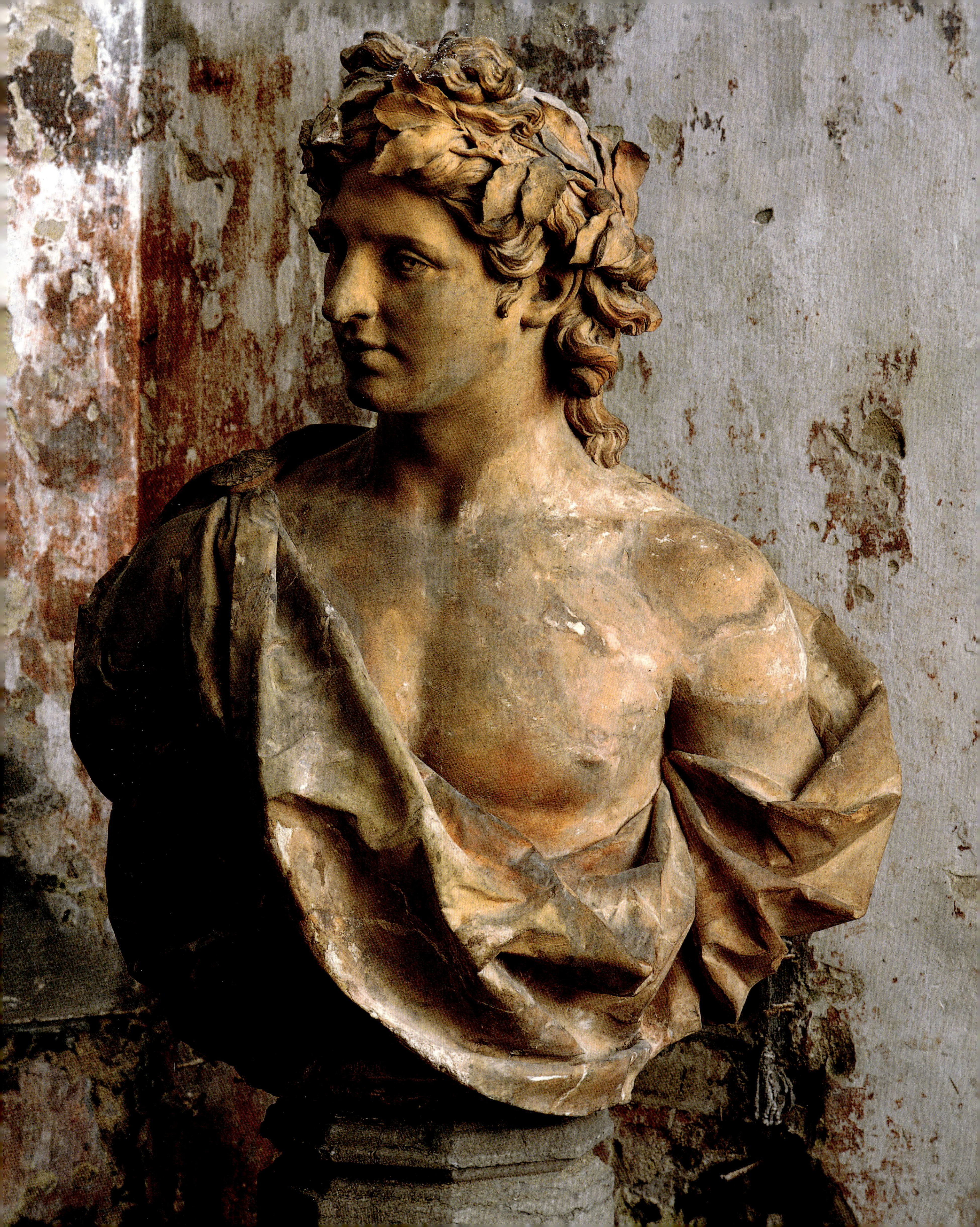

castle

By the mid-1980s, my business life had outgrown the Vlaeykensgang. So I had to find somewhere to live and work which was both larger and a great deal cheaper.

This was a time when I was buying very big collections—often the entire contents of a manor or chateau in France, Italy, or Belgium, plus the finds from my protracted buying trips throughout England—and shipping them back to the houses in the Vlaeykensgang. I've never been frightened of furniture on the very grand scale and am also fond of very large tapestries and pictures, and these were the years when I was discovering just such large-scale pieces. The need to display them in the right amount and proportion of space became an increasingly urgent problem. To do them justice large rooms were required and many more of them than the houses in the Vlaeykensgang could offer.

Although I knew of the Castle of 's-Gravenwezel it had never occurred to me that it might be for sale. It was a sleeping beauty of a castle, twenty minutes from the center of Antwerp, that had been in the same aristocratic Belgian family since 1728.

I heard the castle had been put up for sale by the forty-two heirs to the estate. We were living quite close by at the time and one Sunday morning I decided just to go and see the castle. On the way there I said to myself, "No, don't go. Don't be stupid. You don't need to live in a castle." As I turned back, I collided with another car. My car turned over but I didn't even have a scratch on me. I had a very strong feeling at that moment, as though fate were telling me to go to the castle. So when the police brought me home, I said to May, "We've got to go to the castle and see it." And when we stood on the bridge over the moat and gazed at it, we turned to each other and I said, "There's no choice." Just then the gardener came along and when we told him we were interested in buying the castle he said, "Sorry, it has just been sold."

Desperately trying to find out who'd bought it, I discovered that a Dutch couple had taken a two-month option to buy. The next week, an hour or so before a four o'clock meeting we'd arranged with the sellers, the Dutch couple rang my bell in the Vlaeykensgang and asked me to furnish and arrange for them a triplex apartment they had just bought in a service block. "But, I asked, weren't you also interested in an historical building?" They told me their children were against the idea. I went right off to the four o'clock meeting and found out that the option was still in place. So I waited two months, until it expired, without even telling my mother that we were interested, so that no one would find out.

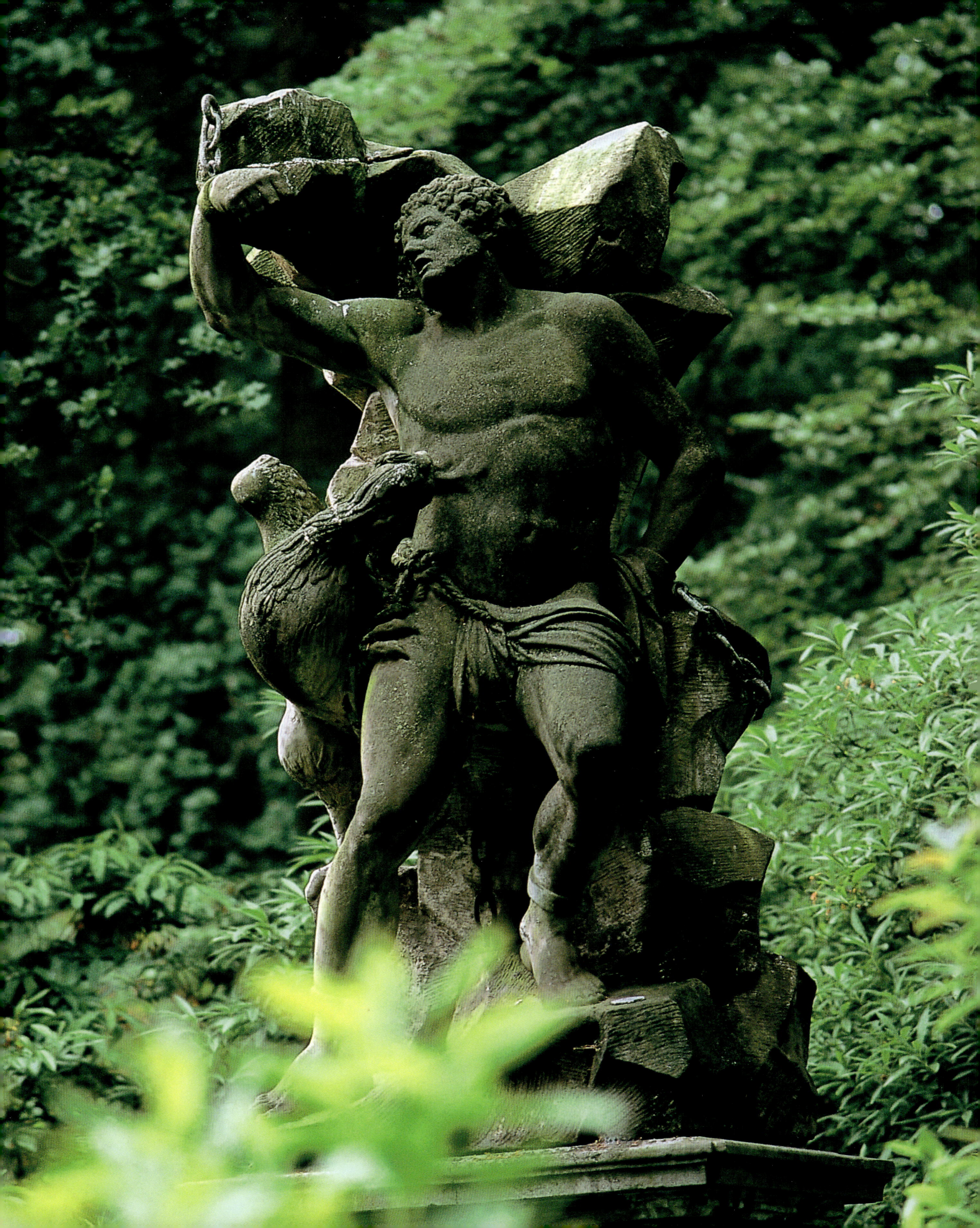

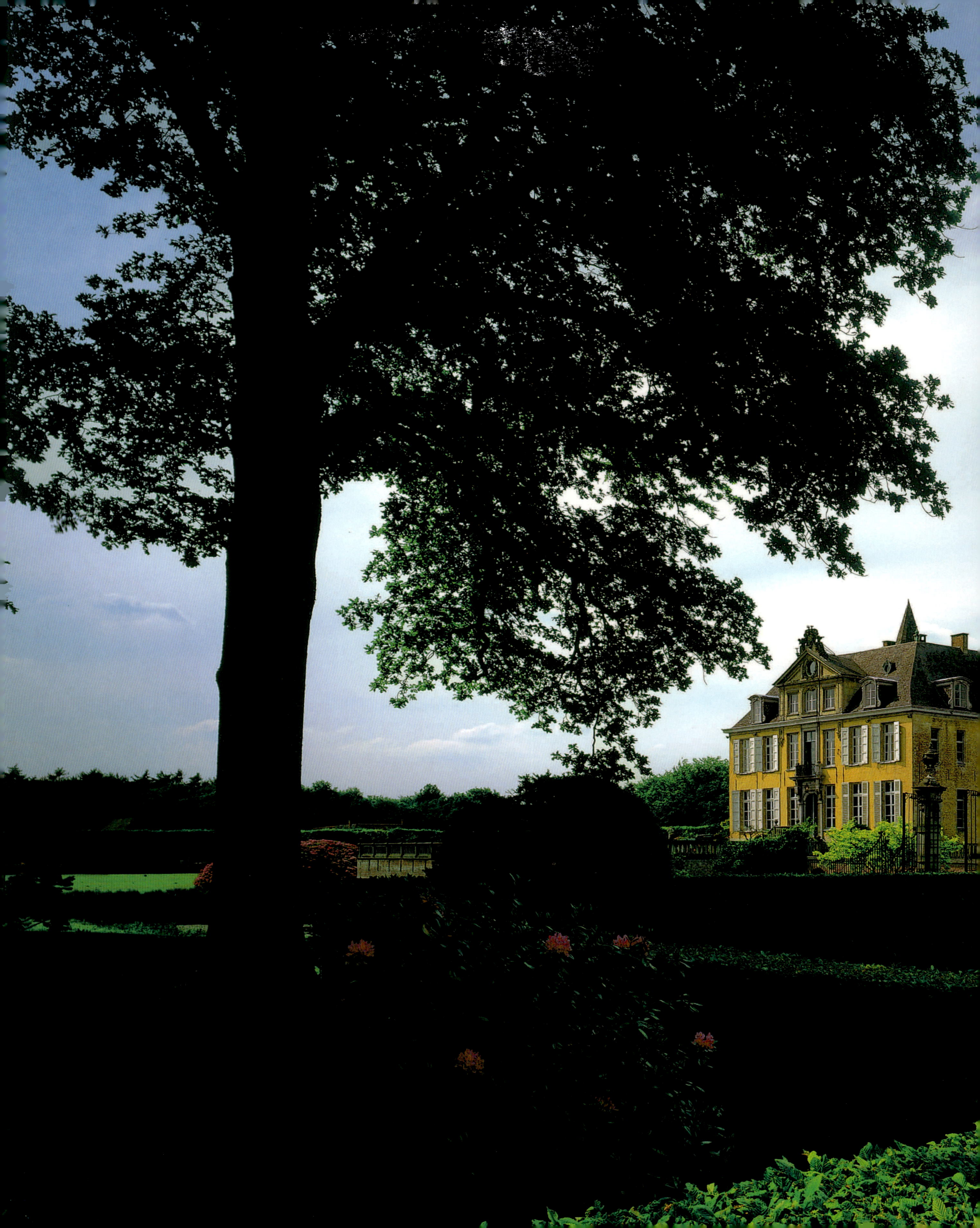

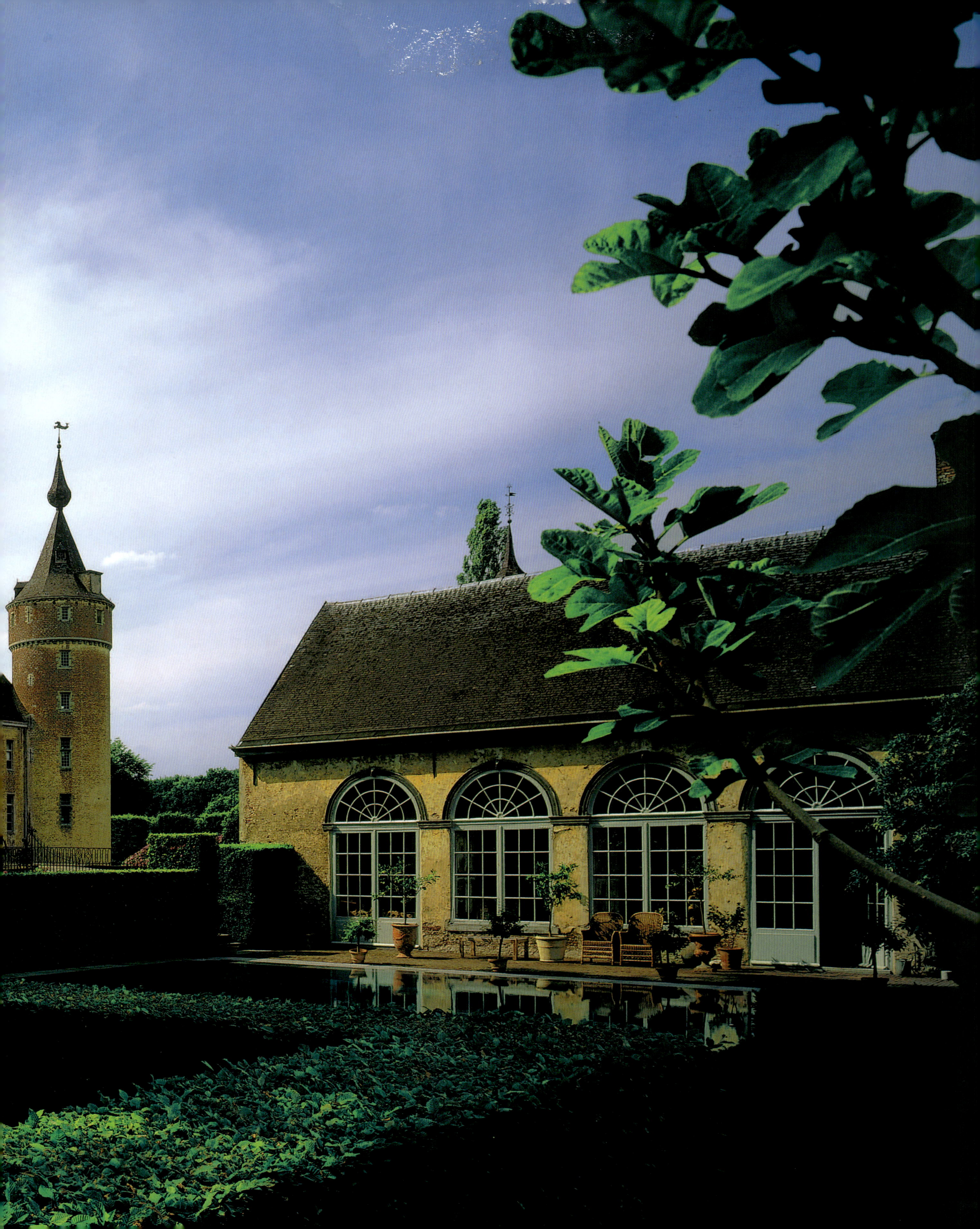

It took over six more months for the forty-two people in the family who had inherited shares in the castle to sign an agreement to sell, but by the end of 1984, Kasteel van 's-Gravenwezel was ours. For me, it's like a present. I really feel I have been chosen to live in the castle.

But you can't possess a thousand-year-old castle. Rather, it chooses you. You can buy it, but you can't own it, you feel like the happy inhabitant, there for only a short period in its long life. Living in something so old and venerable is very different from living in a house you have built yourself.

Good architecture is universal in its appeal. The architects wished to inspire the castle's inhabitants to live as close to God as possible, and I believe they wanted the nine-floor climb up the medieval tower to be a pilgrimage to heaven. The bulbous tops of the turrets are like flames proclaiming the spirit within the house. The specific theological theories behind the stones and mortar may be lost on modern man, but its spirit is not.

As one ascends from the kitchens at the bottom to the heavenly views from the upper floors, one can always tell what floor one is on from the pattern on the ceiling. As fashions changed, subsequent owners clad the house in a rococo façade by Jan Pieter van Baurscheit, one of the most famous architects of that period, who was also a sculptor, an artist, and something of a philosopher, but its roots have never been lost.

When we bought the castle, it was in a fairly bad state of decoration. So, for the first few years we lived in it, the house possessed us. We both felt it was our task to bring it back to life again, to transport it to our own time. The process of restoration was long and laborious and we had only two years before we had to leave our house in Vlaeykensgang, as we had rented it out to a restaurant. So first we studied the history of the castle and scraped every single interior wall to discover the original colors it had been painted. Then we repainted the walls in specially mixed natural paints which echoed the original colors.

For two years over forty people worked on the castle, day and night. May and I often asked each other during those two years how to do it—how to give it harmony, make it a positive place. Inside it was terrible. There was plastic paint on the walls and tiny little moldings all of the wrong scale and probably do-it-yourself. It really was terrible. We had to purify it. We even had to take out things that had been well made because they were wrong—it wasn't easy to decide to go to those lengths. We have restored most of the rooms to what they would have been originally. But some are in our style, the rooms nearest to our hearts, where the architecture is of course original but the decoration has been purified.

When we'd almost finished the work, we gave a big party to celebrate with fireworks. I remember, I was standing on the bridge and, suddenly, seeing the castle transformed, I became one with it.

Today, the almost 1,000-year-old Kasteel van 's-Gravenwezel leads a rich and modern life of a kind the original architects could never have dreamed of. In the whitewashed medieval kitchens overlooking the moat, we give lunch and dinner parties around an oval table that can seat twenty, with a great

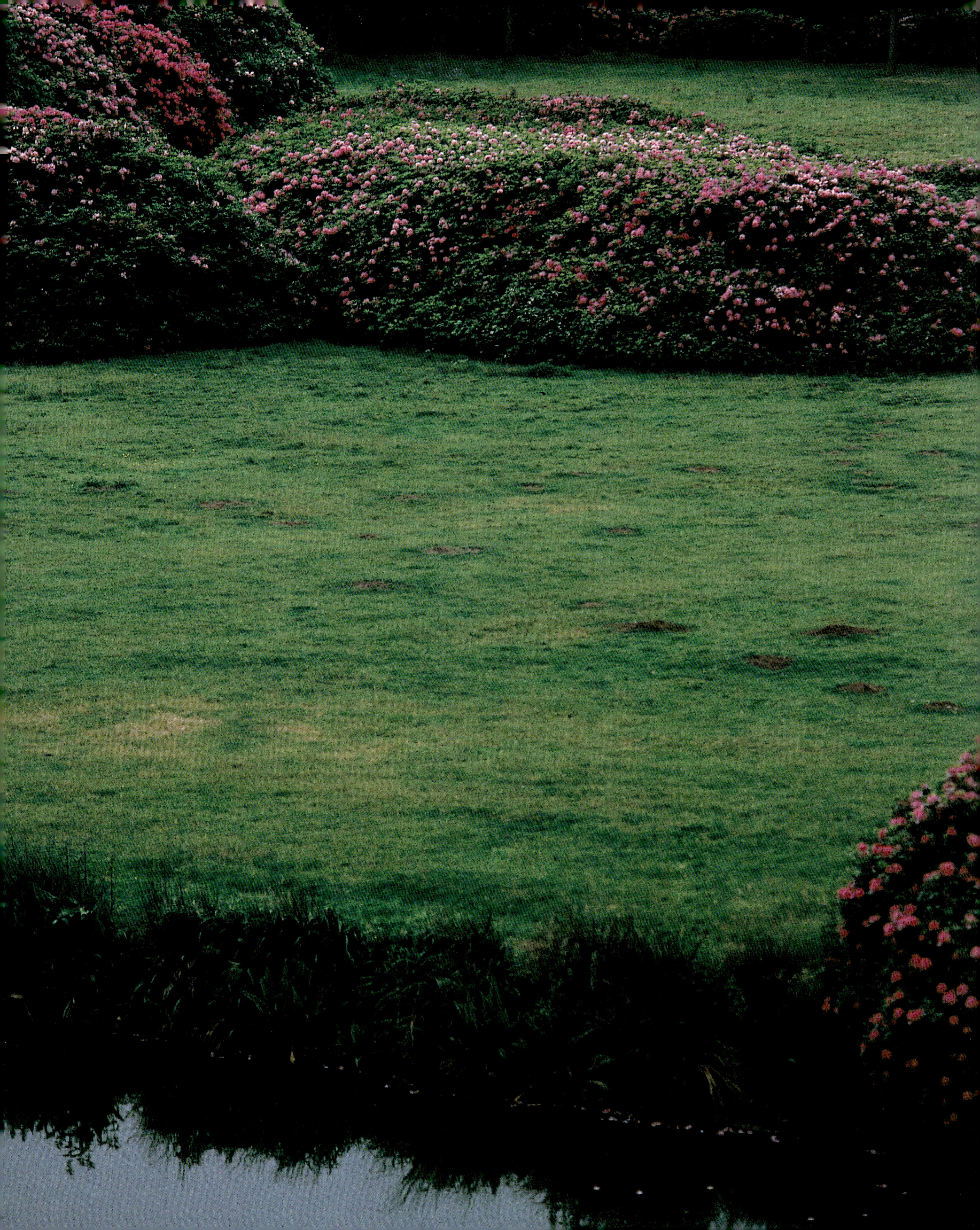

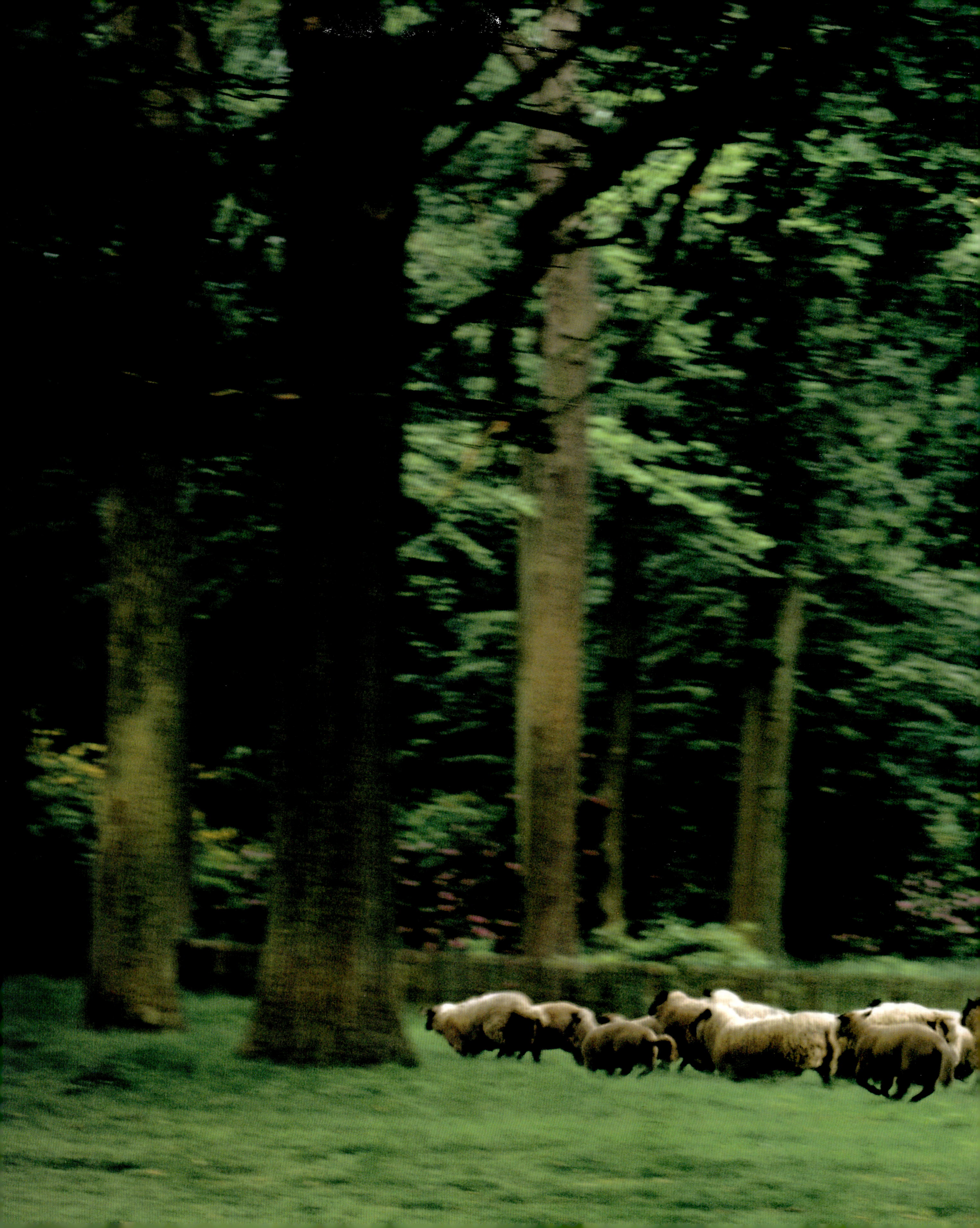

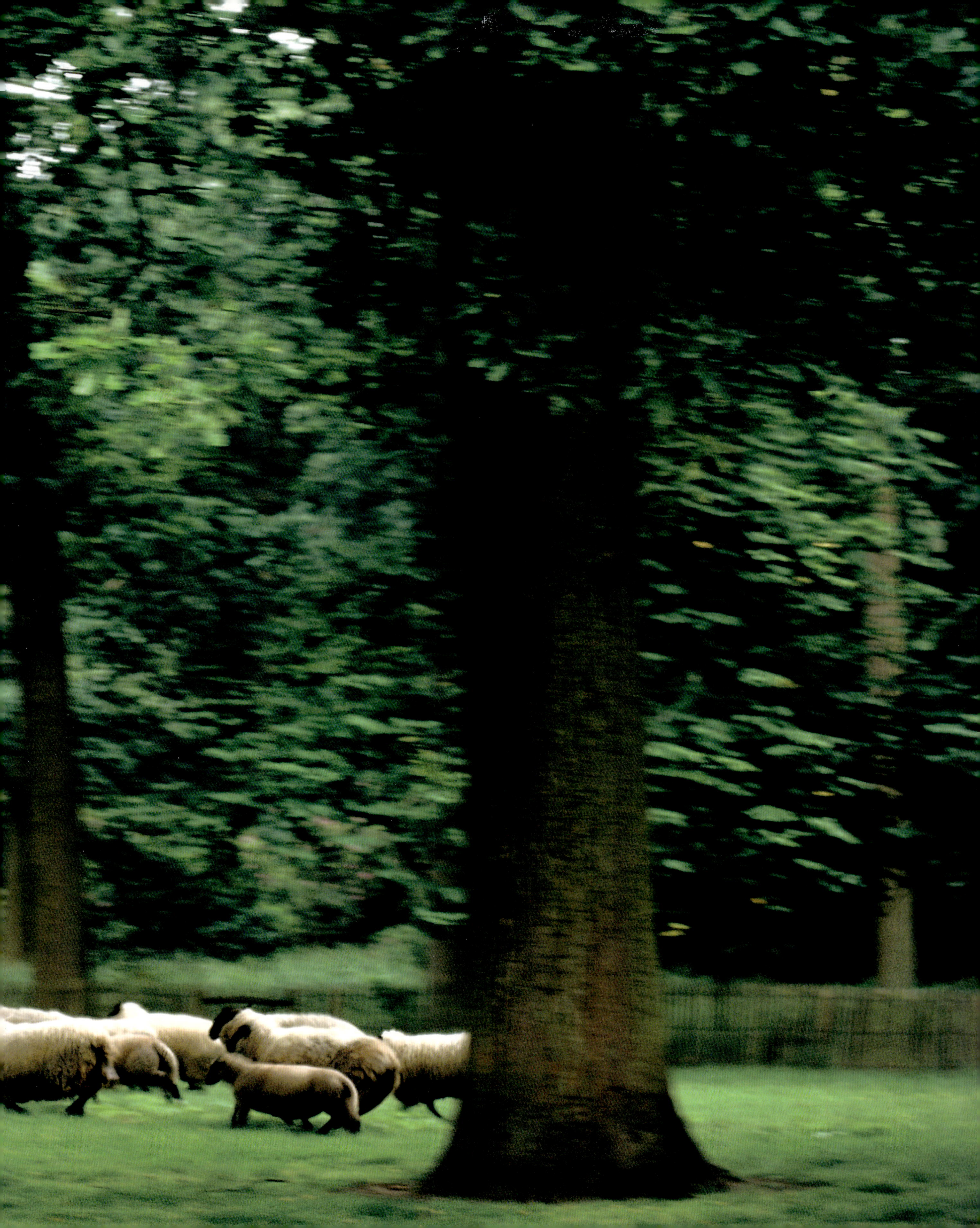

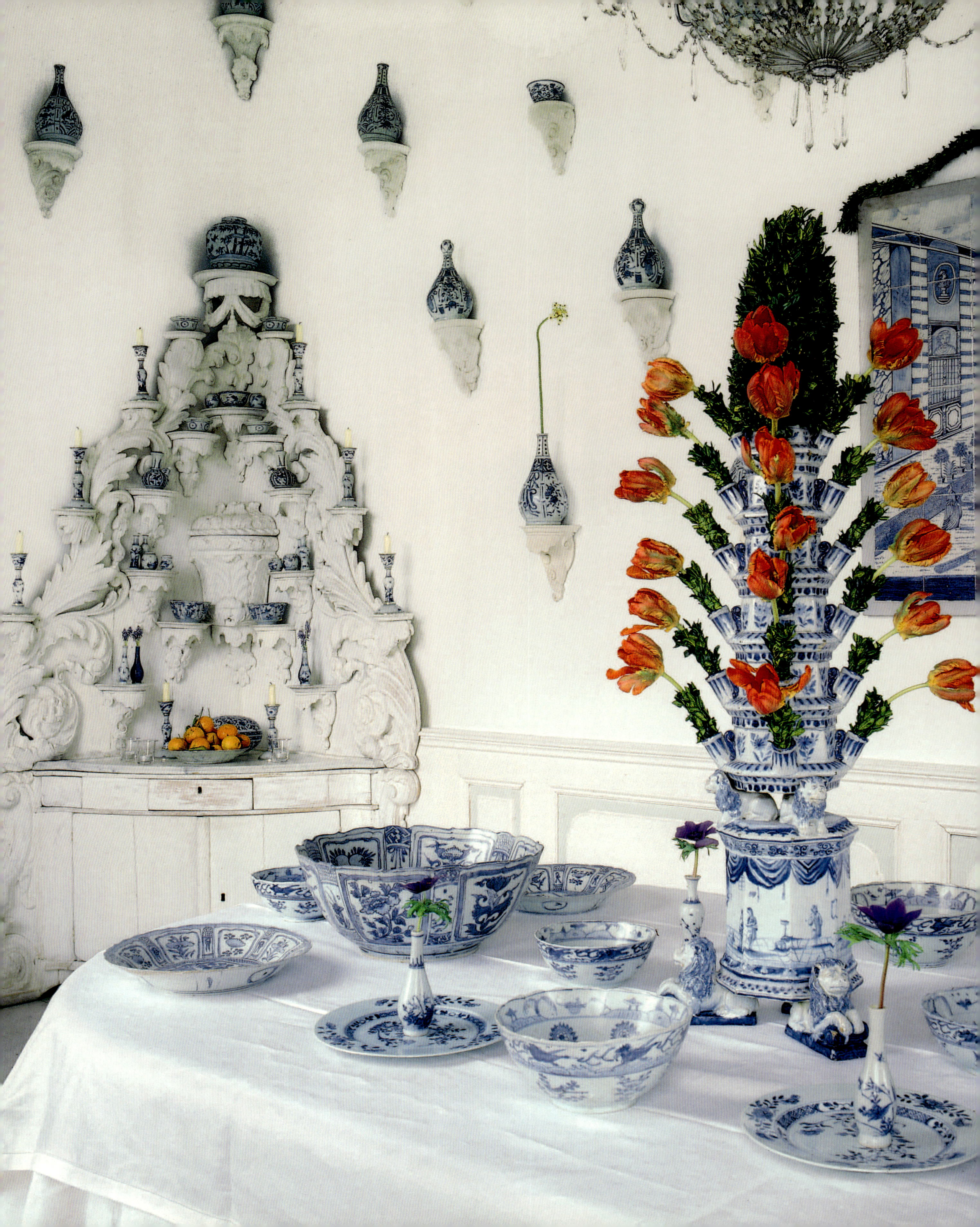

fire burning in the original roasting grate. Above our guests' heads are shaggy clouds of wildflowers from the park that May has arranged in huge lily vases. Royalty, the wealthy, classical composers, contemporary artists, Jesuit professors, captains of industry, neighboring farmers, and friends from all over the world can sit and enjoy both the delicious food May prepares and conversation about music, art, life, everything.

The castle's principal floor, or *piano nobile,* has a central flagstone hall leading to a large library where I work surrounded by massive eighteenth-century bookcases. Behind this is a music room with a table where I can show clients plans and discuss projects. Beyond this, in the base of one of the towers, is a small chapel. Next to the dining room is a large drawing room where I keep some of my most precious smaller objects, such as the sixteenth-century turned-ivory pieces, a fragment of a carved Gothic frieze, and my collection of turned wood. There is also a wonderful collection of sixteenth- and seventeenth-century books on architecture, the first edition of the great *Diderot Encyclopaedia,* which I find inspiring, and many books on how to turn wood and ivory, all of which I use as references in my work.

And then comes a surprise—one of many in the castle—a smaller pure-white dining room with a white corner buffet by Daniel Marot and some of the Hatcher late-Ming and transitional blue and white porcelain displayed on white brackets, again by Marot, on the white walls. This enfilade of rooms is where May and I give our parties, which often, in good weather, spill out onto the large terrace at the front of the castle.

The rooms on the first floor are very different. Here the grand manner gives way to something more contemplative. The "withdrawing" room, as we call it, is another surprise. Here we sit and think, we listen in the silence and the space and we don't talk very much. The floor is not parquetry, nor is it covered in fine silk carpets. The bare, scrubbed boards are silvery in the light. There is no Chippendale in this room. A Ming chair of abraded elm, remarkably modern in design, sits beside the simple opening of the fireplace. One plainly plastered wall is dominated by on important abstract painting by Antoni Tàpies, bought in Paris twenty years ago after I had seen it in Belgium at the "Europalia" exhibition on Spain. It was the only contemporary painting in the show and hung in a room with some wonderful Zurbaráns. Sitting on the boards below this is Fontana's 1959 *Concetto Spaziale Natura,* a round, roughly sculptured bronze that looks as if it might be a meteor just landed from outer space.

Behind a big minimalist sofa of our own design, covered in white cotton duck, is a well-worn shepherd's table from the Alps. And in front is another *arte povera* table, showing signs of the work and wear of centuries past. On another wall is a Chinese calligraphic scroll dating from 1376 and the Egyptian vessels I added recently to make the room more universal. The walls are painted with chalk mixed with brown earth from the park, because I wanted it to have an earthy feel. In this room there are none of the pretty bouquets from the garden or park that May arranges everywhere else in the castle. Here, only a spray of branches is permitted, sometimes flowering cherry, sometimes chestnut with the pale sharp green leaves of early spring. It is the room in the castle which, above all, represents my typical personal taste. Of all my many

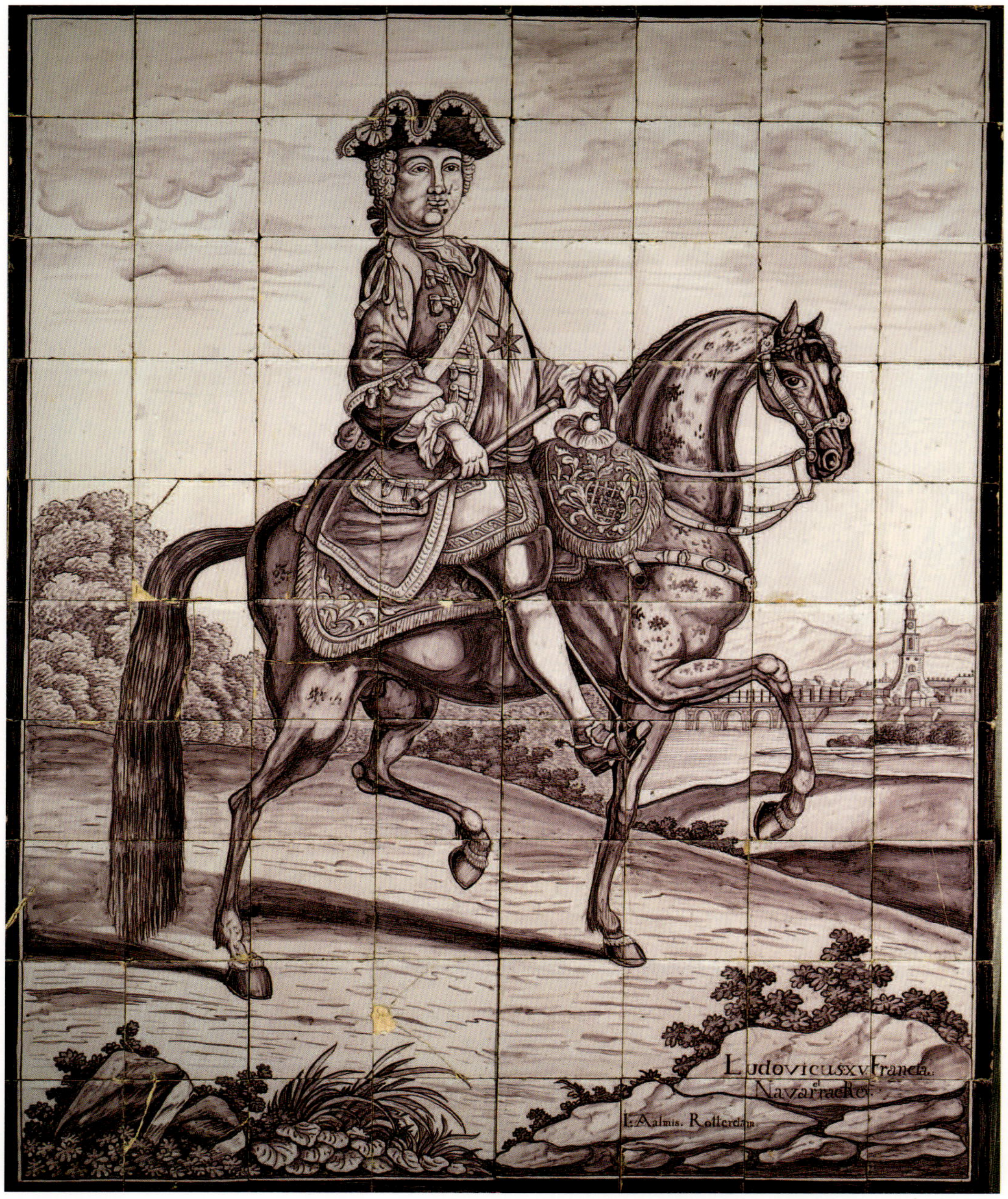
Ludovicus xv Francia.
Navarrae Rex.
I. Aalmis. Rotterdam

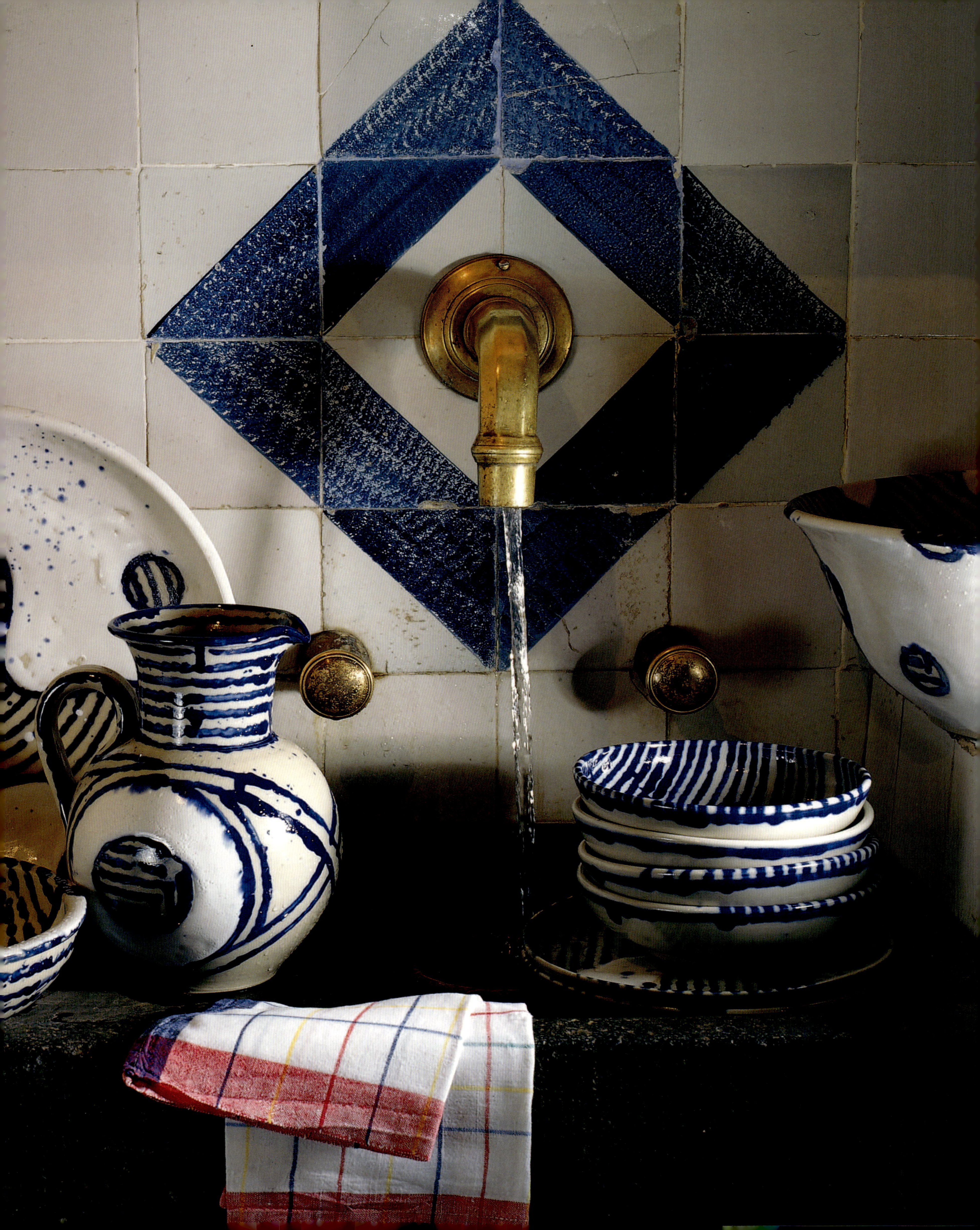

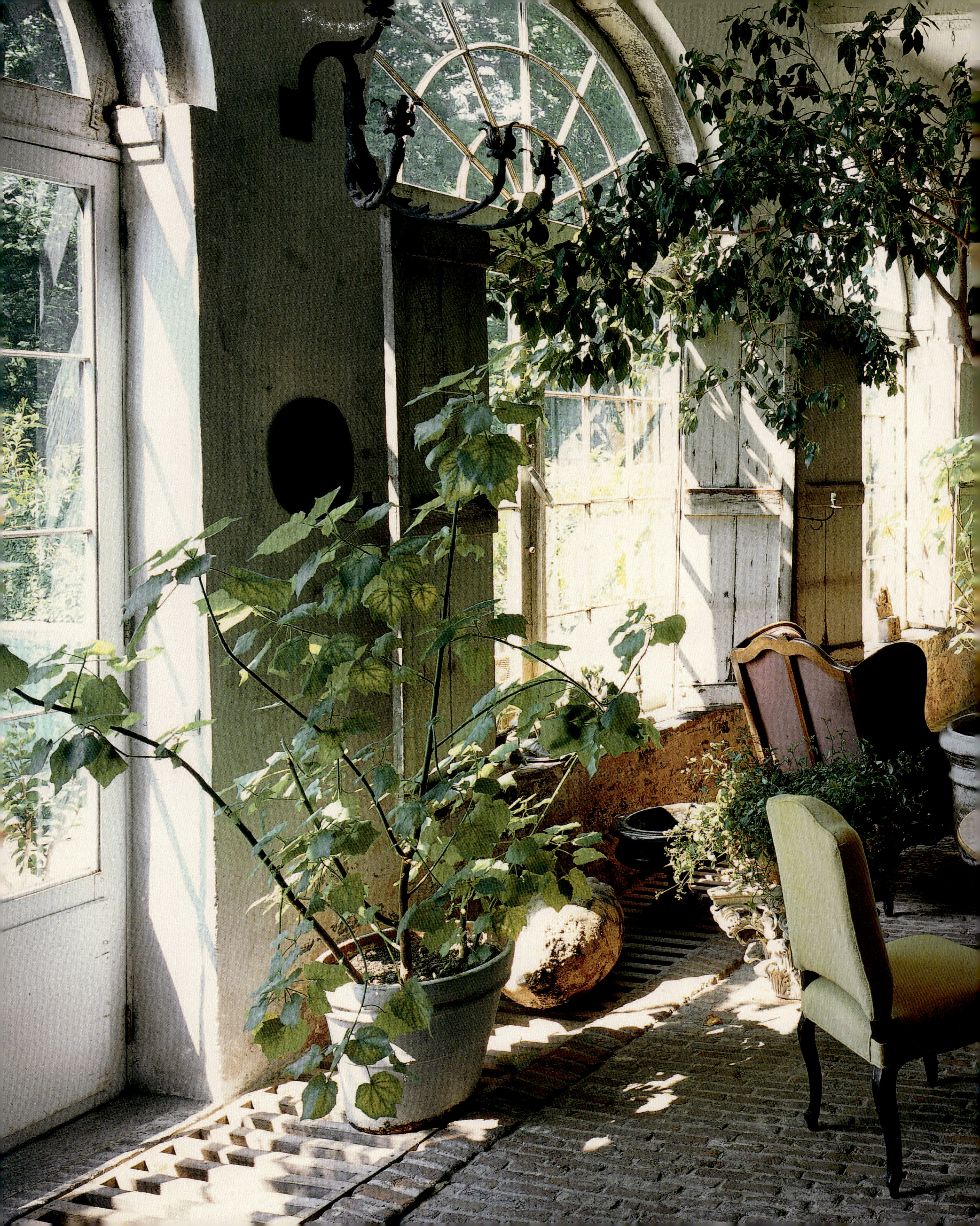

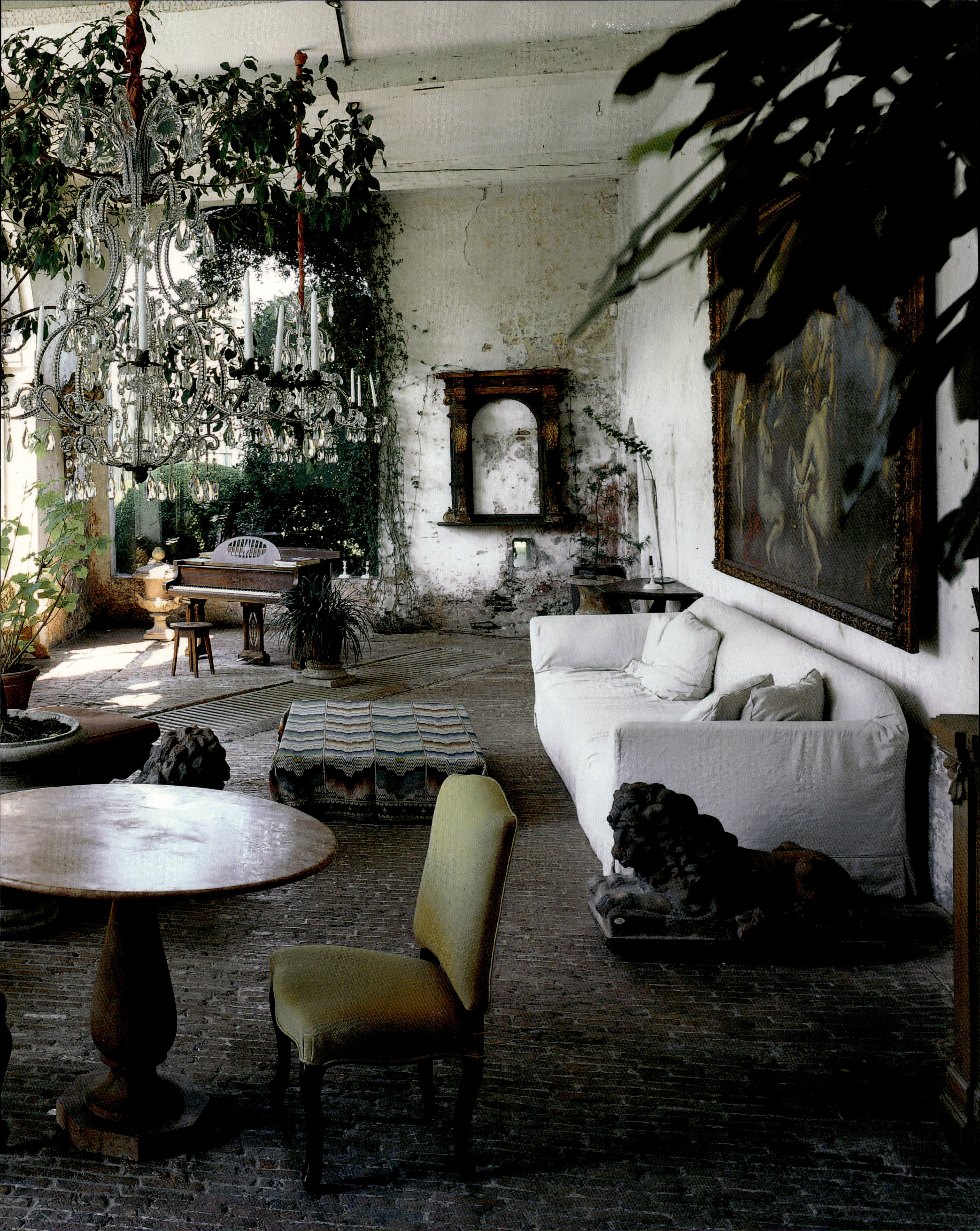

rooms it is the truest to my central beliefs about the life we should live and about contemporary taste. I believe in space. Real space is very important in the twenty-first century. The world has become so small and space so scarce, you have to create it without limits within a limited space. If the baroque library is yin, then this room represents the other side of my life, the yang of Zen.

Our bedroom next door contains our favorite works of art, including our best abstract painting by Jef Verheyen called *Espace Idéal*. There is also a very beautiful Zen screen with a very simple stone design, on which is written a poem—I have never seen anything approaching it in beauty. Then there is a very early Romanesque chest, the earliest piece of furniture I have ever owned, on top of which sits a Japanese Shigarake vase, the earliest Zen pottery in existence. It is extremely rare and I bought it twenty years ago because it looks as if it had been made yesterday. It looks extremely simple but it has a primitive power you just do not see in any other ceramic. Then there are about twelve pieces of Han pottery with a pearly skin, an iridescent effect on the patina due to a millennia-long burial in the soil. On an ivory "Bargueña" chest, one of the first pieces May and I bought together in Sussex, is a collection of white ceramic pieces of all periods.

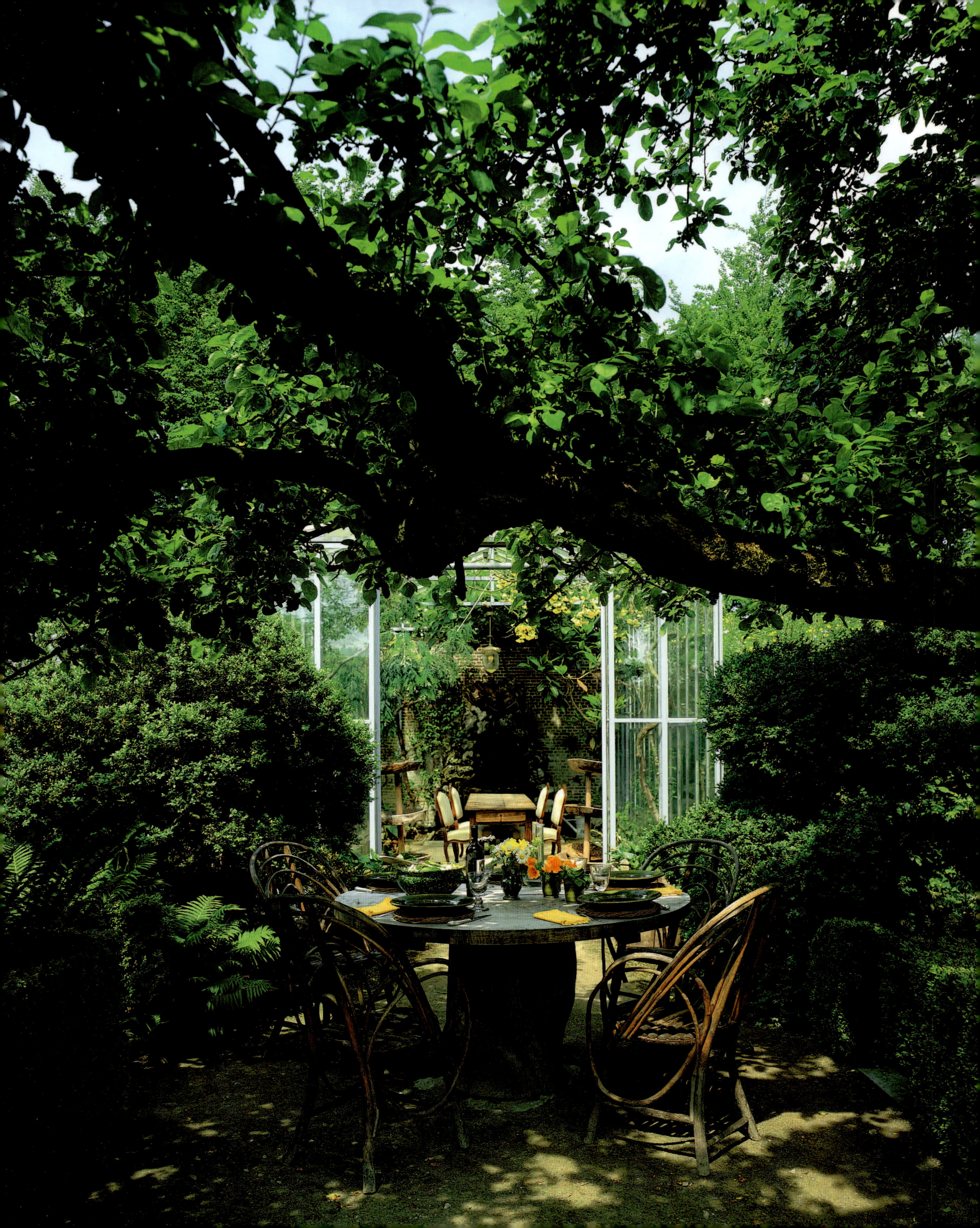

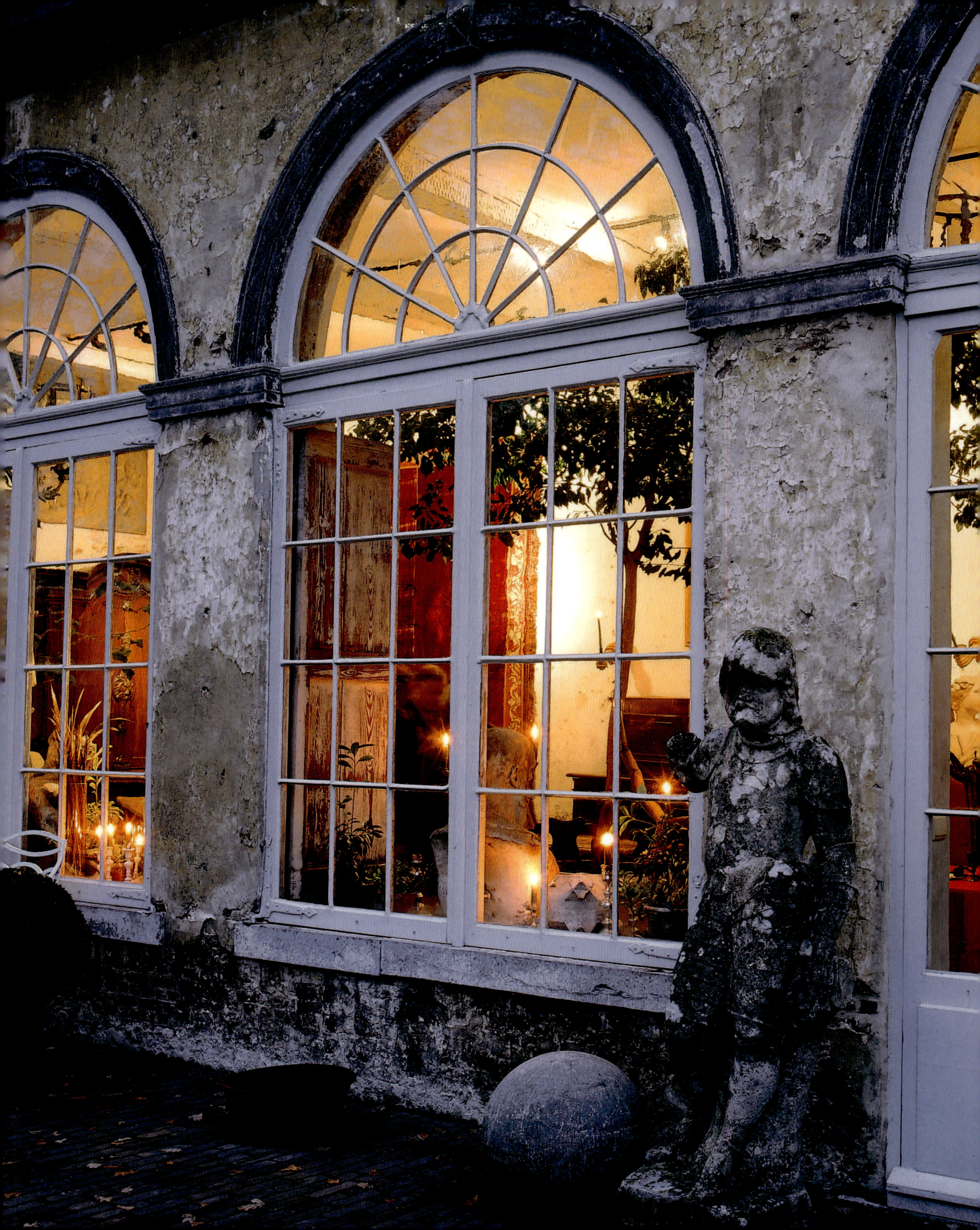

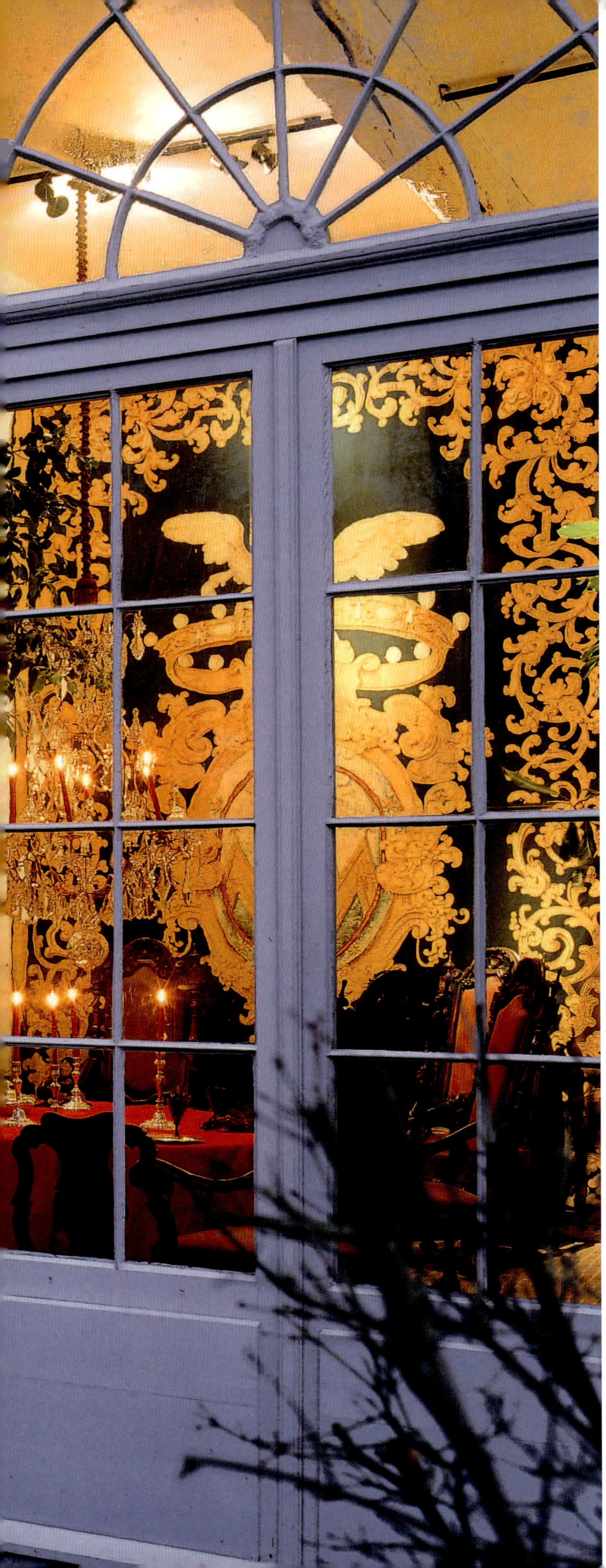

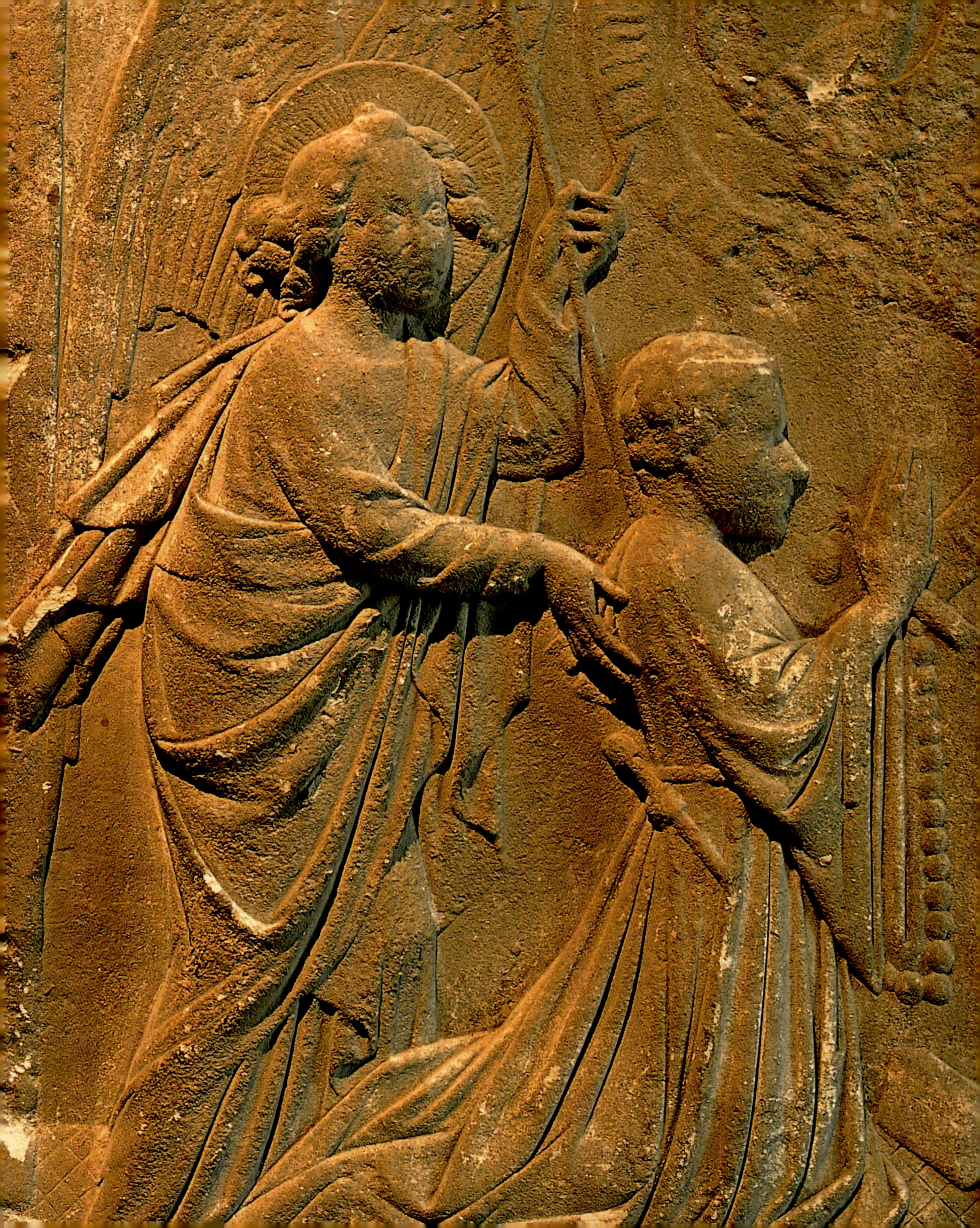

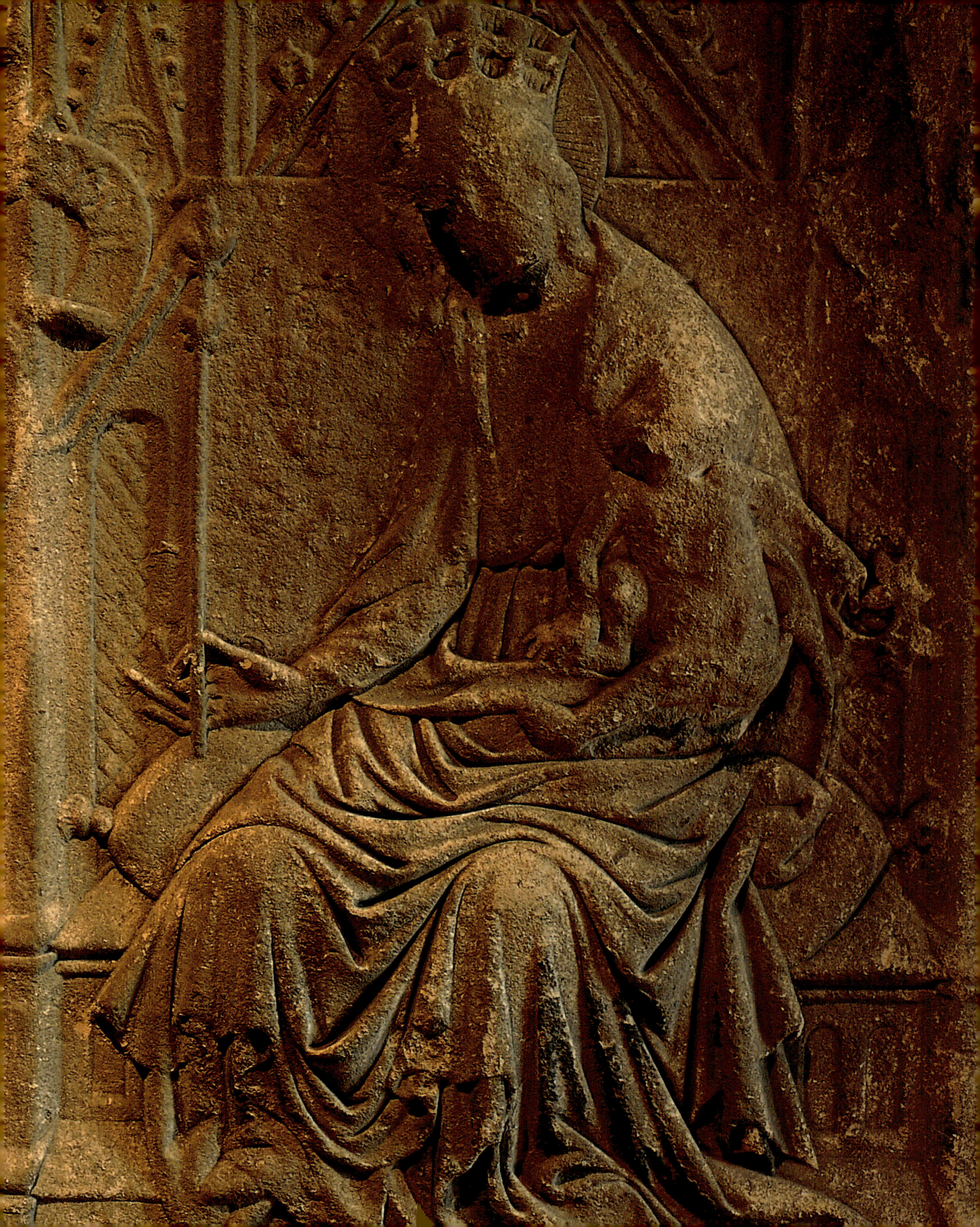

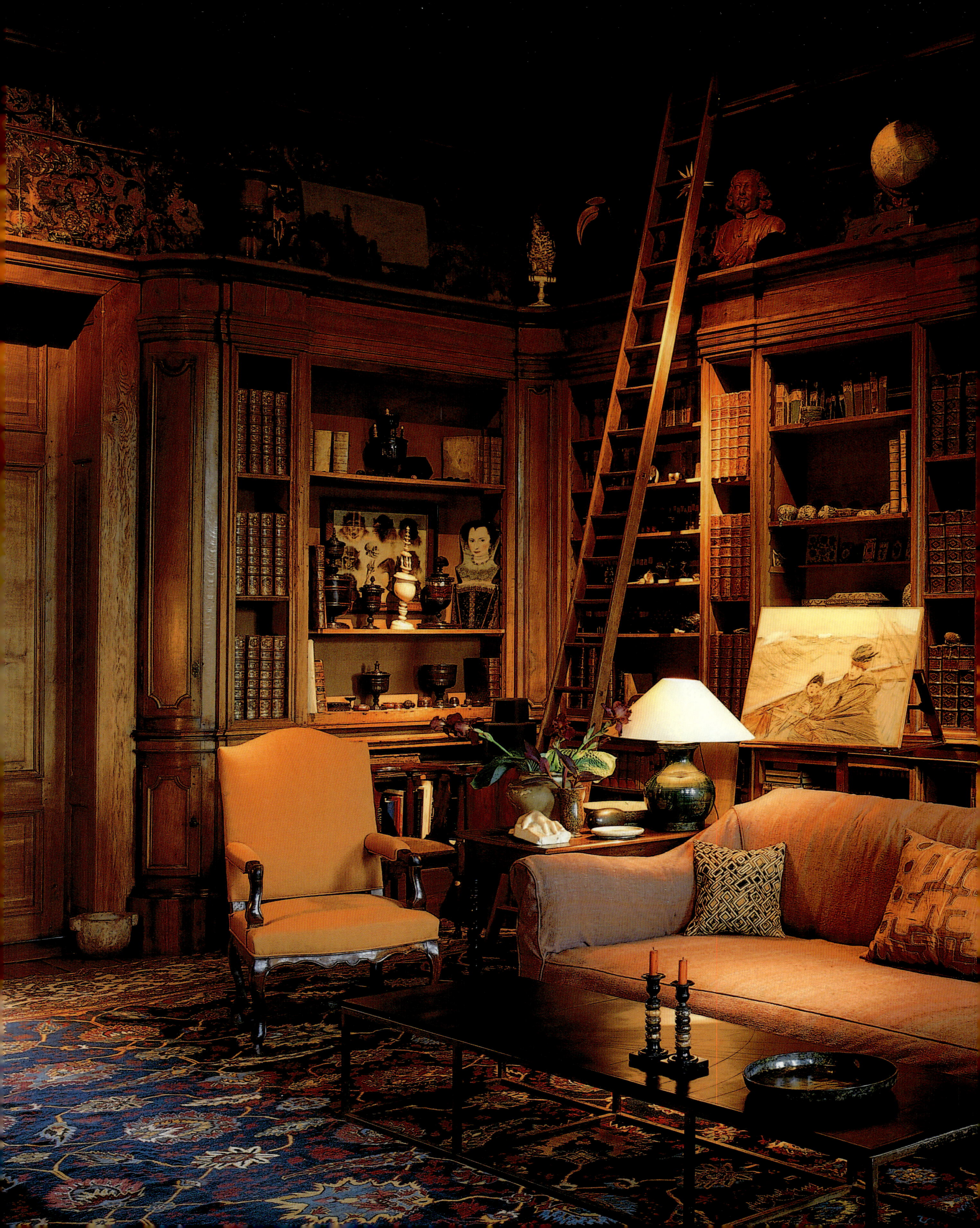

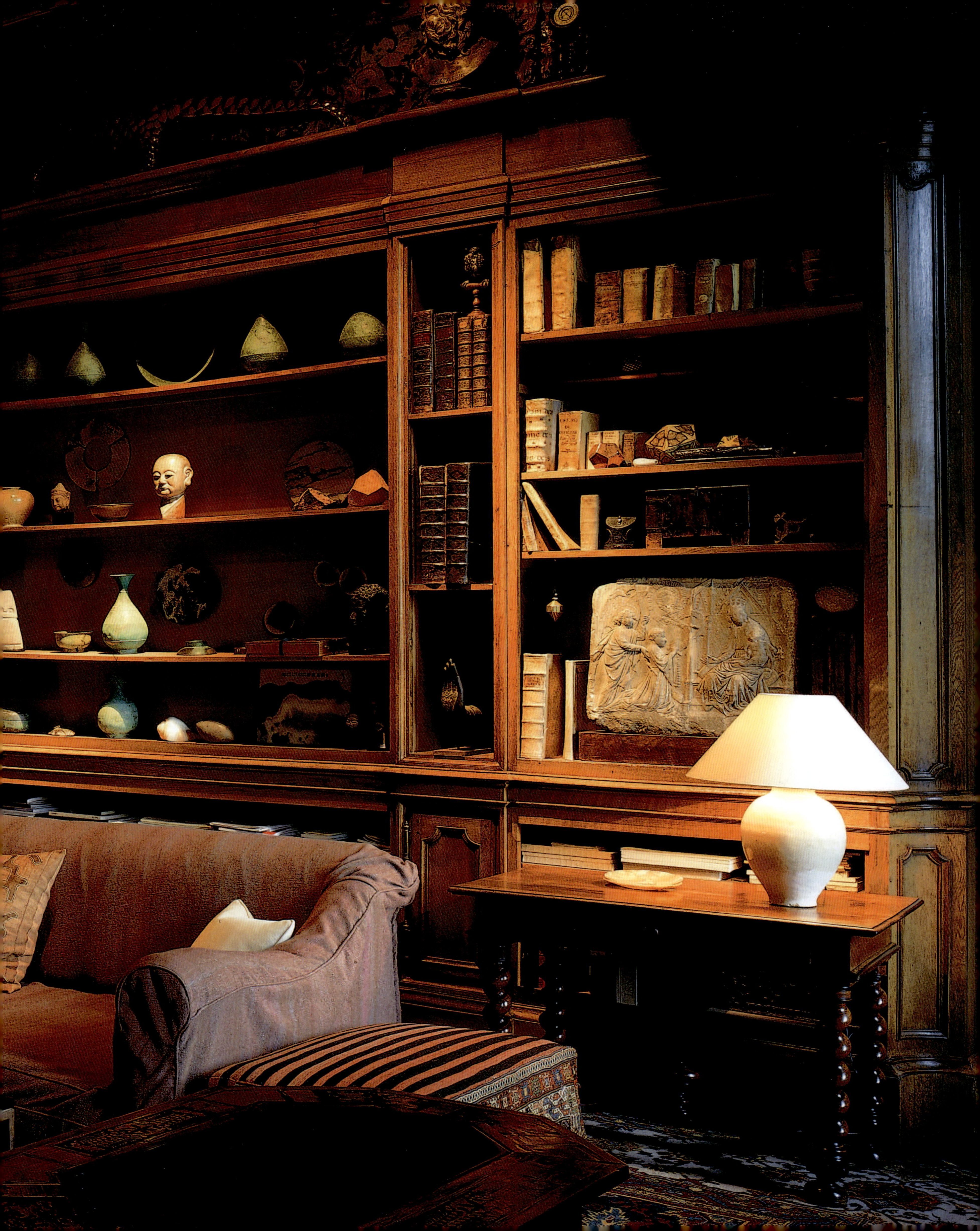

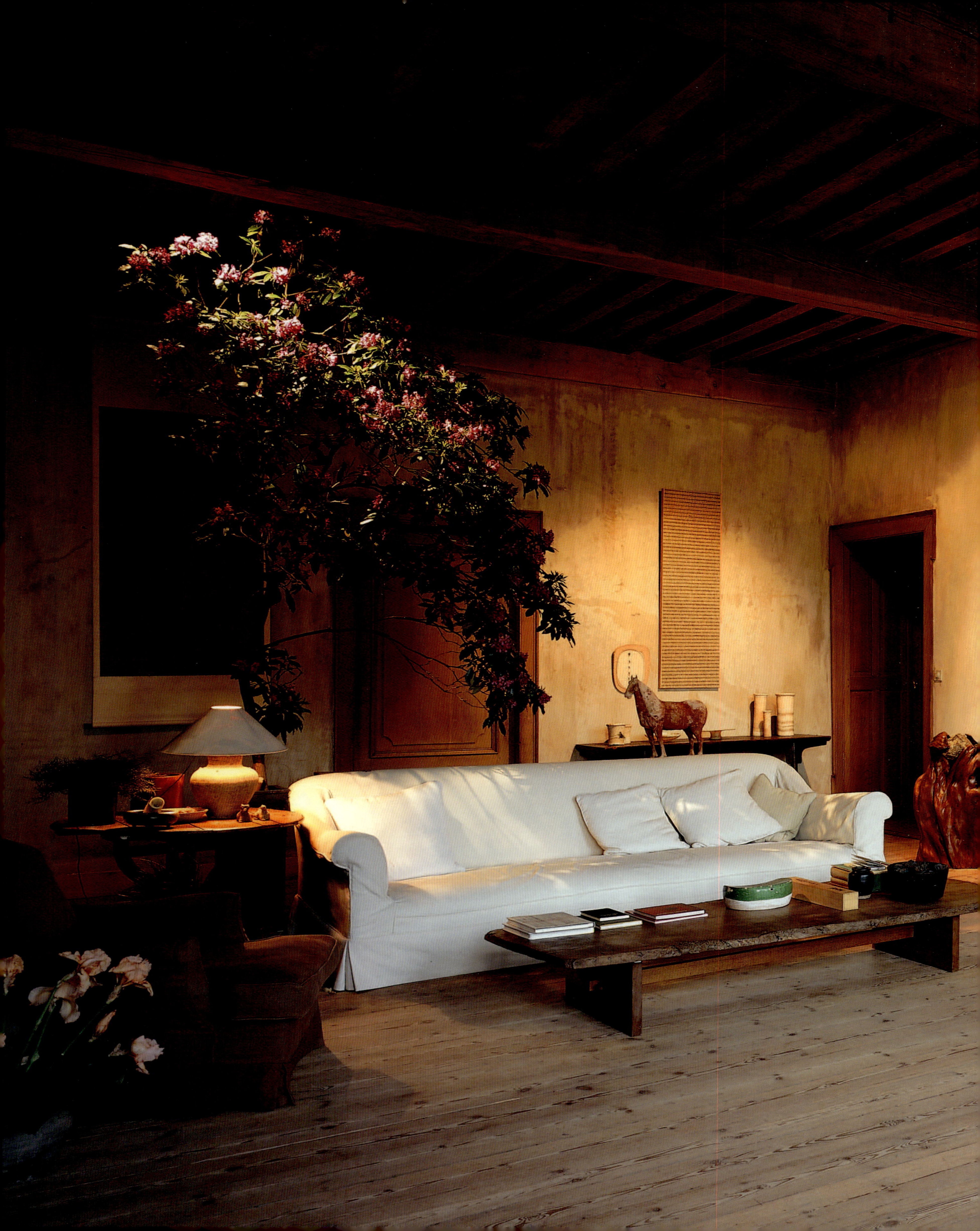

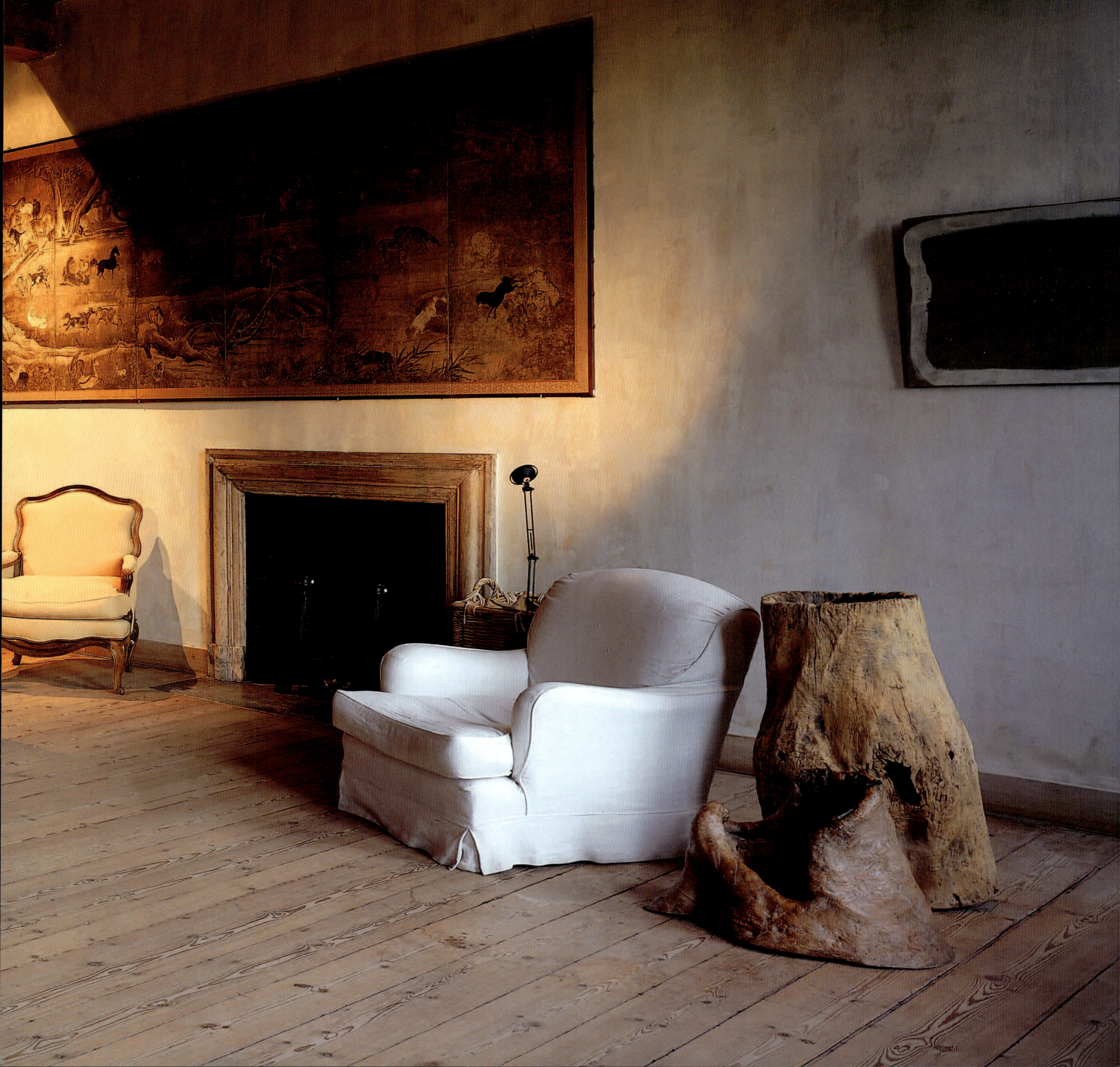

"There have always been good and bad paintings...in art, however, the terms ancient and modern have no place."

Hsieh Ho

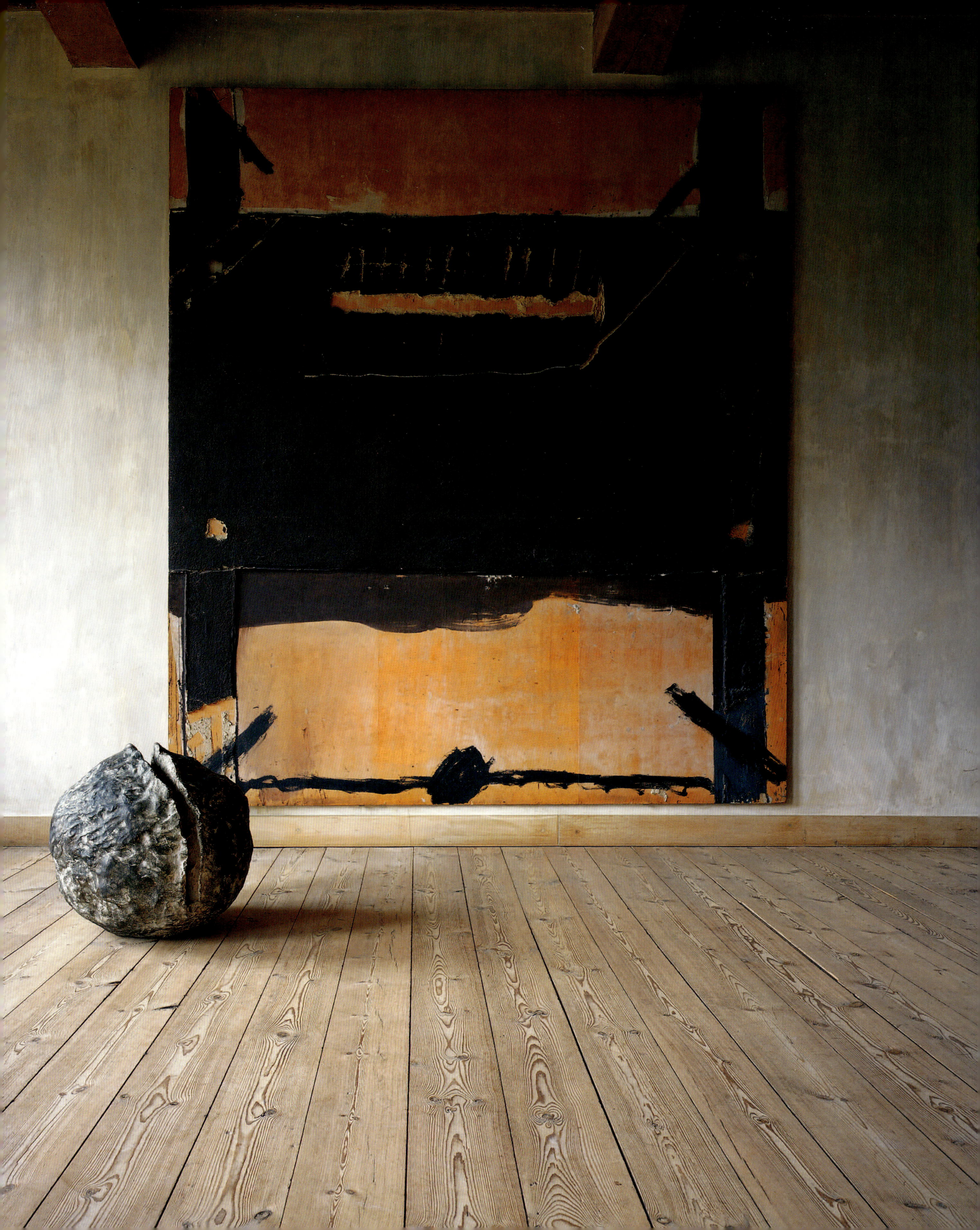

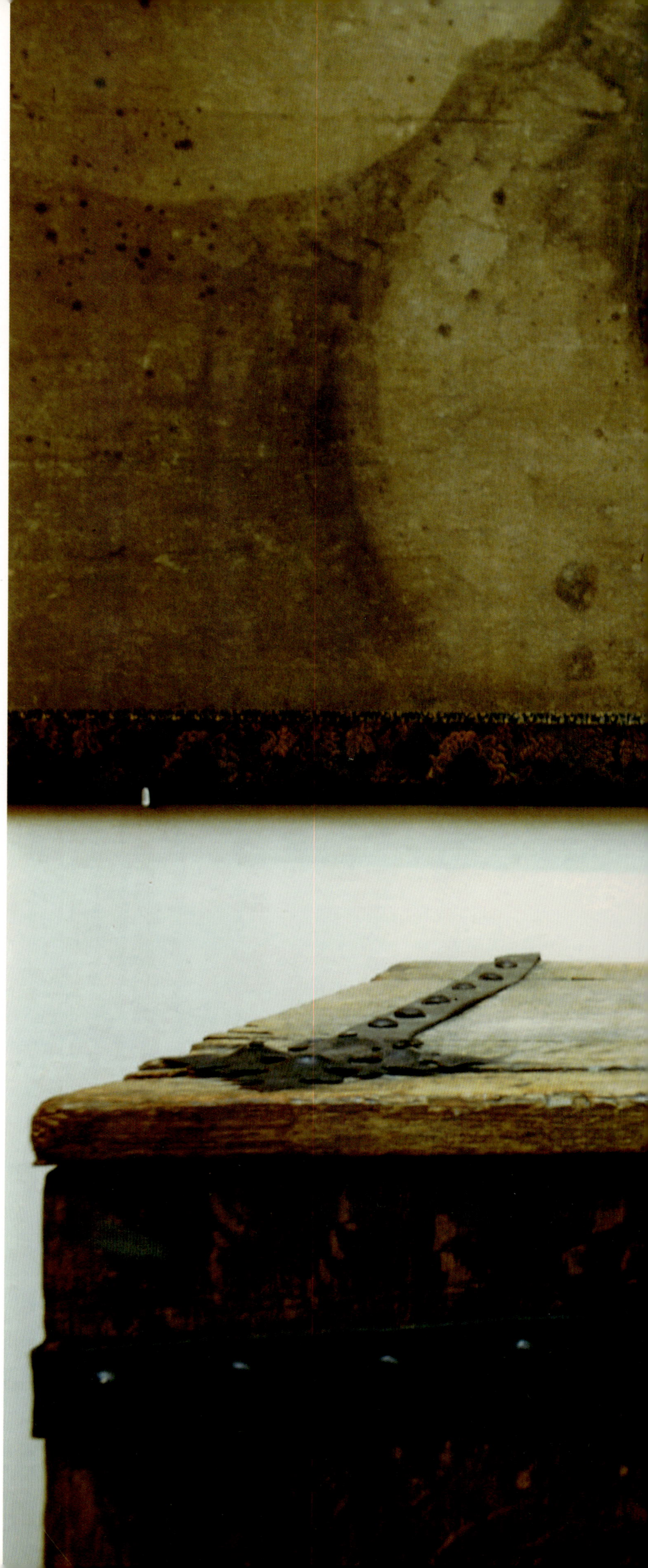

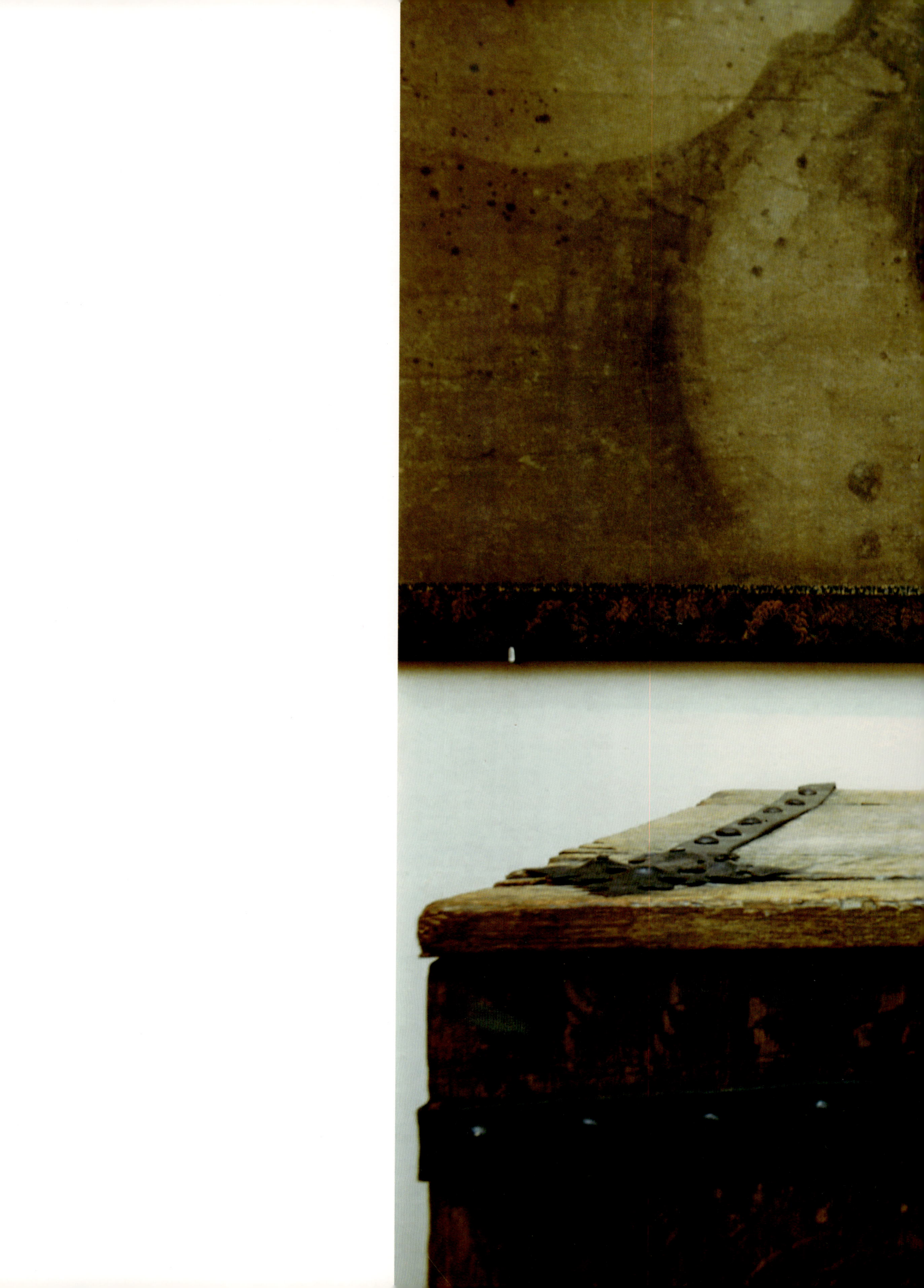

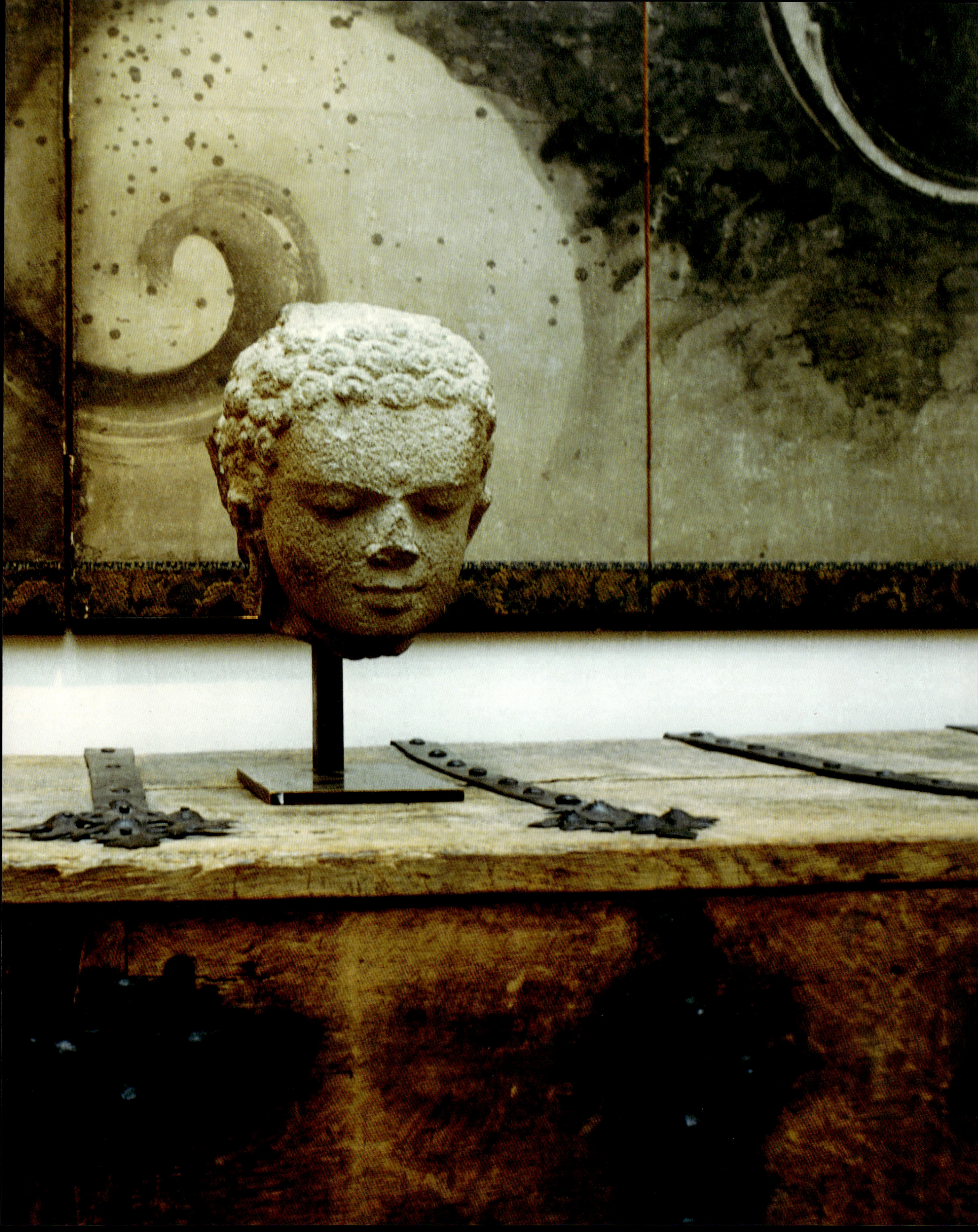

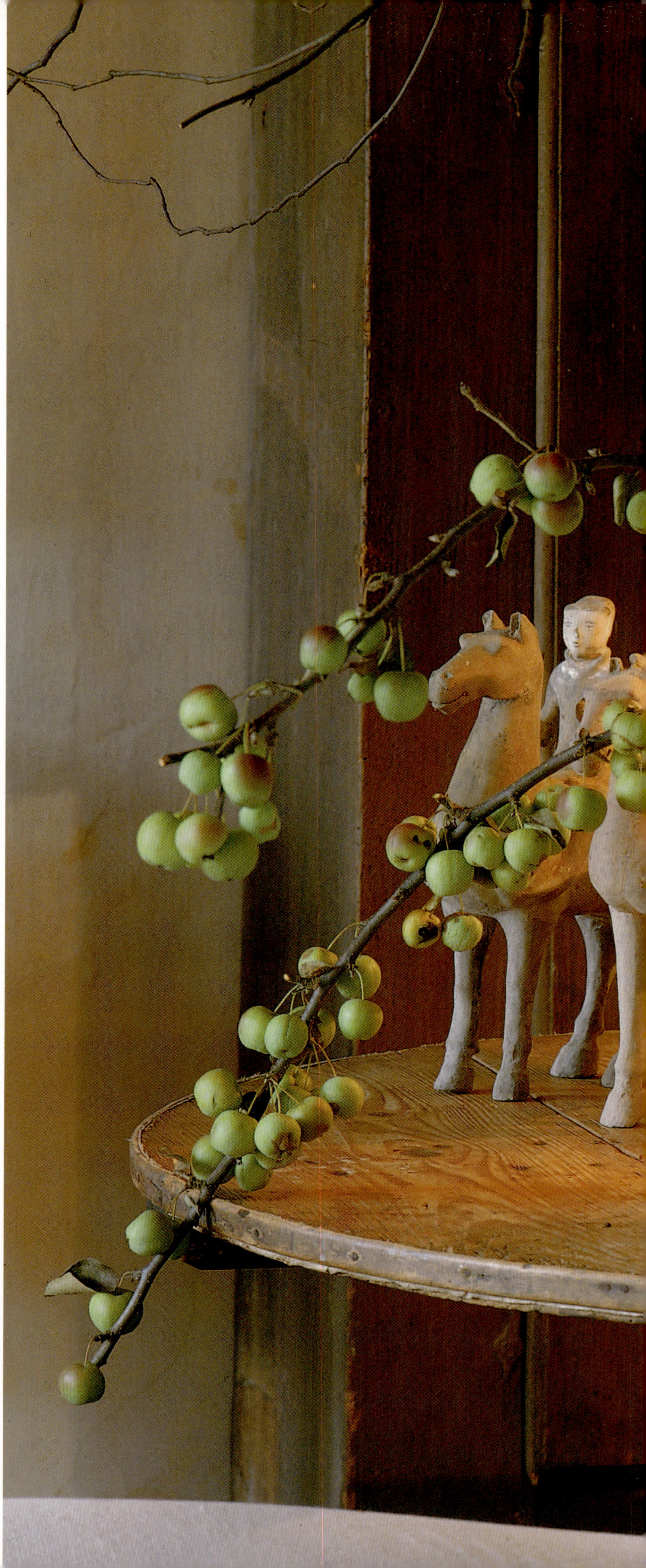

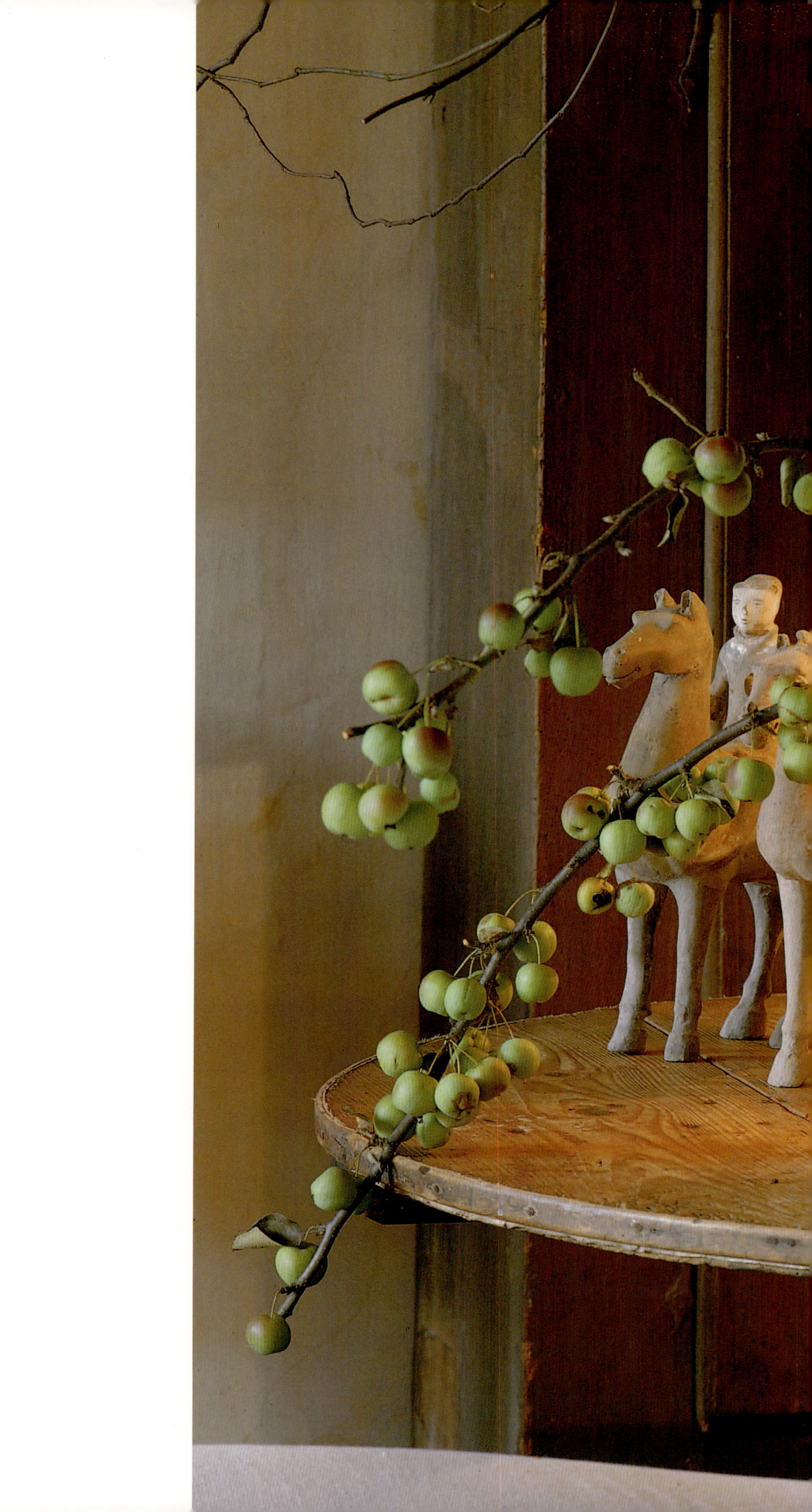

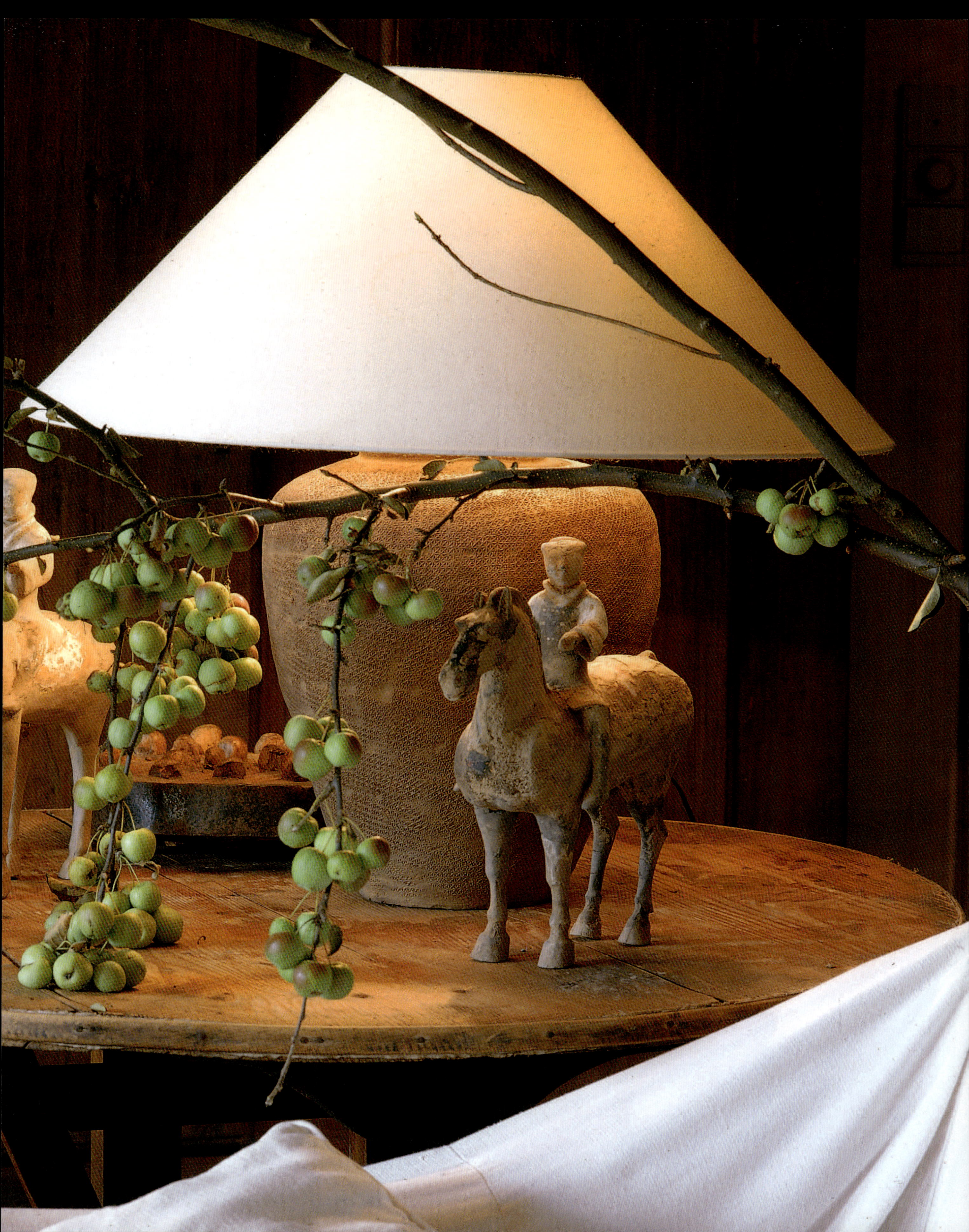

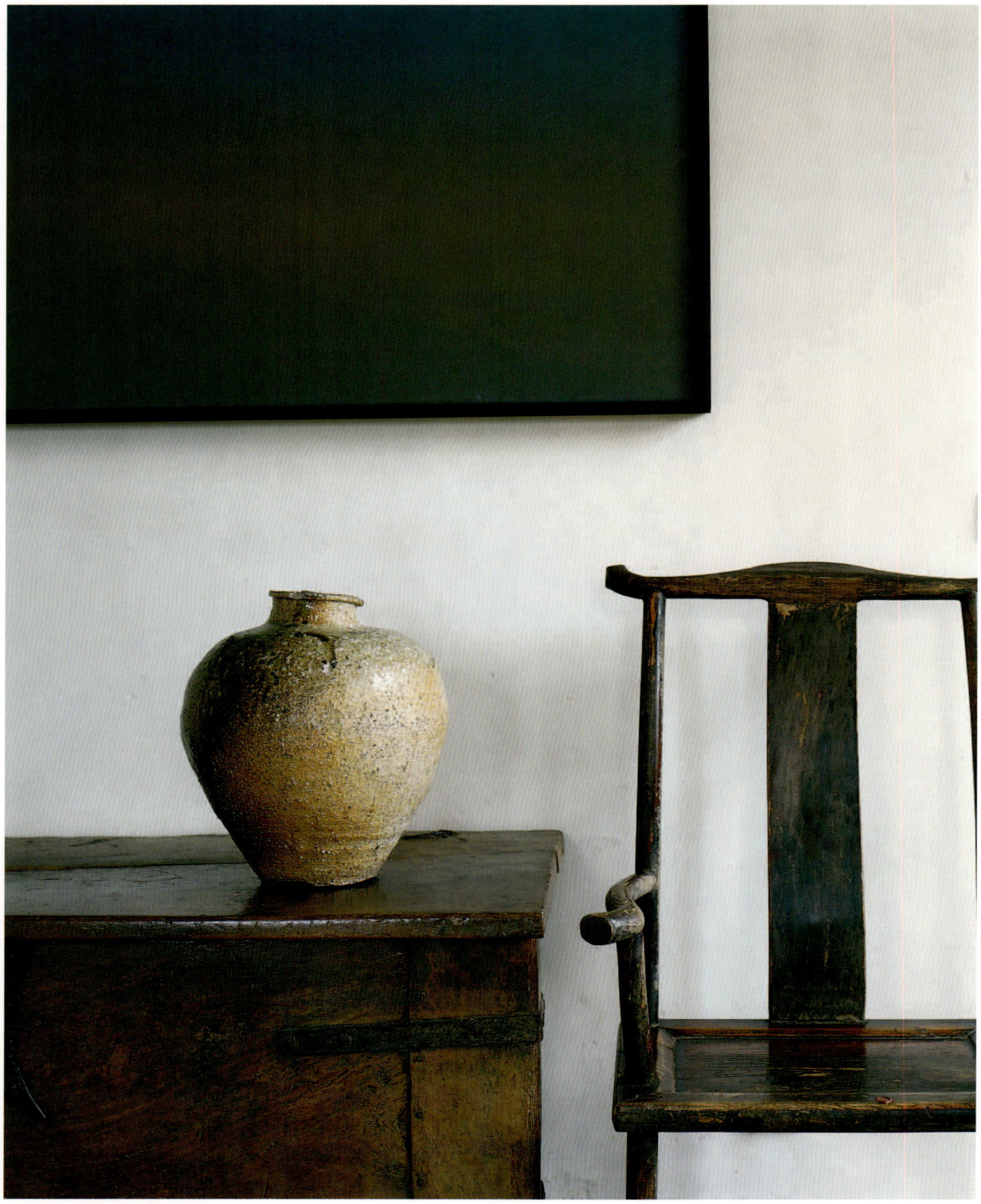

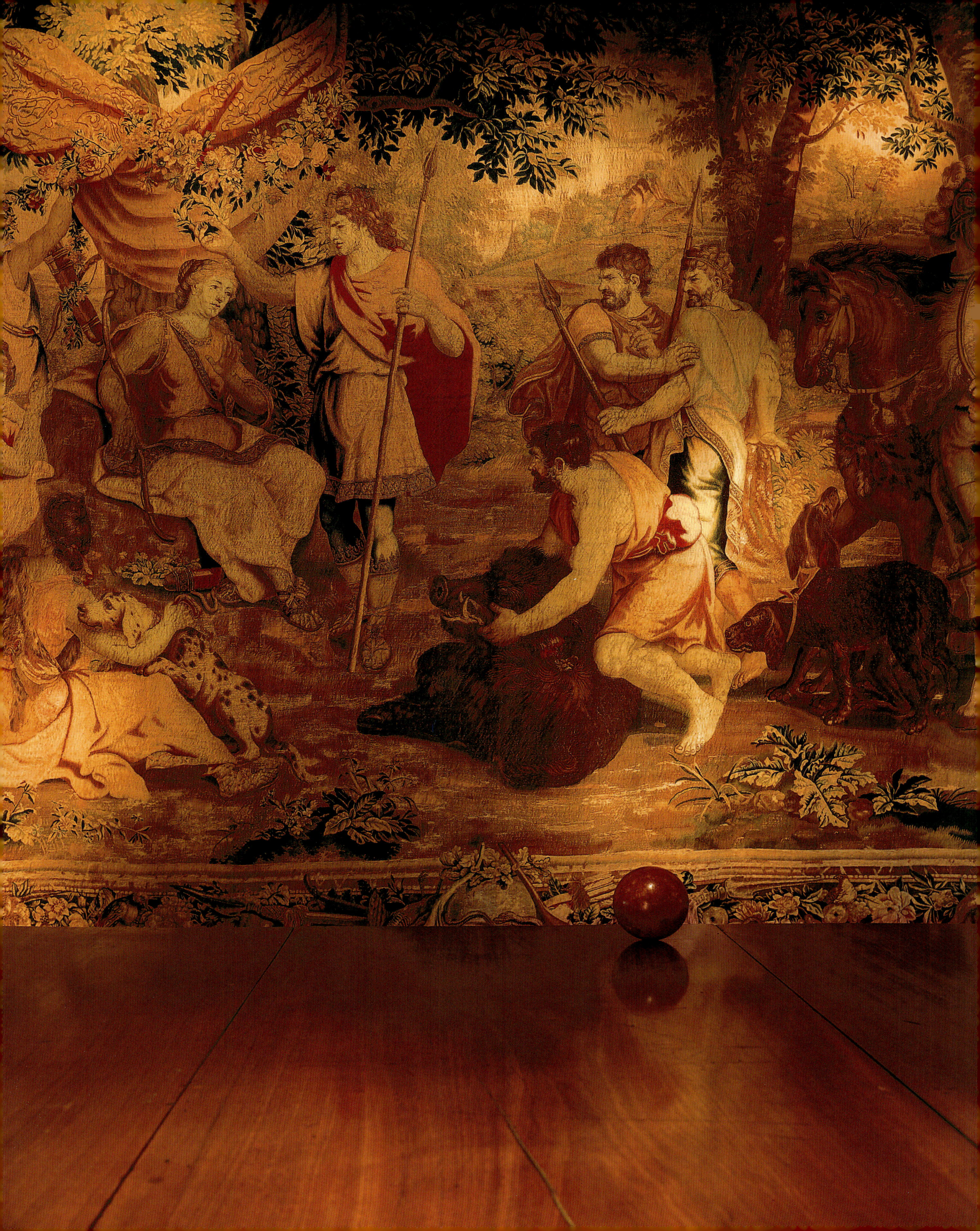

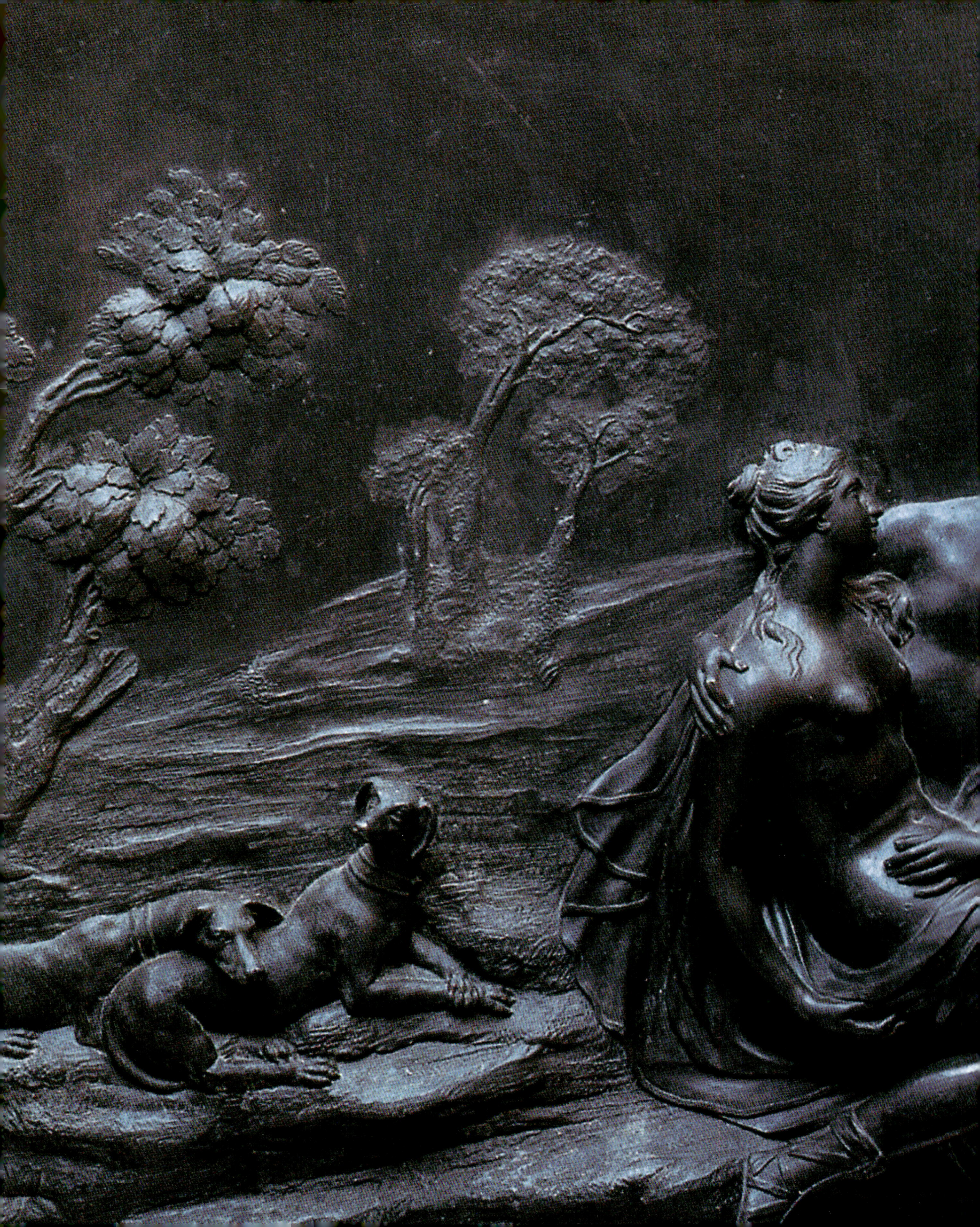

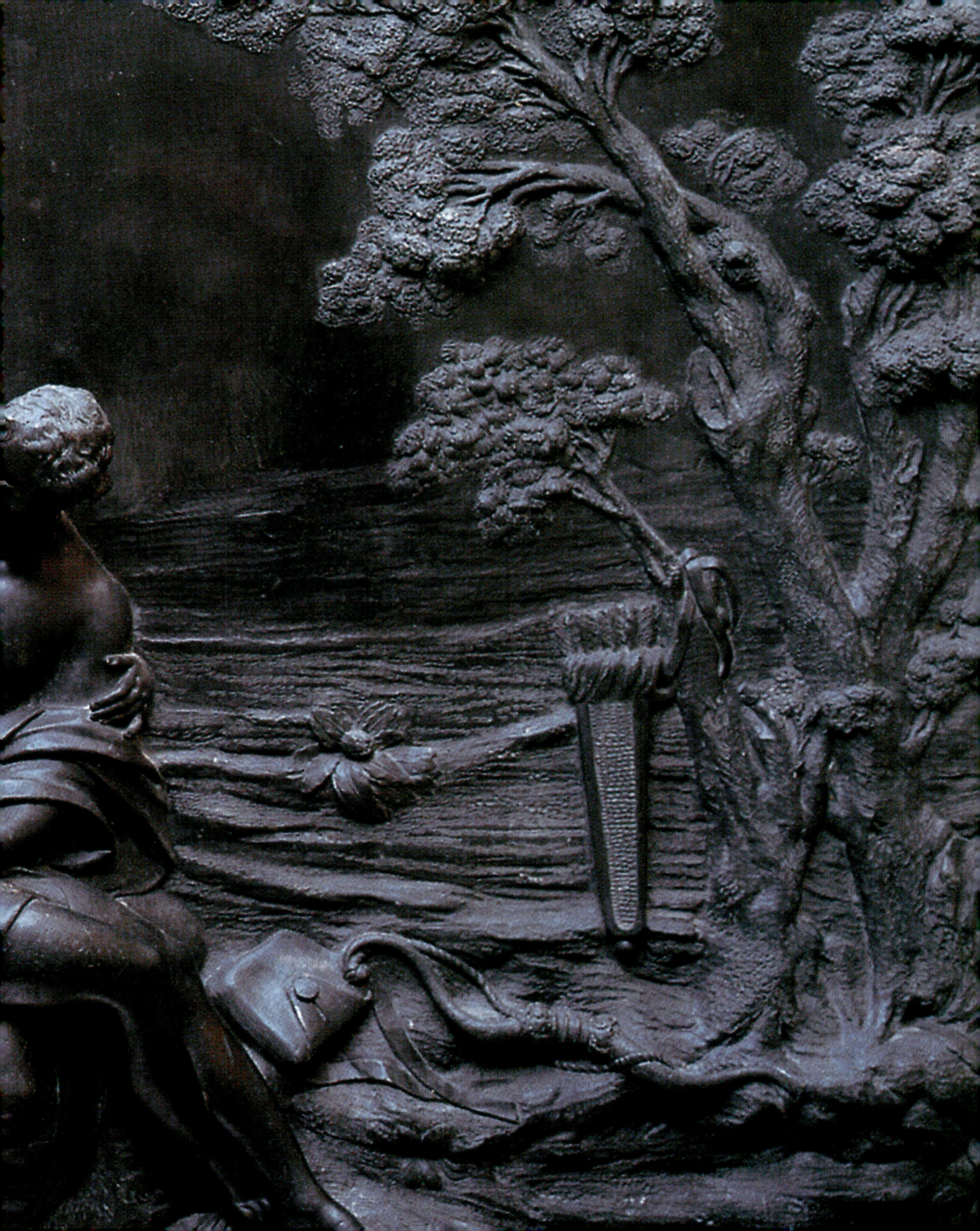

"Art comes to you frankly to give nothing but the highest quality to your moments as they pass, and simply for those moments' sake."

Walter Pater

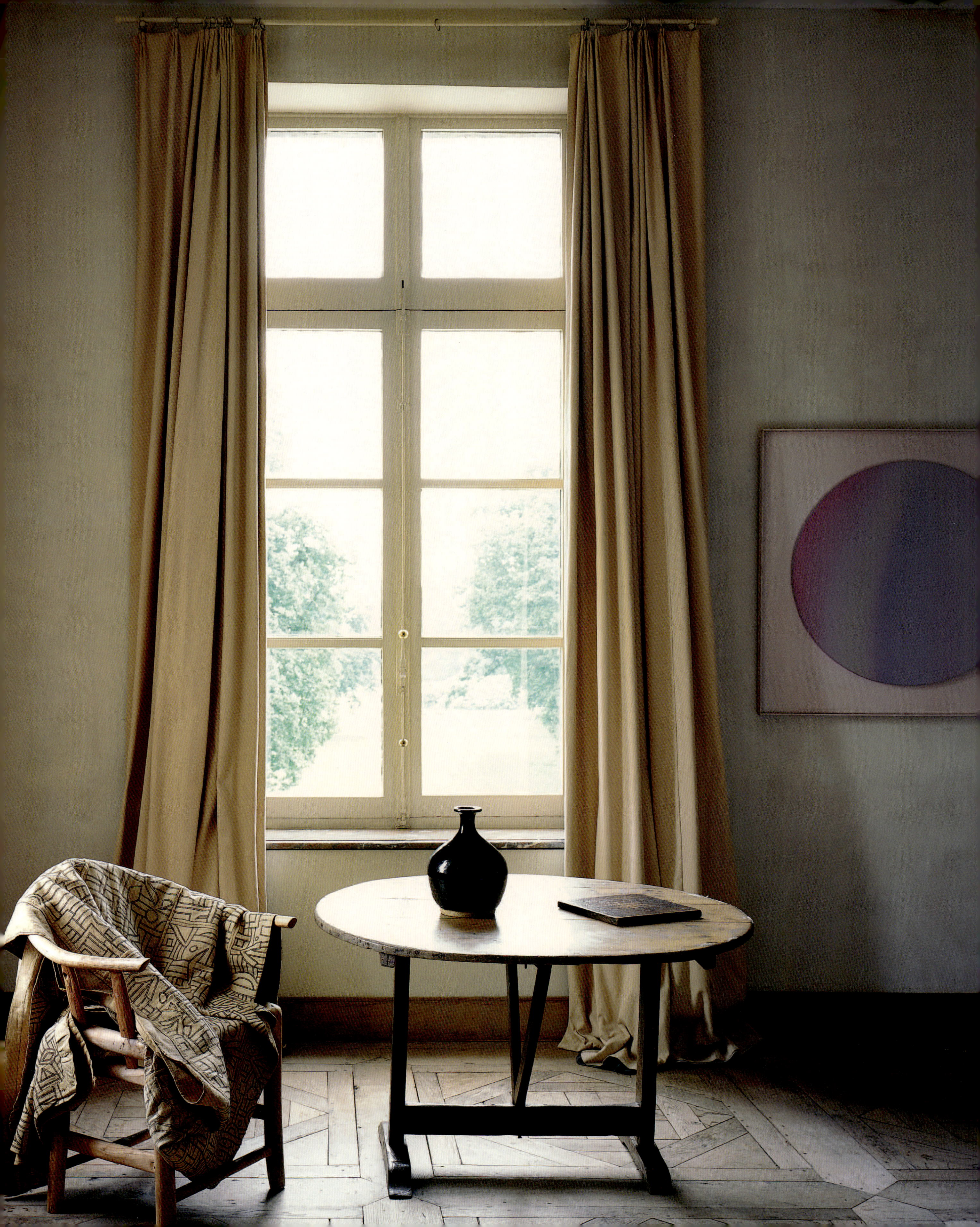

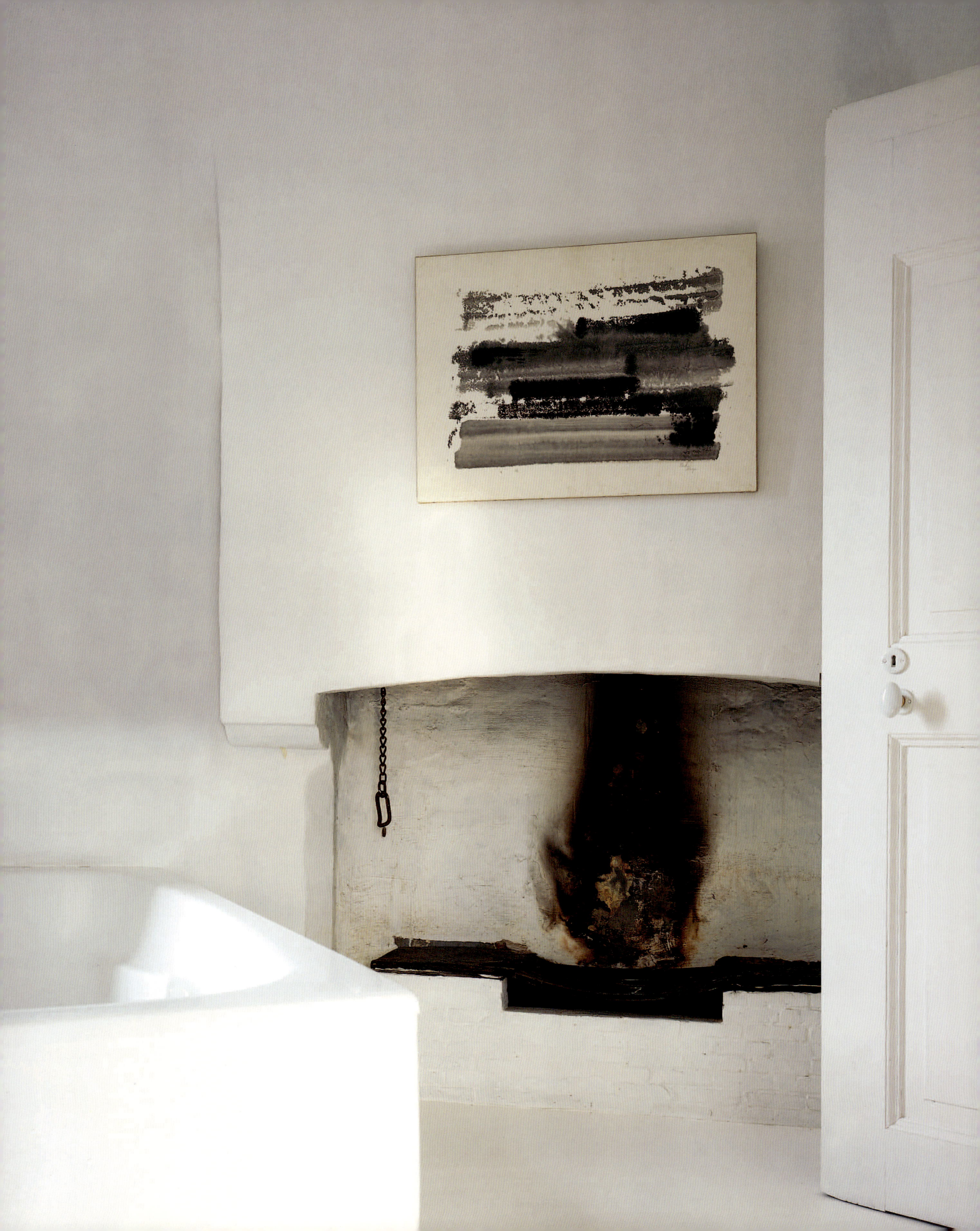

kanaal

The private rooms in the castle that May and I decorated for ourselves, where the clocks were not turned back to the castle's heyday, represent everything I believe in. Of all the rooms I have lived in, they are the truest to my ideas about the life we should live and the direction in which contemporary taste should develop. To demonstrate this new way of looking at interiors, to explain and promote this vision of limitless spatial purity, I needed to find another, very different environment. So, about six years ago, I began to look for an industrial building to buy near Antwerp to strip down to a minimalism inspired by the loft we had created in the Vlaeykensgang in 1973 when we were just married.

On the edge of the huge shipping canal leading to the port of Antwerp, some fifteen minutes' drive from the castle, there is a vast industrial site, a conglomeration of industrial buildings that we found and decided to turn into the Kanaal gallery. It took us a long time both to find and to acquire the site, because everyone had different ideas for its future. The city wanted to build houses on it, and there were also plans to appropriate the land for a business park or to keep it as an industrial site. But in the end we were the only ones interested in it and prepared to risk it. Now that it is complete, everyone supports what we have achieved with it.

The site had two parts. First, a series of nice old brew houses dating to the early nineteenth century and built of the traditional narrow red brick as seen in paintings by Pieter de Hooch. Then, in the middle of these attractive red-brick buildings, looms a towering prestressed concrete grain dryer built in the 1950s when the site became a grain store.

The Kanaal now looks virtually the same outside as when malt was being brewed there. But inside it's a very different story. Working very closely with my colleagues and my sons, Boris and Dick, we have restored these remnants of another time by stripping them right down to their essential architecture. The floors are bare—the original sanded wooden board or poured cement. The walls are exposed brick or whitewashed cement blocks. Iron beams and girders are left exposed. Staircases are cement.

In these lofty industrial chambers, I have furthered my ideas of how we might wish to live in the twenty-first century. Here—seen at first from a distance in the sun-filled spaces—one might find a collection of seventeenth- and eighteenth-century library steps and ladders, which look quite different taken out of their original context. By being displayed like this they have become sculpture, true works of art.

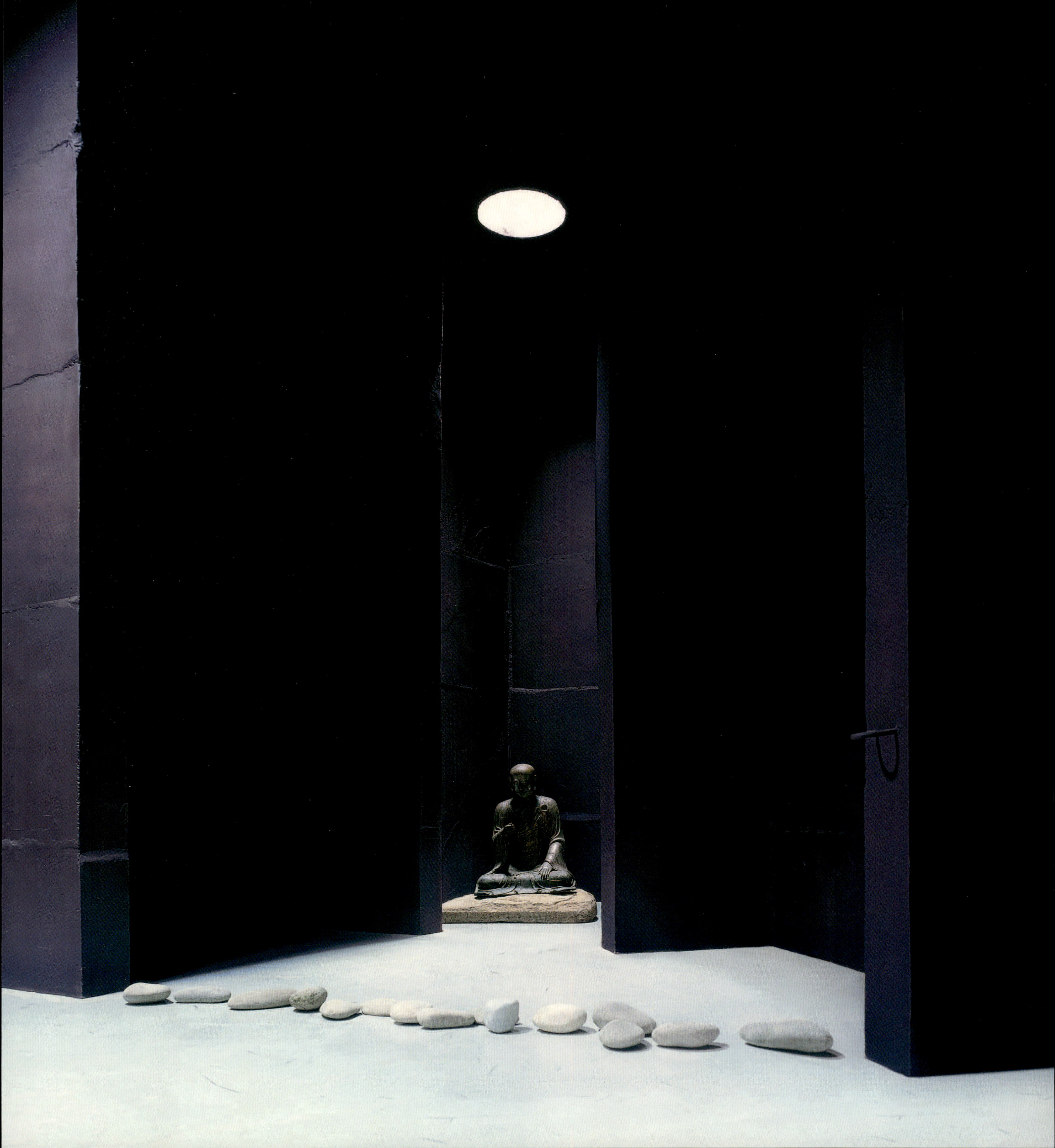

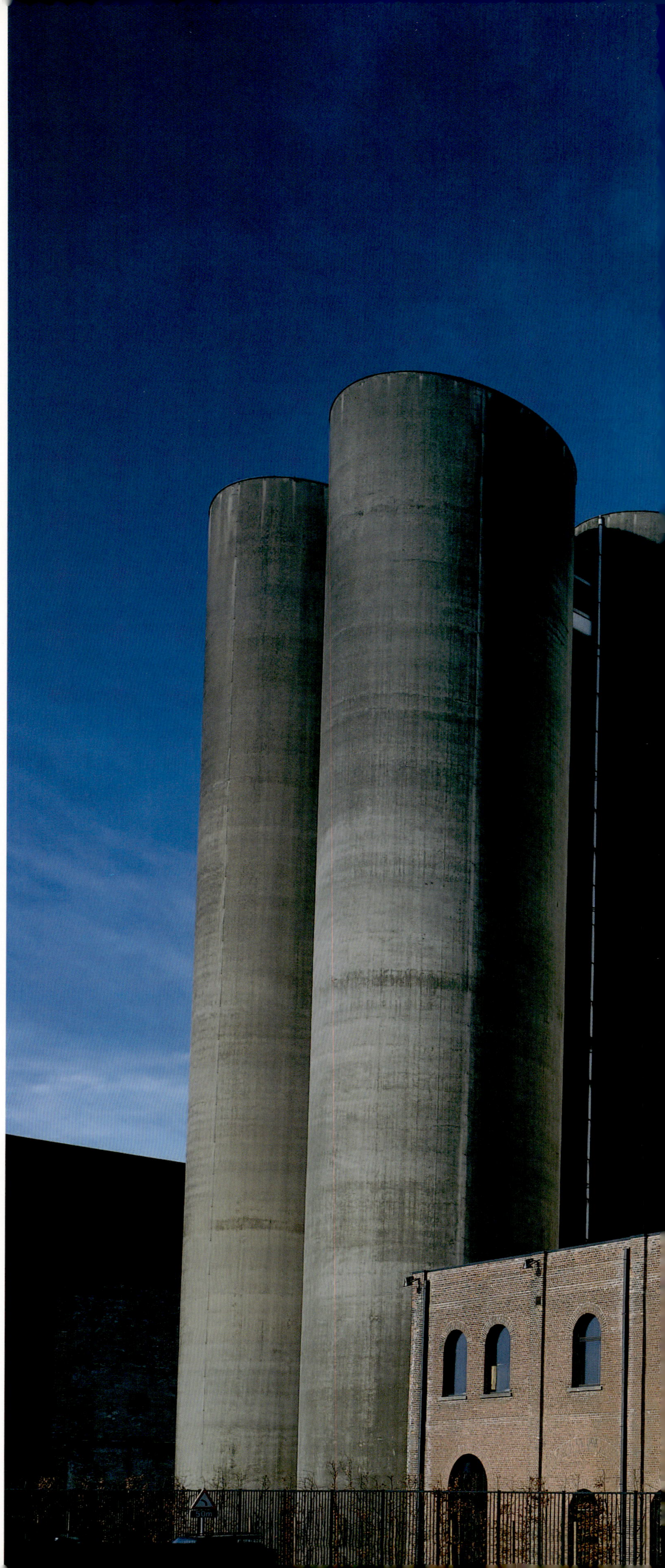

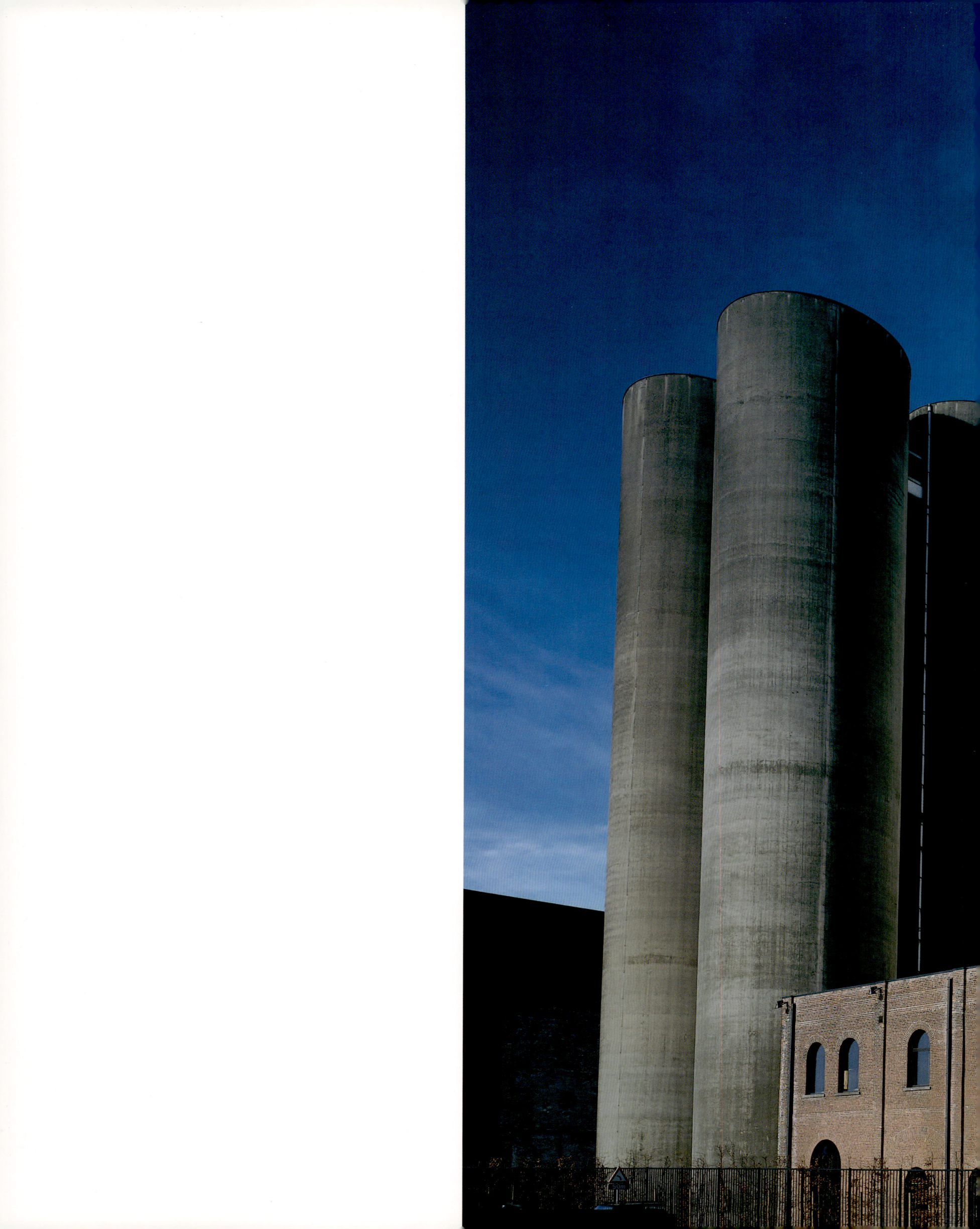

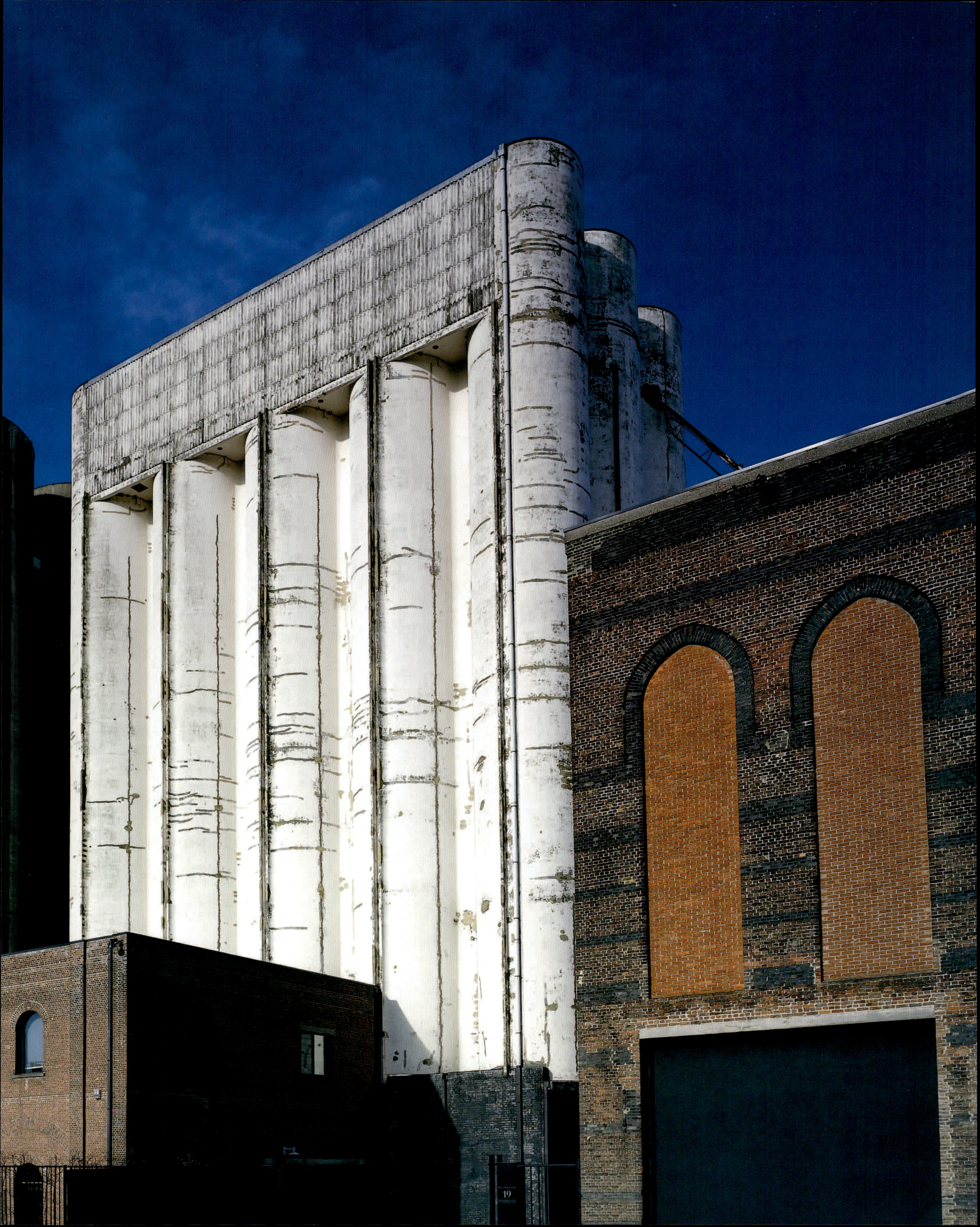
19

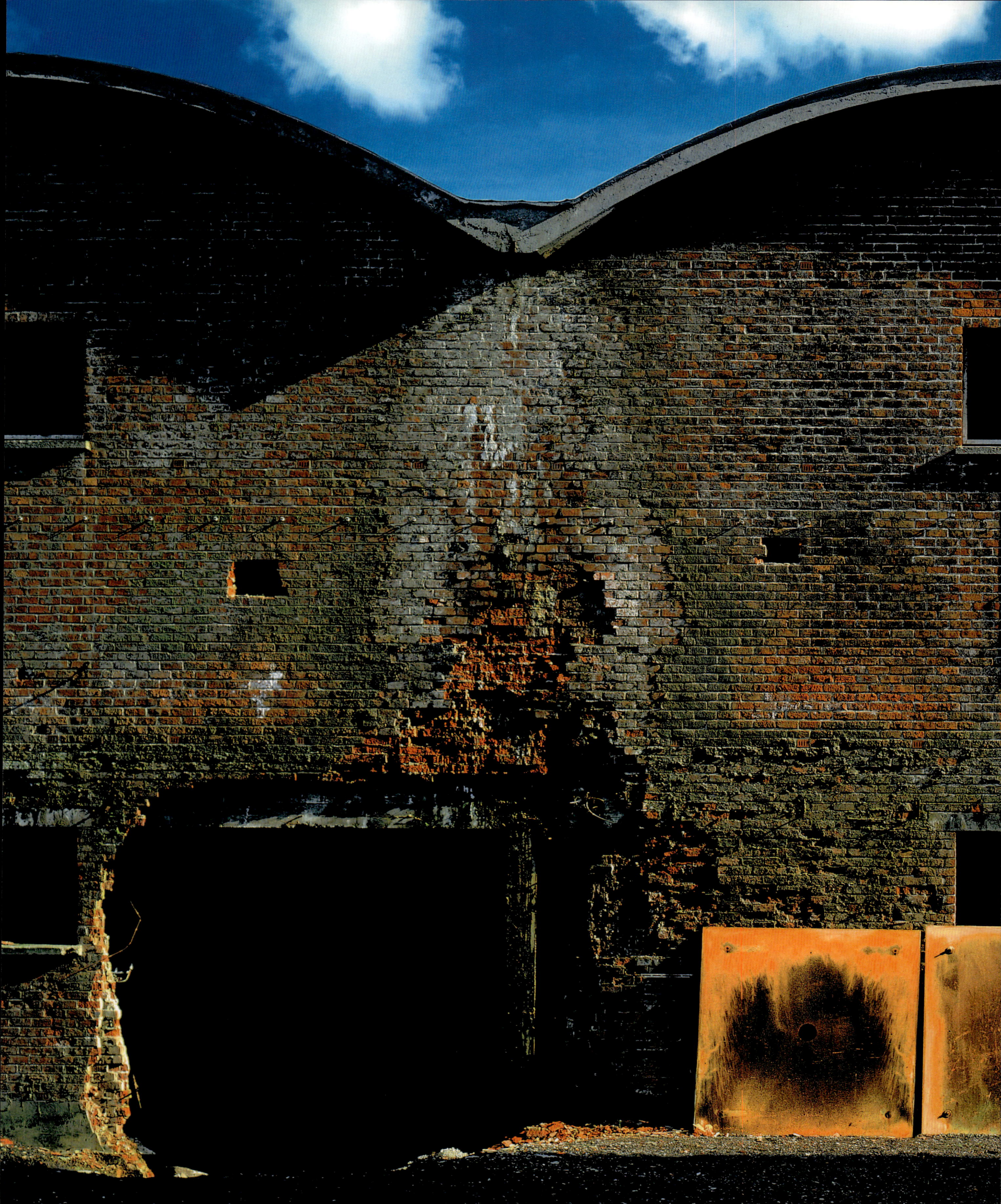

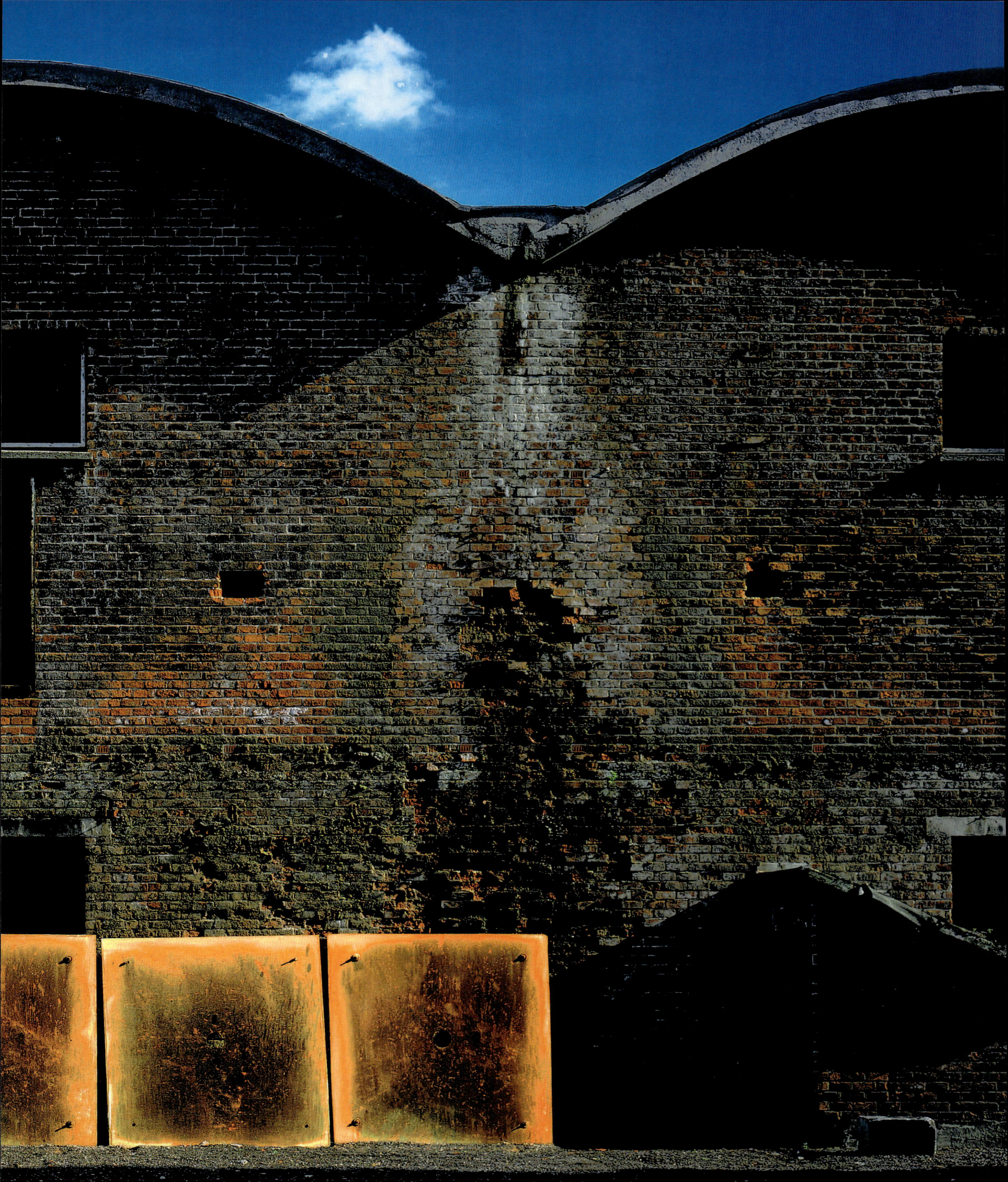

"To me, there is no past or future in art. The art of the Greeks, of the Egyptians, of the great painters who lived in other times, is not an art of the past; perhaps it is more alive today than it ever was."

Pablo Picasso

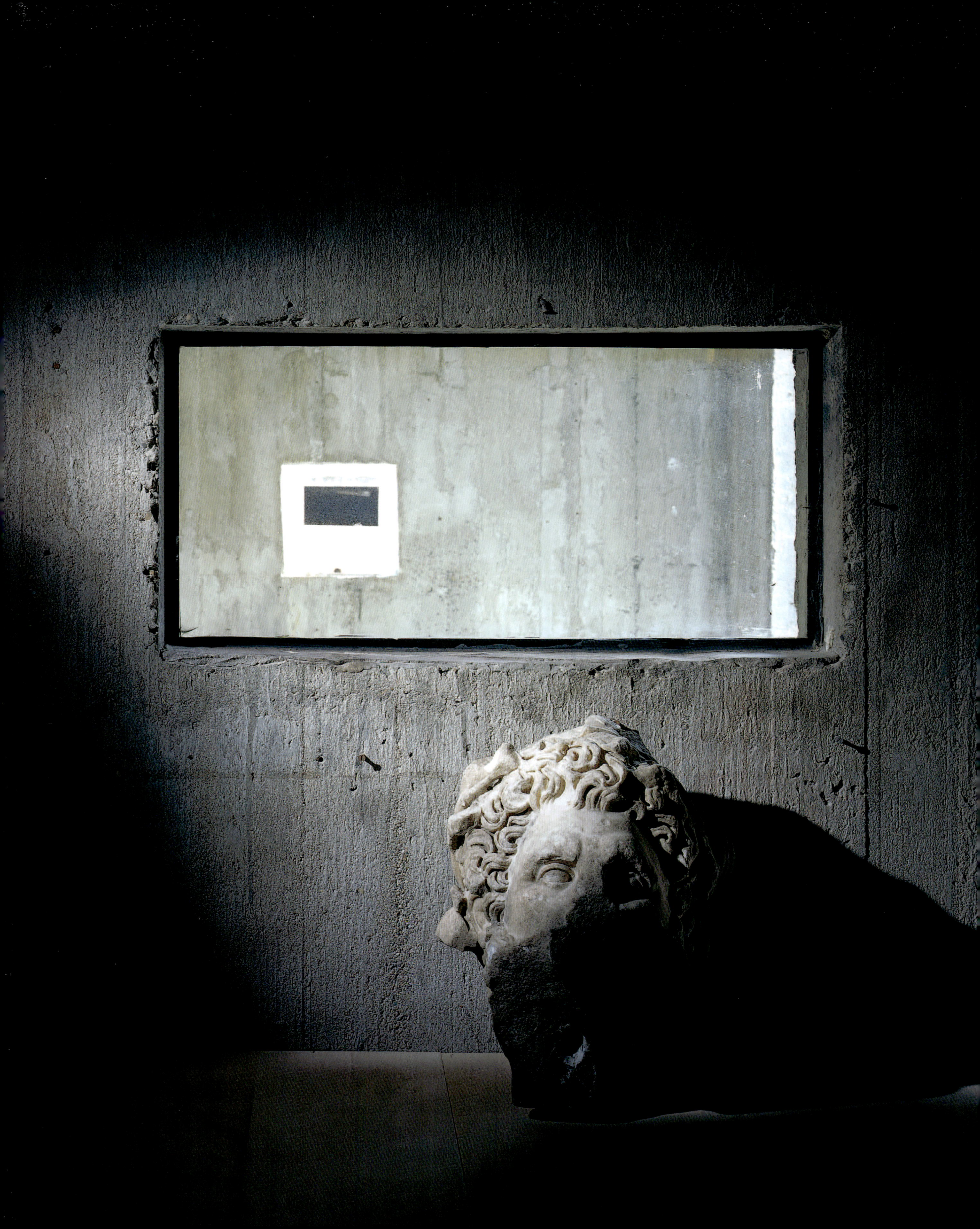

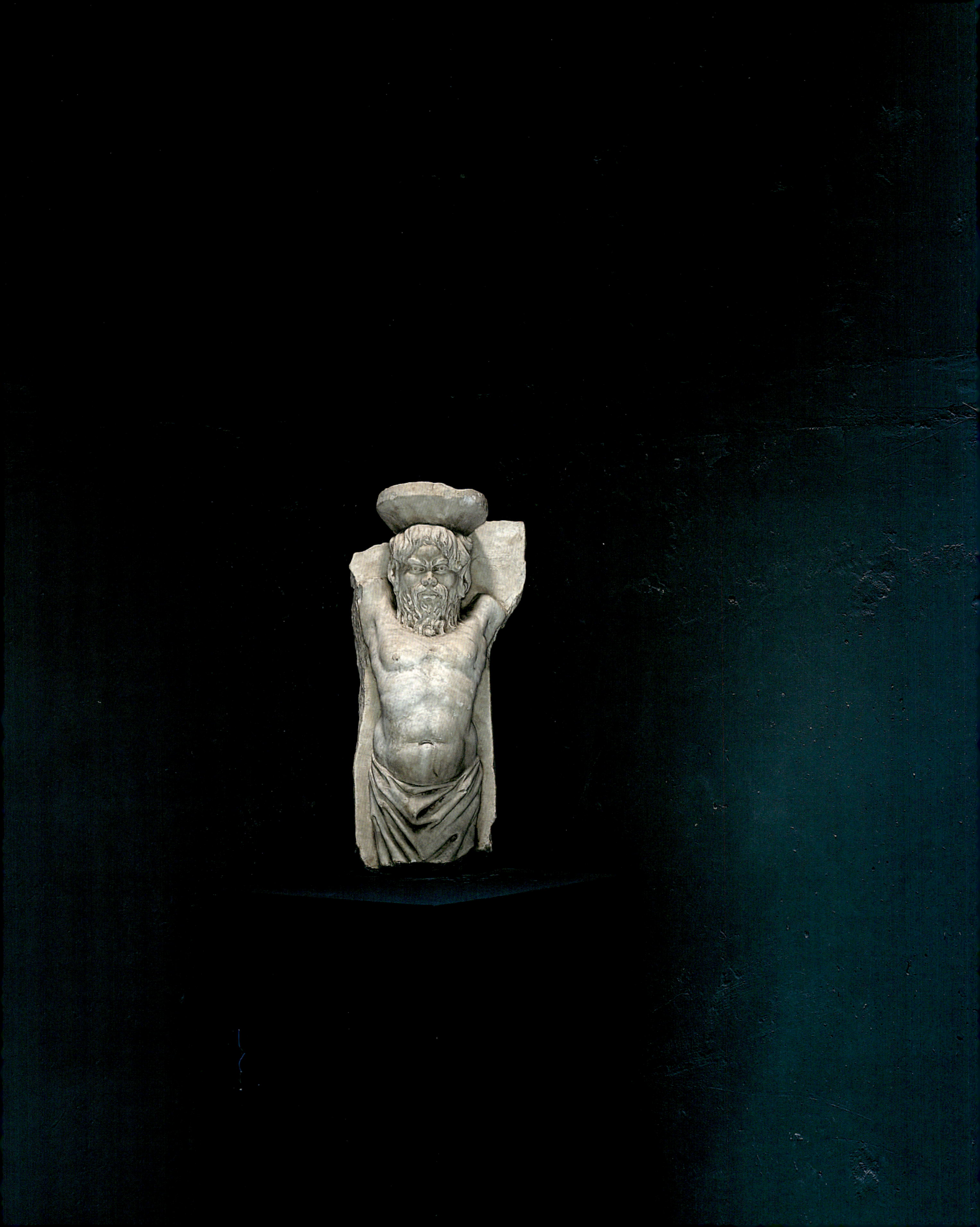

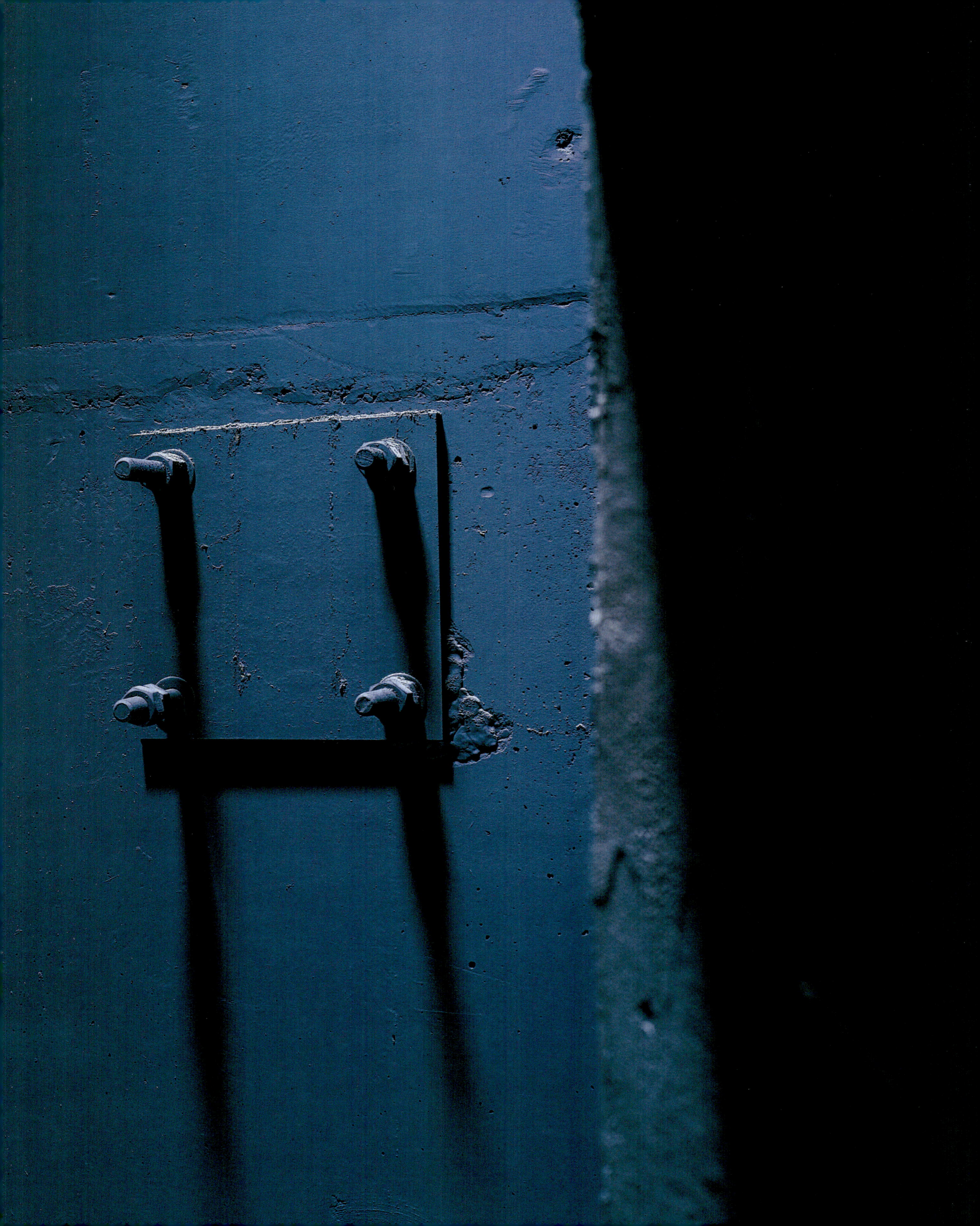

Against an exposed brick wall might be two elaborate silver candelabra by the renowned silversmith Paul Storr. Again, taken away from some princely eighteenth-century dining table, they become not table decoration, nor emblems of wealth and power, but strange and beautiful abstract objects. Massive antique Greek and Roman marble busts, portraits of long-dead notables, baroque gods culled from noble Italian gardens, they all look very different sitting on a poured-cement floor—especially when viewed to the haunting and abstract accompaniment of contemporary compositions by John MacLaughlin, Koen Kessels, Salvatore Charino, or John Cage.

But perhaps the cement grain dryer is truest to my vision of the future. The original rough beaten-earth floor has been left as it was. Simple duckboards lead the visitor through a forest of cement pillars. Soaring into the sky against these pillars, and against walls which still bear blurred and faded marks from the days of grain deliveries, stands the collection of Mon Dvaravatti statues made between the sixth and eighth centuries AD by Indian monks who brought Zen Buddhism to Thailand. It's a challenging new context in which to reconsider these spare exercises in form from an earlier age and a different culture.

I love the Kanaal—the enormous spaces, the total purity, the total lack of decoration, just the necessary architecture and beautiful things. In these rough, empty spaces an old piece of furniture becomes like a contemporary piece of furniture. To me, this makes it like a contemporary piece of art—as long as you don't restore it to make it pretty. Once you restore something too much, it loses its soul. When I discover something, or save it, and it has a patina, I keep it that way. Yes, you might restore an object and adapt it to your own time, but in my opinion you lose something very precious by doing this. If you accept a thing as it comes to us today, it is like a contemporary piece of art that took 350 years to make. Think about it. It takes time to grow the wood. It embodies the spirit of the people who made the piece, the people who used the piece. It gets lost in an attic somewhere. And then it comes to life again when it is rediscovered and used in another sort of environment in a different way.

You can call it contemporary because life is like this today. This piece of furniture, this statue, was not viewed in this way 100 years ago. It is the same piece, but it has a different spirit and we observe it differently with eyes that are seeing things now, not as we would have seen them even 100 years ago.

I find everything I like has a timeless quality. They are what they are, they've got a strong expression, they are made with the right spirit of respect and love and they are made to live for a long time. But I also like things that are created in an instant; I like pictures by Rubens where he has applied the paint with one stroke, like an action painting, and I also like Zen paintings, where a monk might have prepared his painting in his mind for

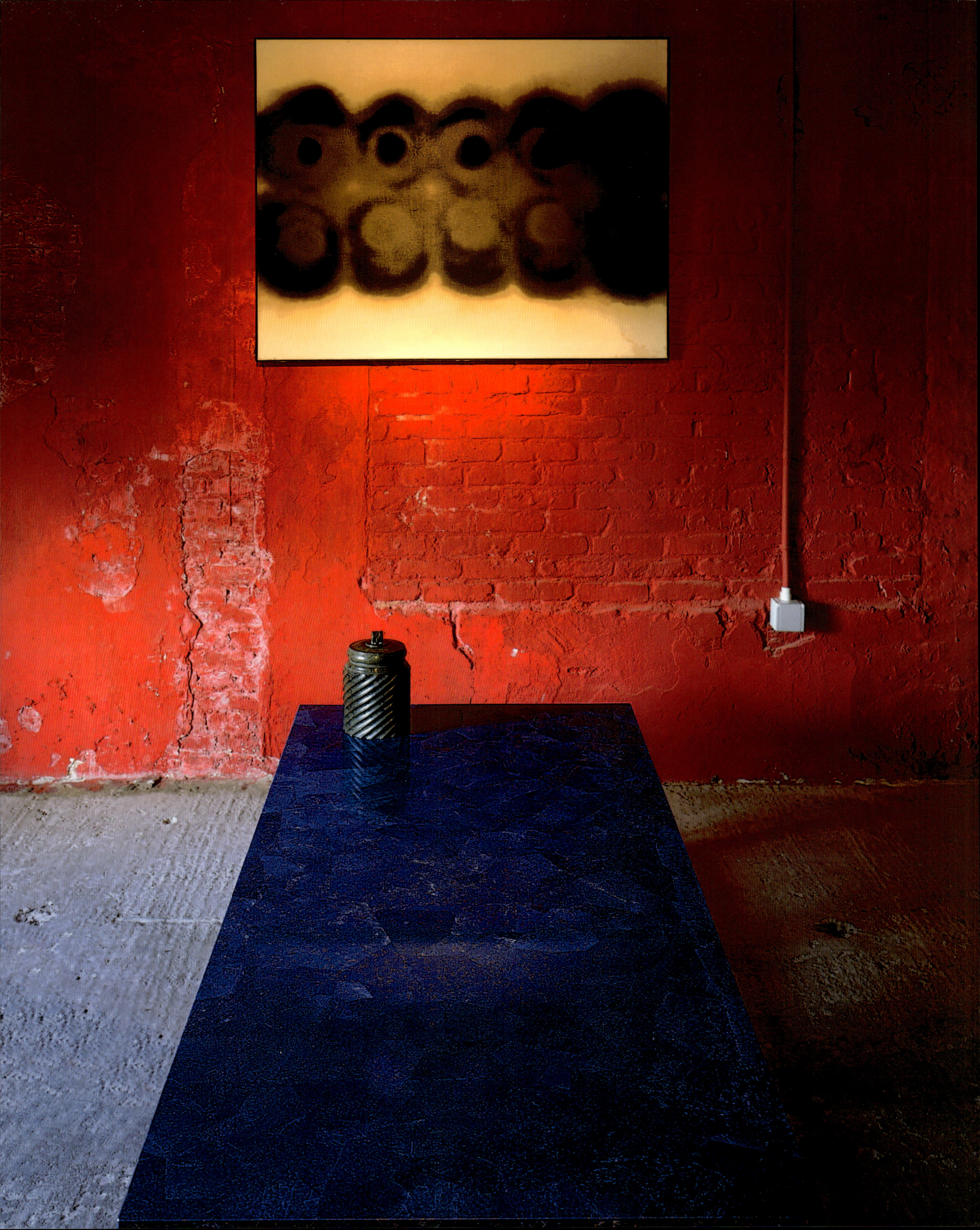

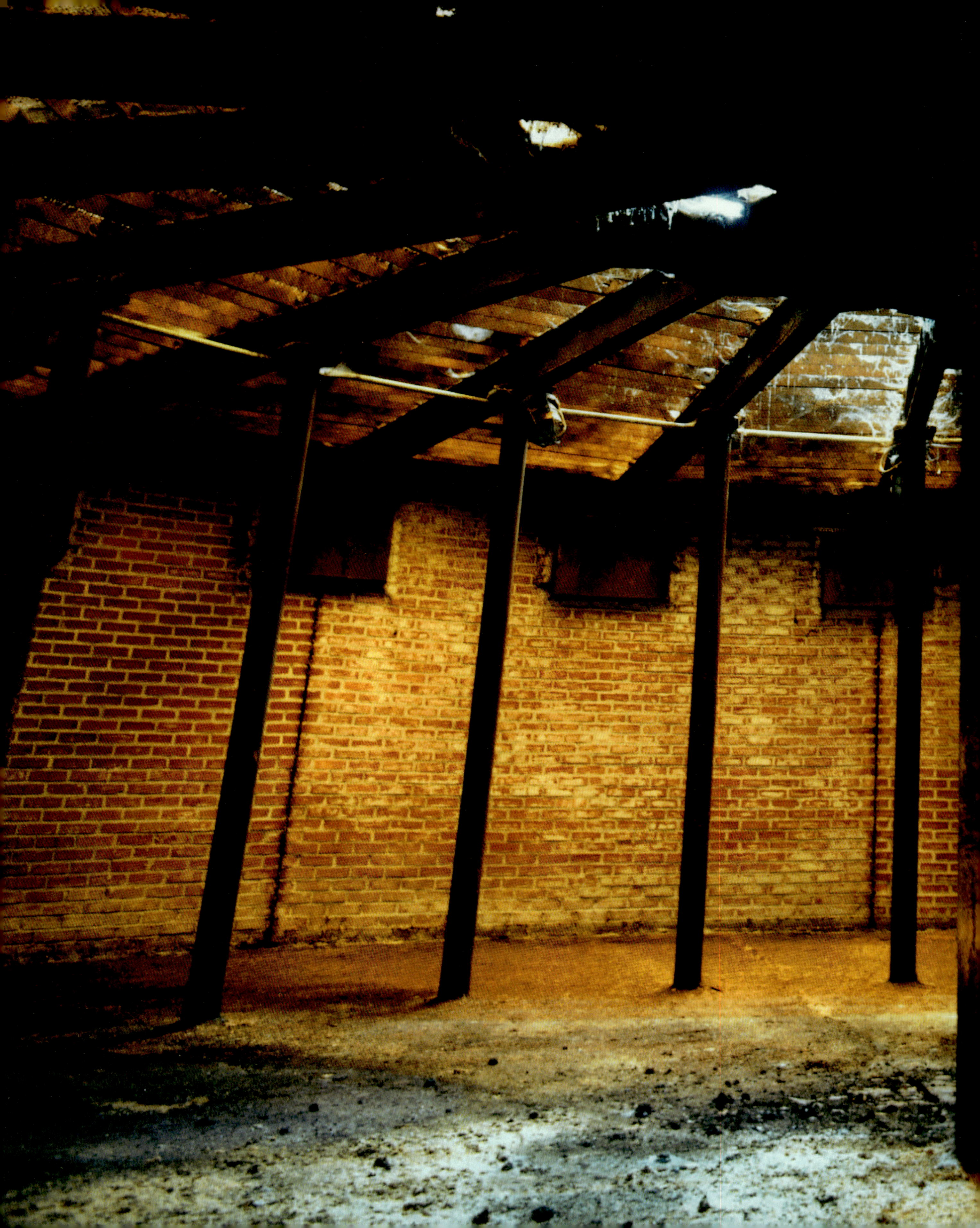

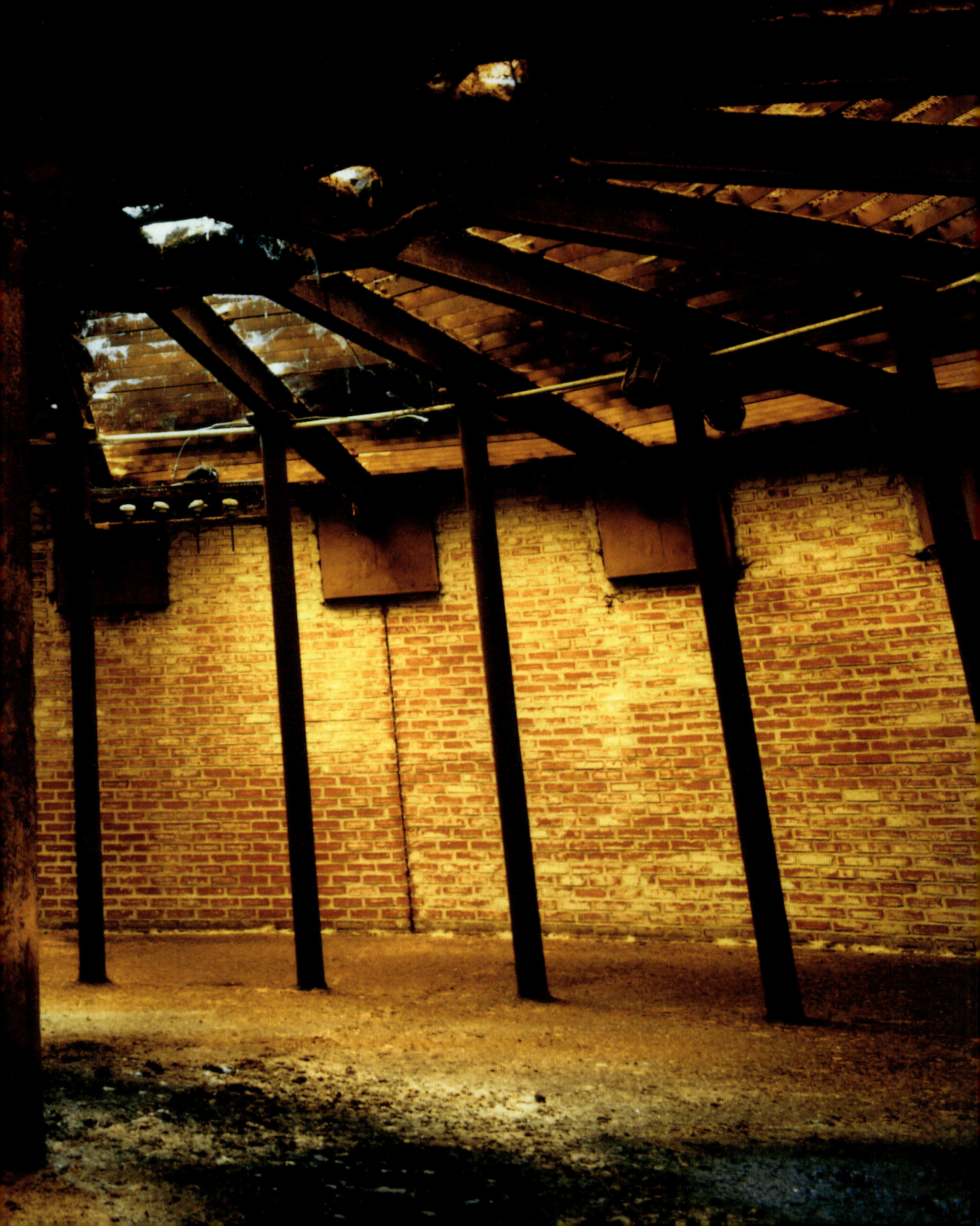

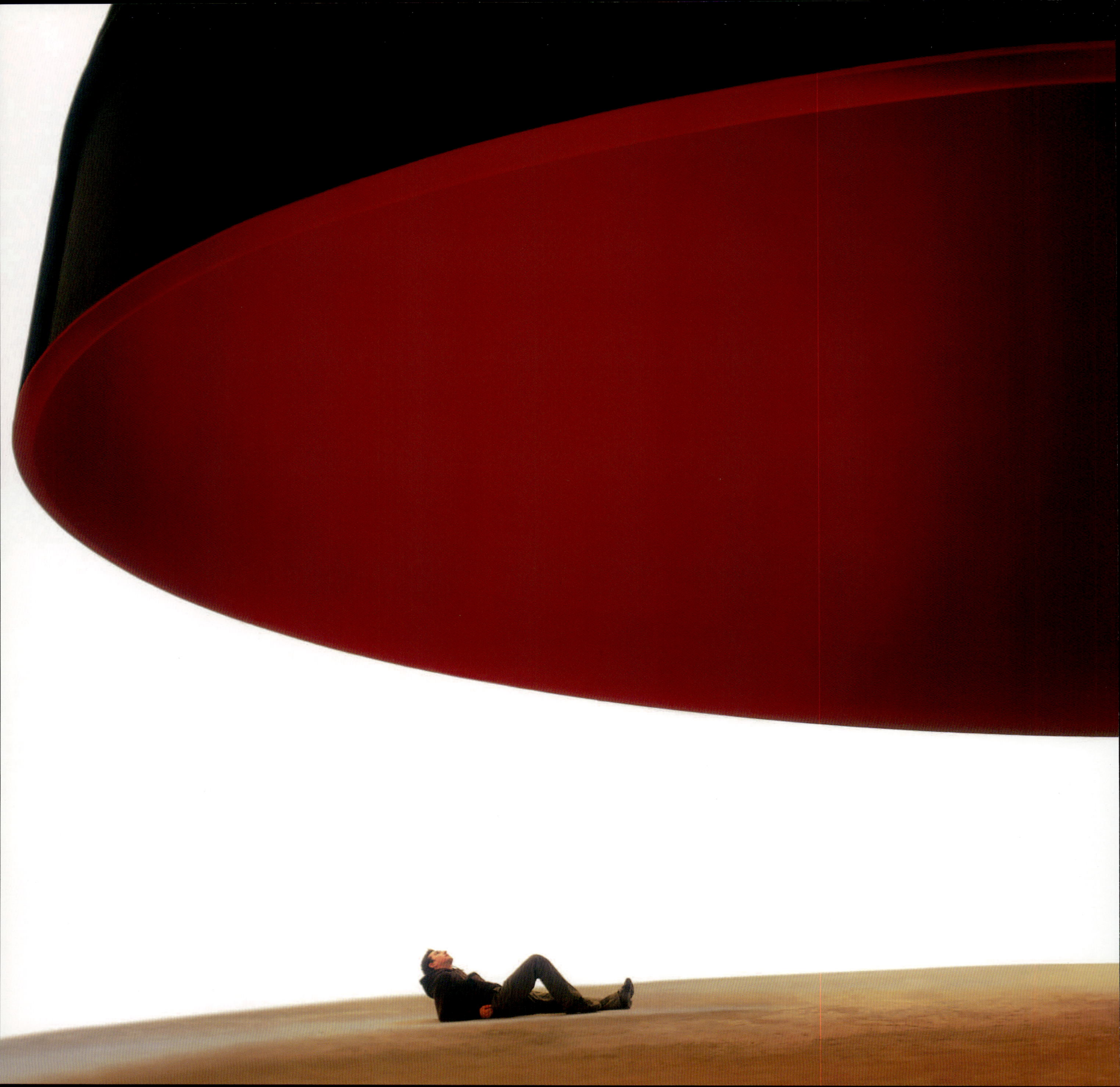

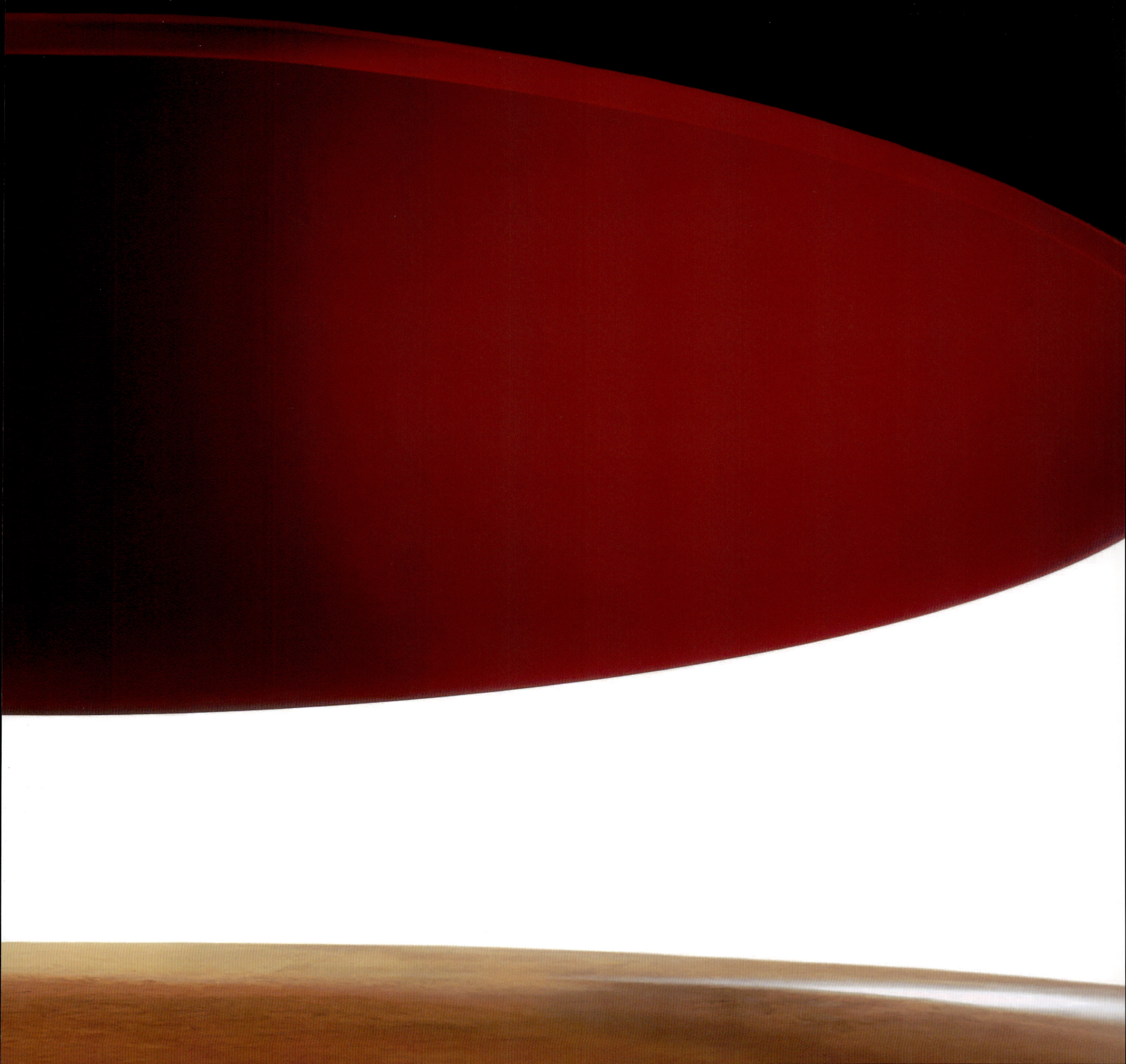

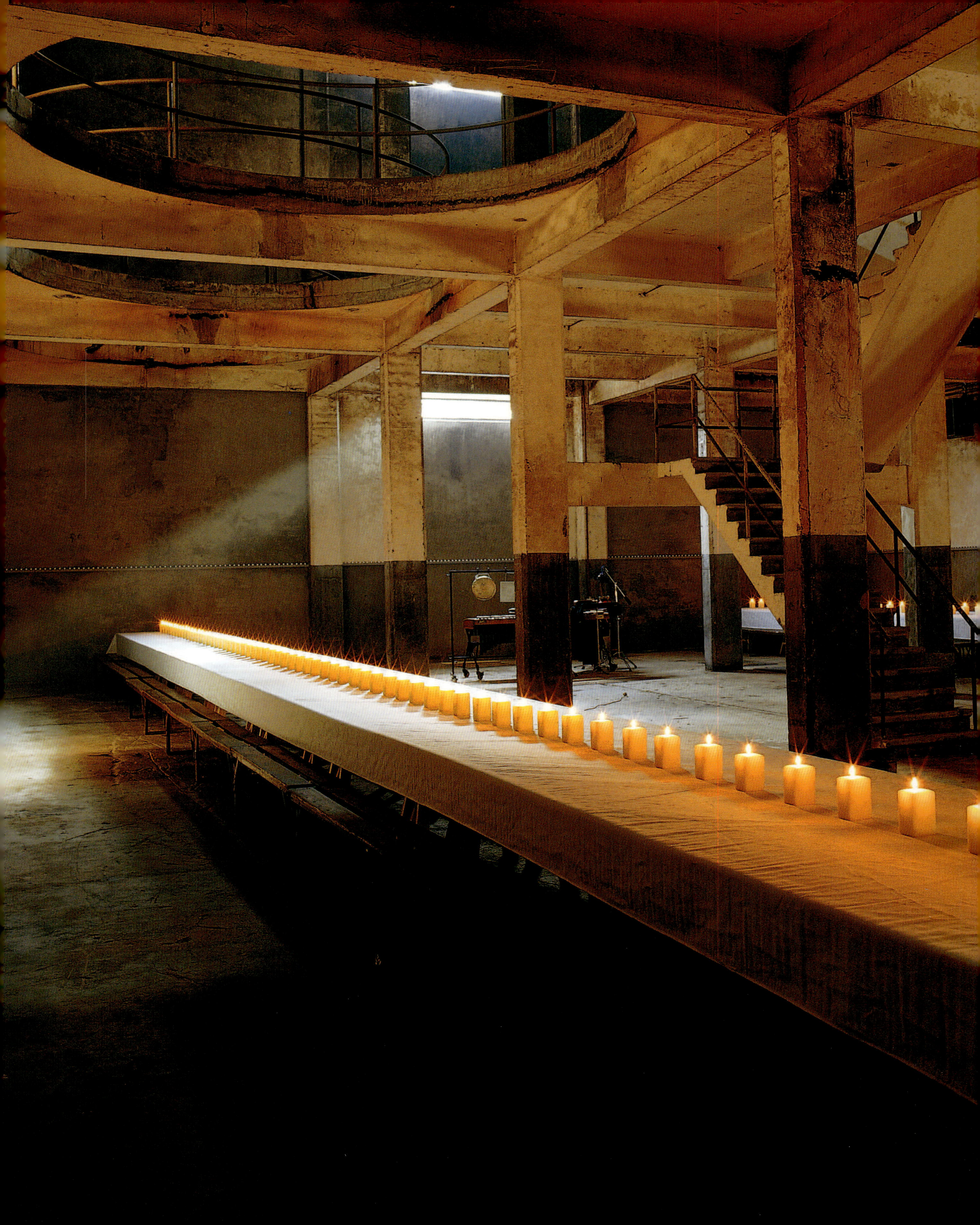

many years and then executed it in one second. I also love the impermanent; flowers, the seasons, and things that have died. I love a day when it is sunny because you know that soon it will be grey.

I felt I needed to give the Kanaal another dimension in its new life. We decided to buy a major contemporary work of art to be displayed there—partly as a gift for the future. Now, in the old circular brew house—stripped of the metal brewing vats, freshly whitewashed with a dark polished cement floor—hangs Anish Kapoor's majestic circular sculpture installation *At the Edge of the World* (1998). The visitor enters through a tiny vestibule and through a small door into another world. Step under the sculpture. Stand in its center. Look up into it, and you are lost in the cosmos, in a dark space without end. As the eye becomes more accustomed to the dark, one begins to perceive the sculpture's a deep, deep red color.

To me it is like existing at the beginning of the world…it's like a heart, moving with the earth. In fact, I don't need to look at it all the time. The fact that it is there, in the Kanaal, means I possess it in my heart. It is very important and I hope it is going to stay there for many generations.

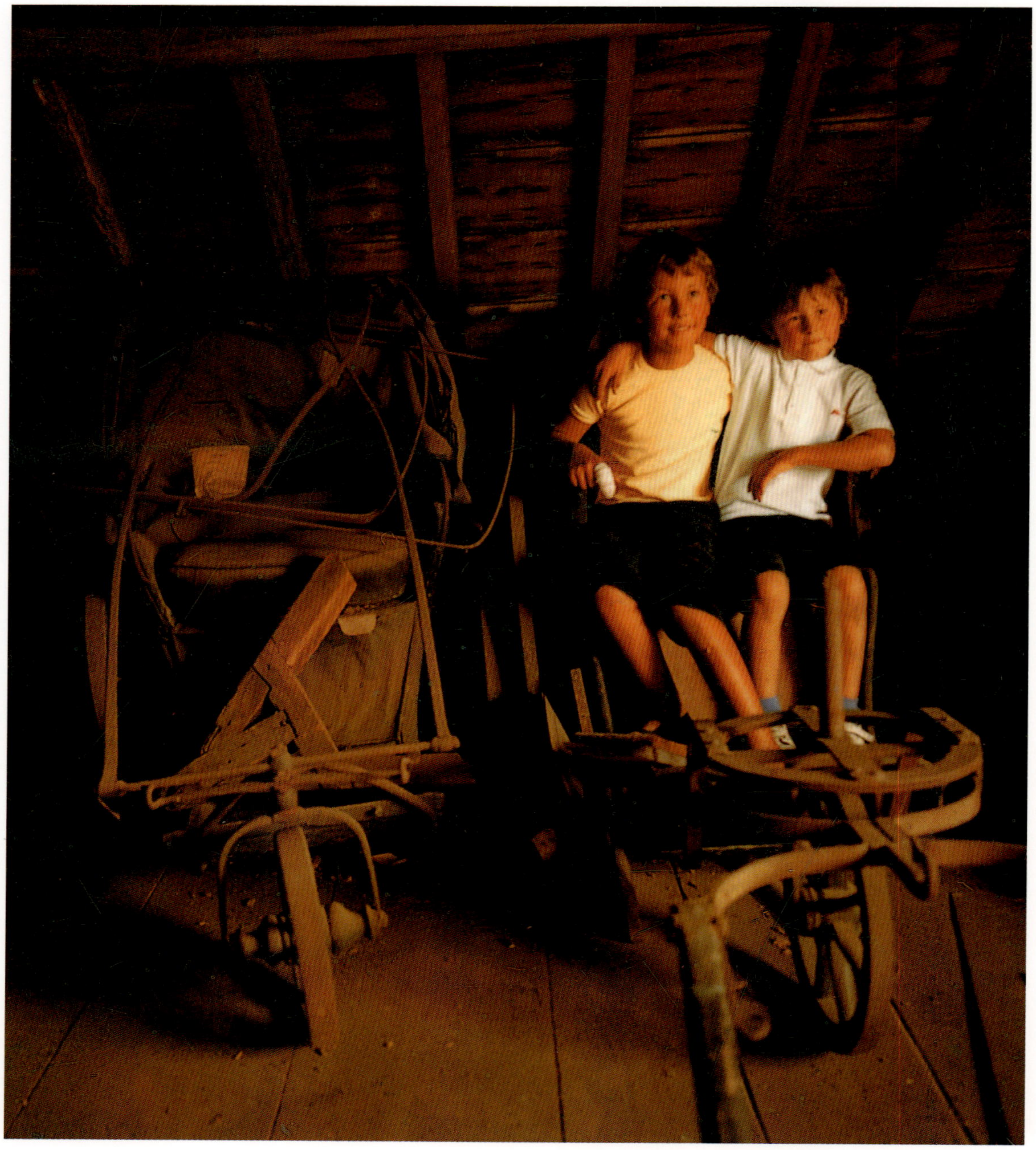

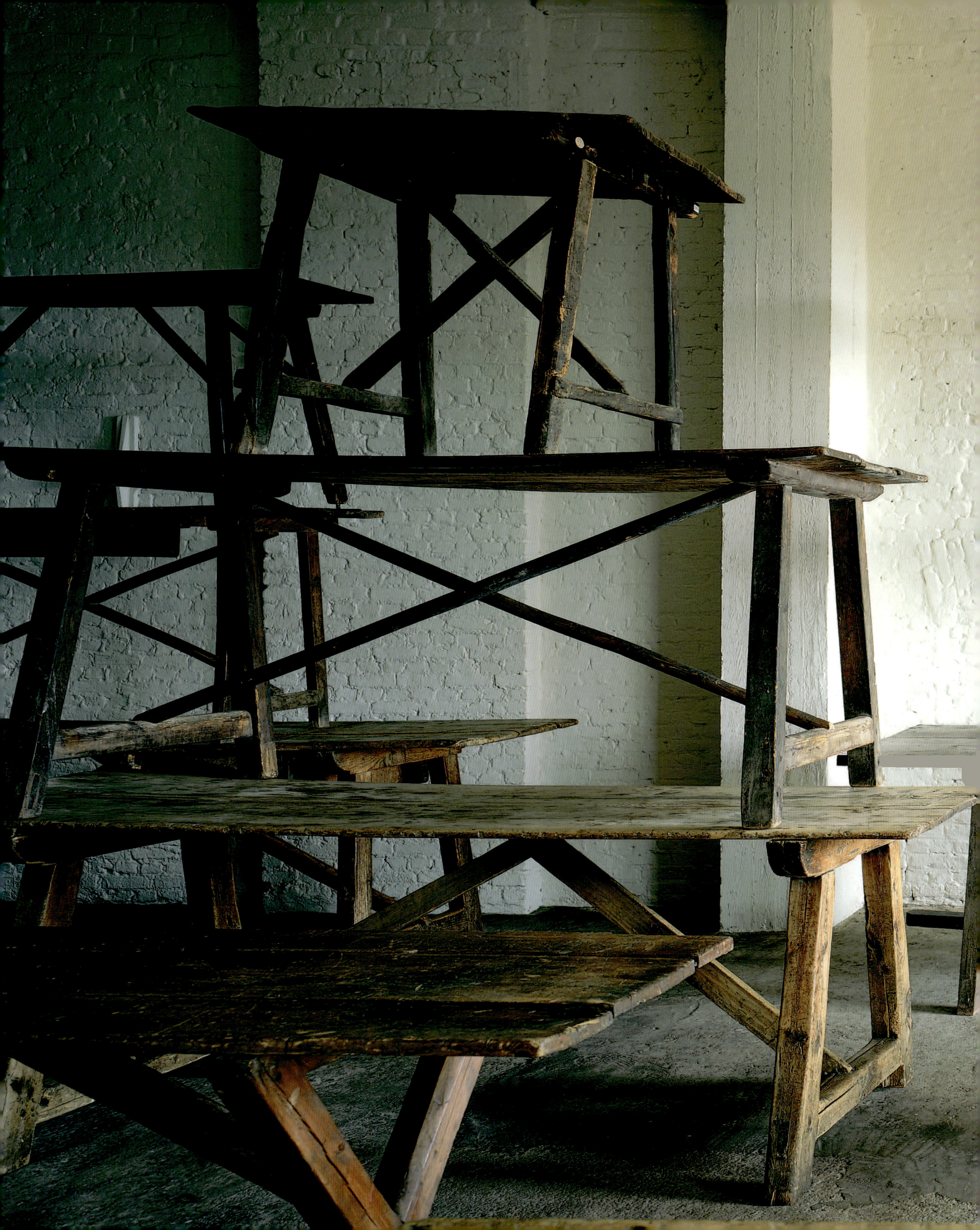

volledig

To me, *volledig,* the Flemish word I use a great deal to explain the philosophy on which I have founded my life and work, means "the fullness of emptiness." Conjuring the space of the future out of the fullness of past taste. Keeping the very best and eliminating all but the essentials. According to Tibetan tradition, the philosopher-leader's mind should be wide enough to embrace paradox and contradiction, polarity and ambiguity, conflict and incompatibility.

My task, as I have seen it from a very young age, has been to rediscover beautiful works of art, to save them for the future, to reveal them for what they are, to show them at their best, to give them a better place in the world—and, perhaps, by doing this, to create harmony and find new ways of expressing the inner life.

I have long believed that the economy of the twentieth century was very wasteful, based as it was on the idea of using something once and then throwing it away. In the twenty-first century, recycling is the spirit of the time. Think of conceptual art—many artists are working and reworking plastics and other objects. When I see the work of Joseph Beuys, for instance, it inspires me. To me, antiques are also part of this movement—reusing old wood, rediscovering old furniture, valuing it and giving it new life by putting it into a new context.

There are probably paradoxes and contradictions in my view of my métier. I don't, for instance, mind if something I discover is "ugly"—the spirit of things is more important to me than how they look. To see the essential harmony in an outwardly ugly object is very important for understanding the fundamentals by getting closer to mankind's beginnings.

What interests me most in my discoveries of old things is understanding how they are the precursors of our present day—of the "contemporary." I need these things for inspiration more than I need to possess them. If I were to live in a smaller house, I would take very few of my possessions with me—some of my modern pictures, some Oriental art. I might take some Egyptian pieces and beautiful, simple things to use in wood. I would take nothing that was there to show richness or exterior wealth, I would only take things that have an internal life and an interesting spirit. I would, for instance, take fabulous sixteenth-century silver because it is very plain and looks like nothing, but is, in reality, very valuable. But value doesn't matter to me, I like things which are pure.

To me it is important to love and to know the past, so I can help create the future. I've never wanted to hide myself in the past. I've never had the feeling, "Oh, I wish it was the seventeenth century," or

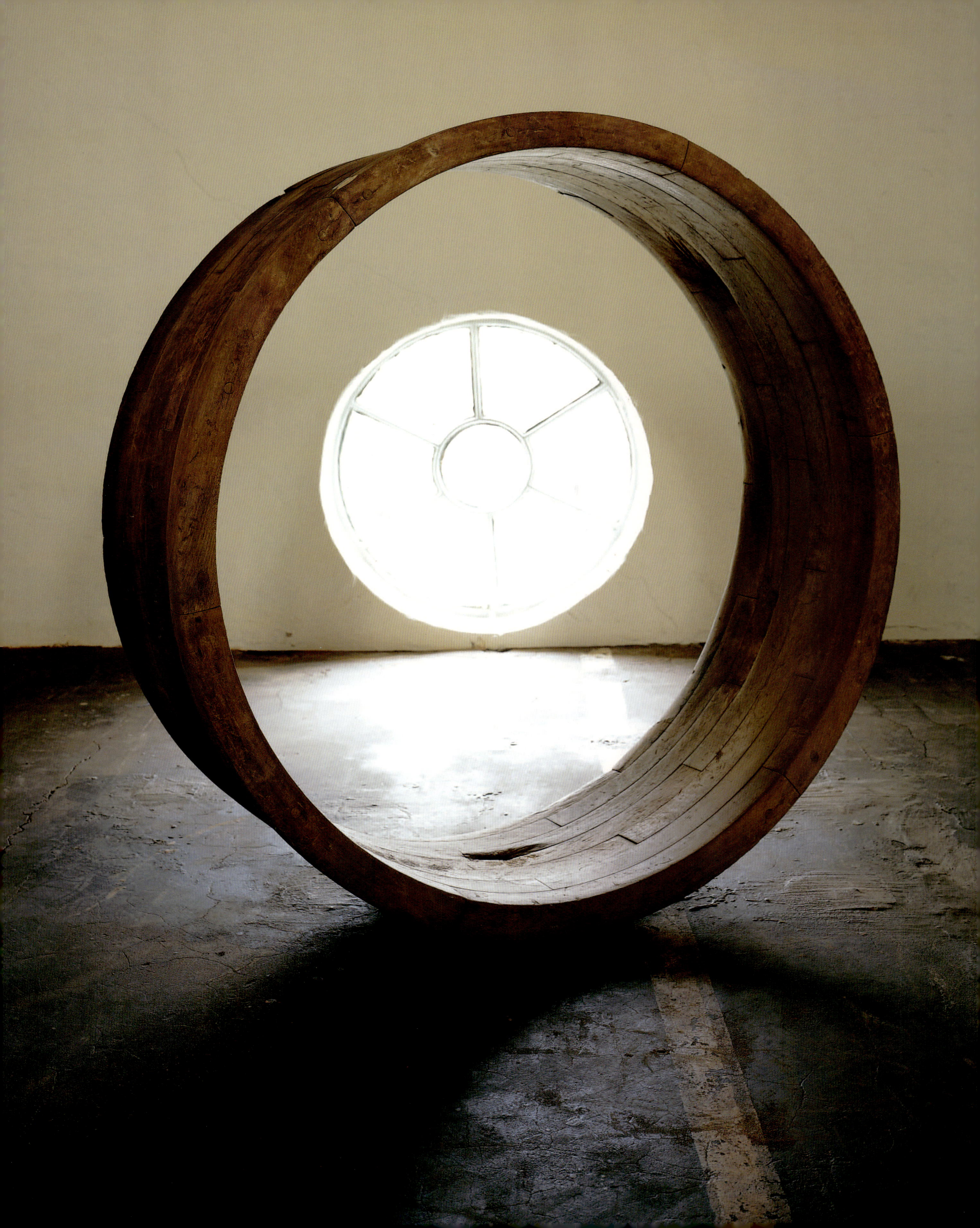

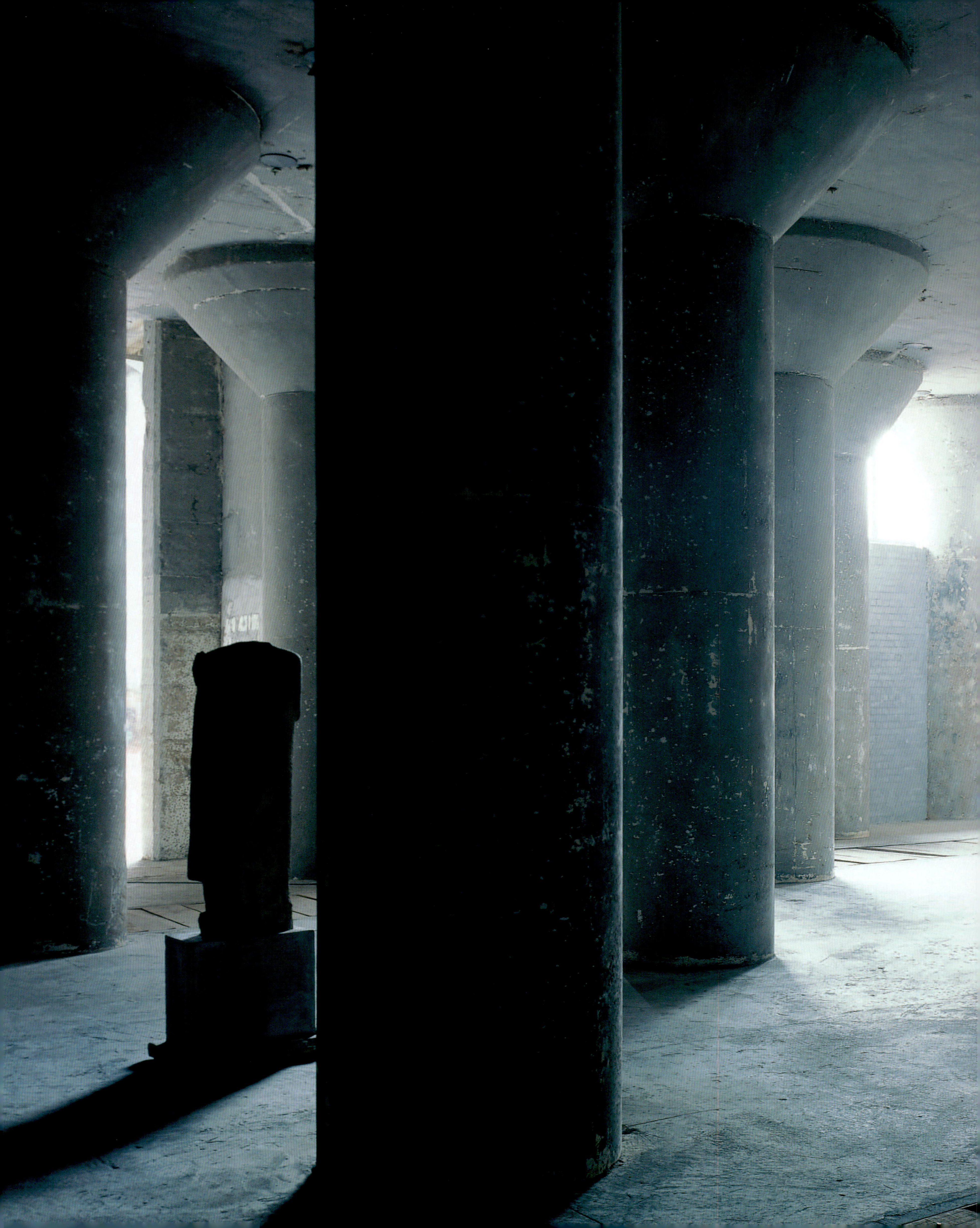

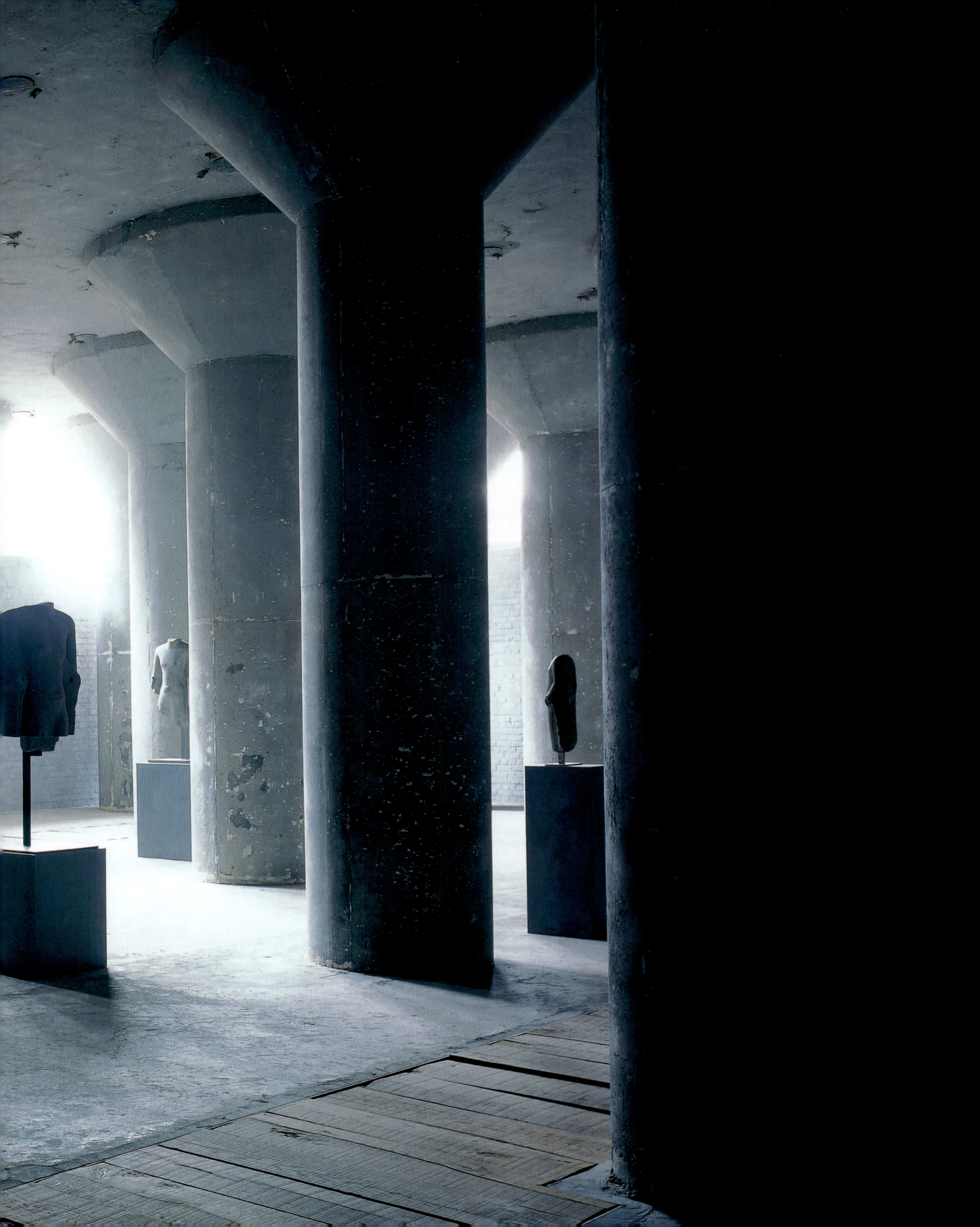

"The history of art
is the history of revival."

Samuel Butler

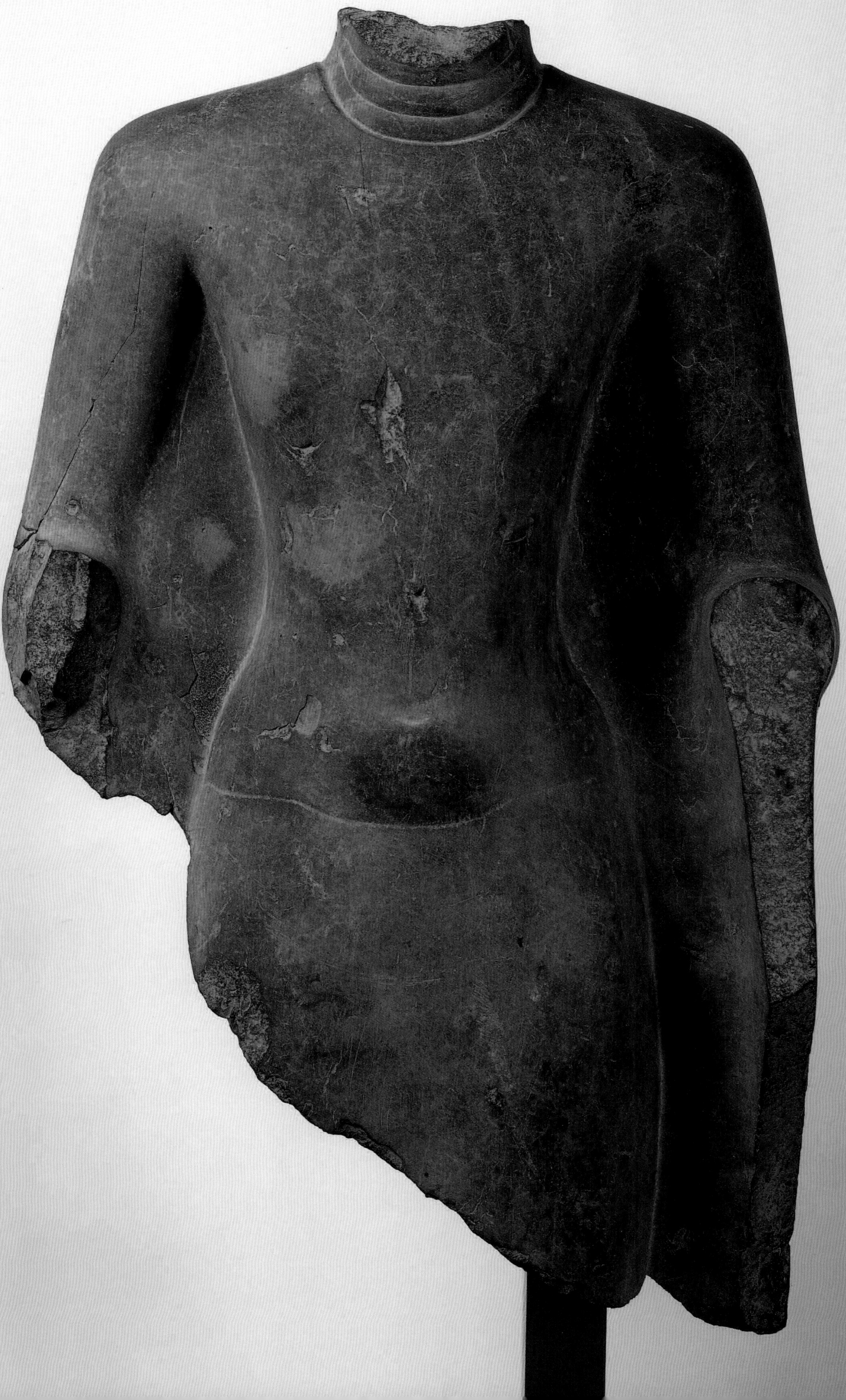

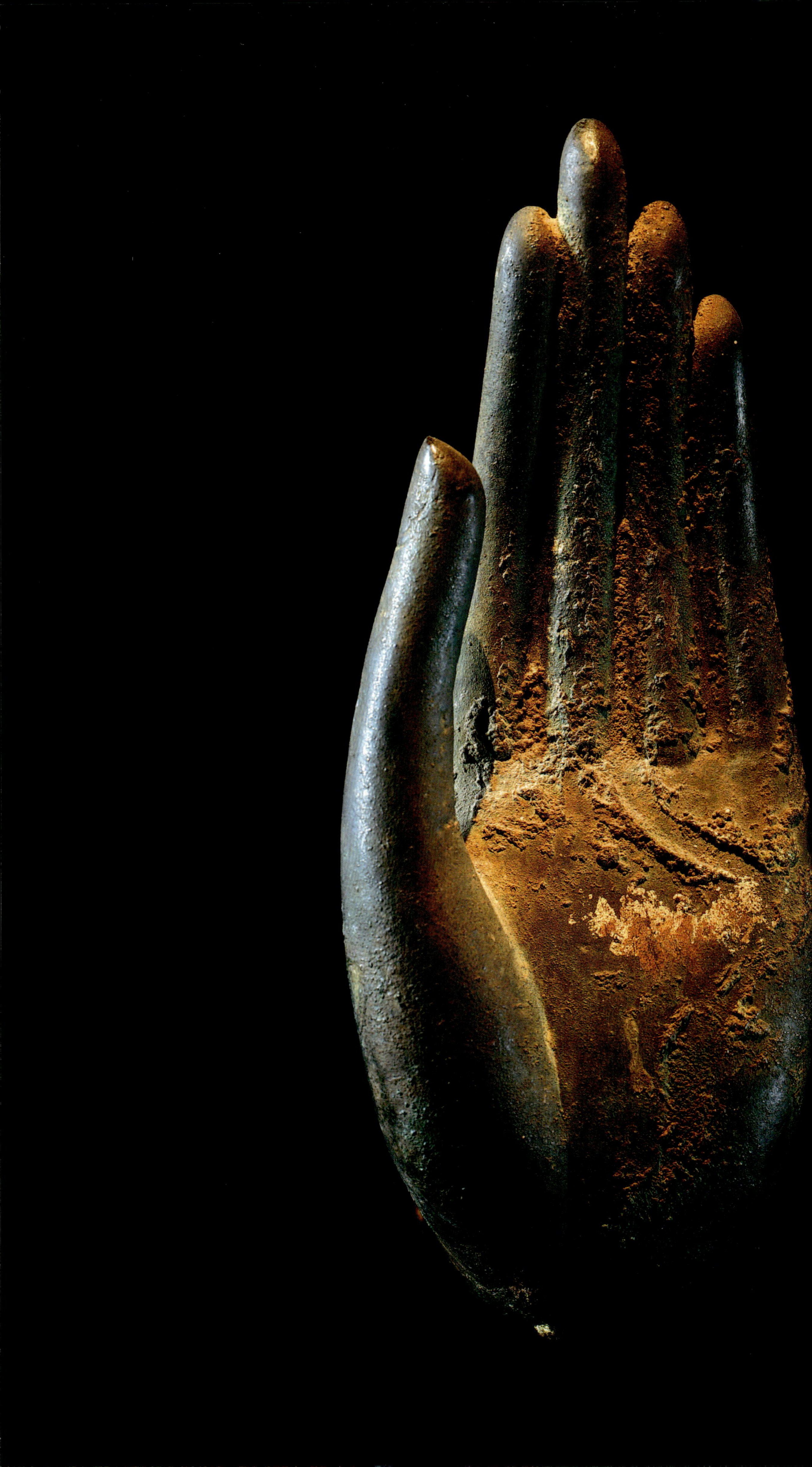

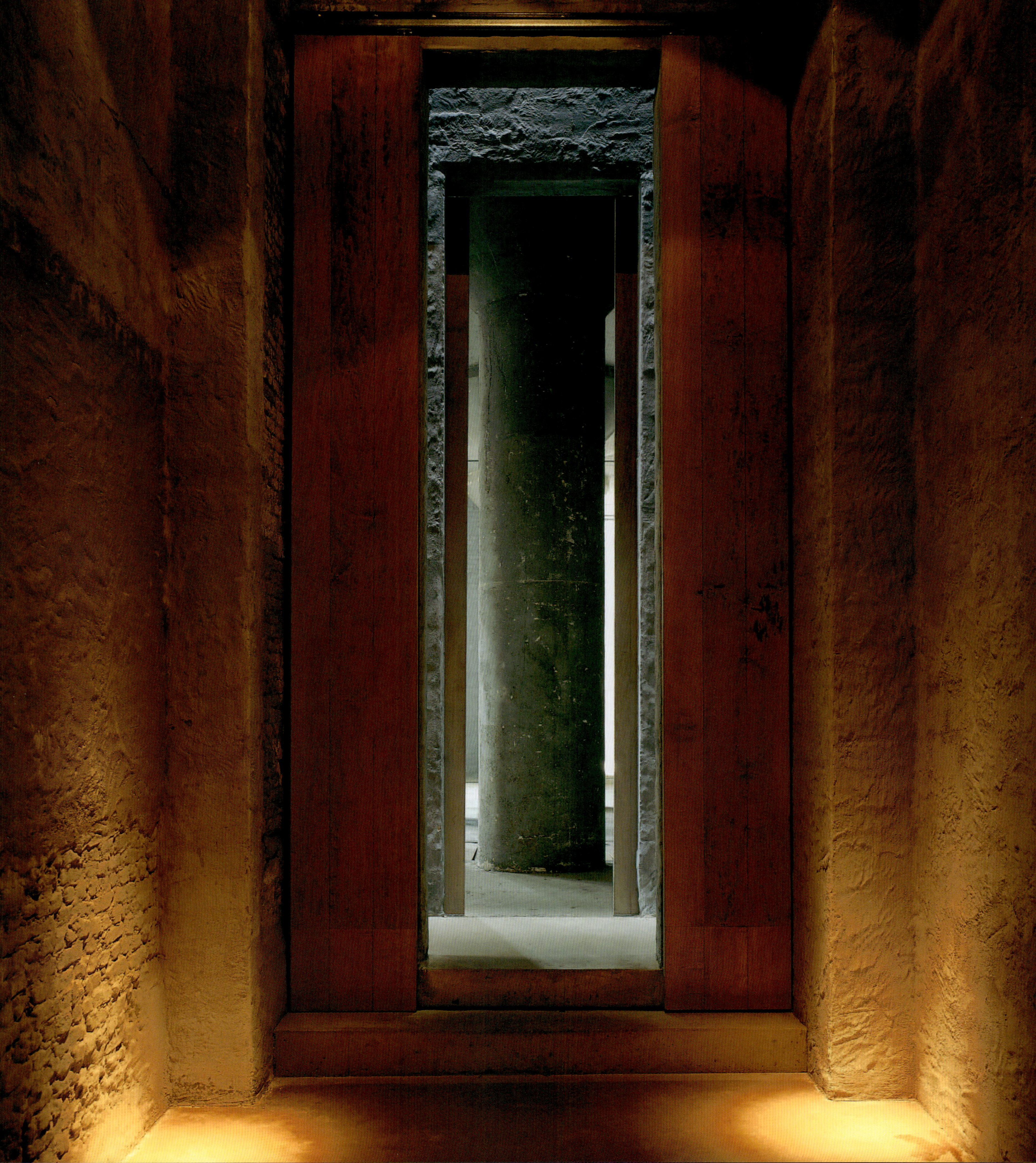

"How nice it must have been to live in England in the eighteenth century." I am very happy with today.

I consider myself a very eclectic collector and dealer. I treasure the timeless and disdain the trendy. My taste spans centuries, cultures, continents, and economic strata. I have never liked flashy or ostentatious interiors. Each room must have its own essential identity. I love the tension between different objects and different cultures and I always let the space I am restoring inspire me. In decorating a house it is as exciting for me to bring out its history as it is to suit the character of the present owners, who must, of course, feel comfortable in their home. Above all, my task is to give things and people a better place in the world.

Purifying houses, giving them humanity, making them livable is what I try to do. So many people have beautiful houses and yet don't live in them properly. They live in corners—they live in the tiniest room where the television is, or part of the kitchen, and everything else is just dead space. I try to persuade people to live everywhere in their house; in their library, the drawing room, the study, in the big, warm, happy kitchen, and I try to make every room interesting in a different way so every person in the family finds his space somewhere in the house, and they are not all crowded into just one corner. What is the point of living in a big house if you don't like every room and you don't use it all?

To create a house in a particular style is like interpreting a passage of Bach, Mozart, Schubert, or Shostakovich. In the world we now live in, the world of the third millennium, the idea of a style "for the times" will, I believe, become more and more relative. One's state of mind will inform the times and style in which one lives. Everyone has her own personal choice. In music, as in style, it is always a question of how to balance and harmonize taste.

For thirty years I have been interested in developing an art of living which can transform the ordinary object into an objet d'art and the everyday gesture into perfection—the fullness of emptiness.

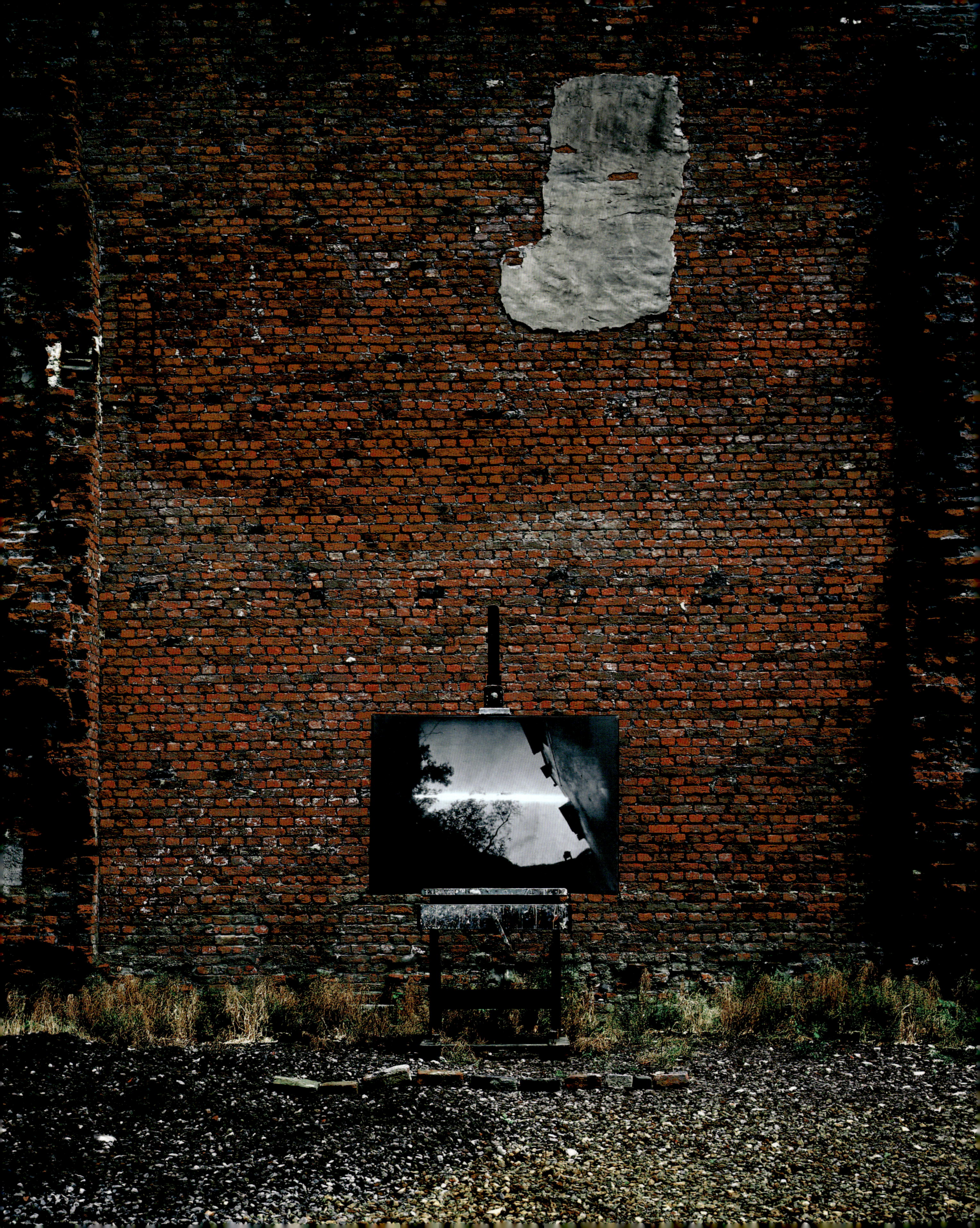

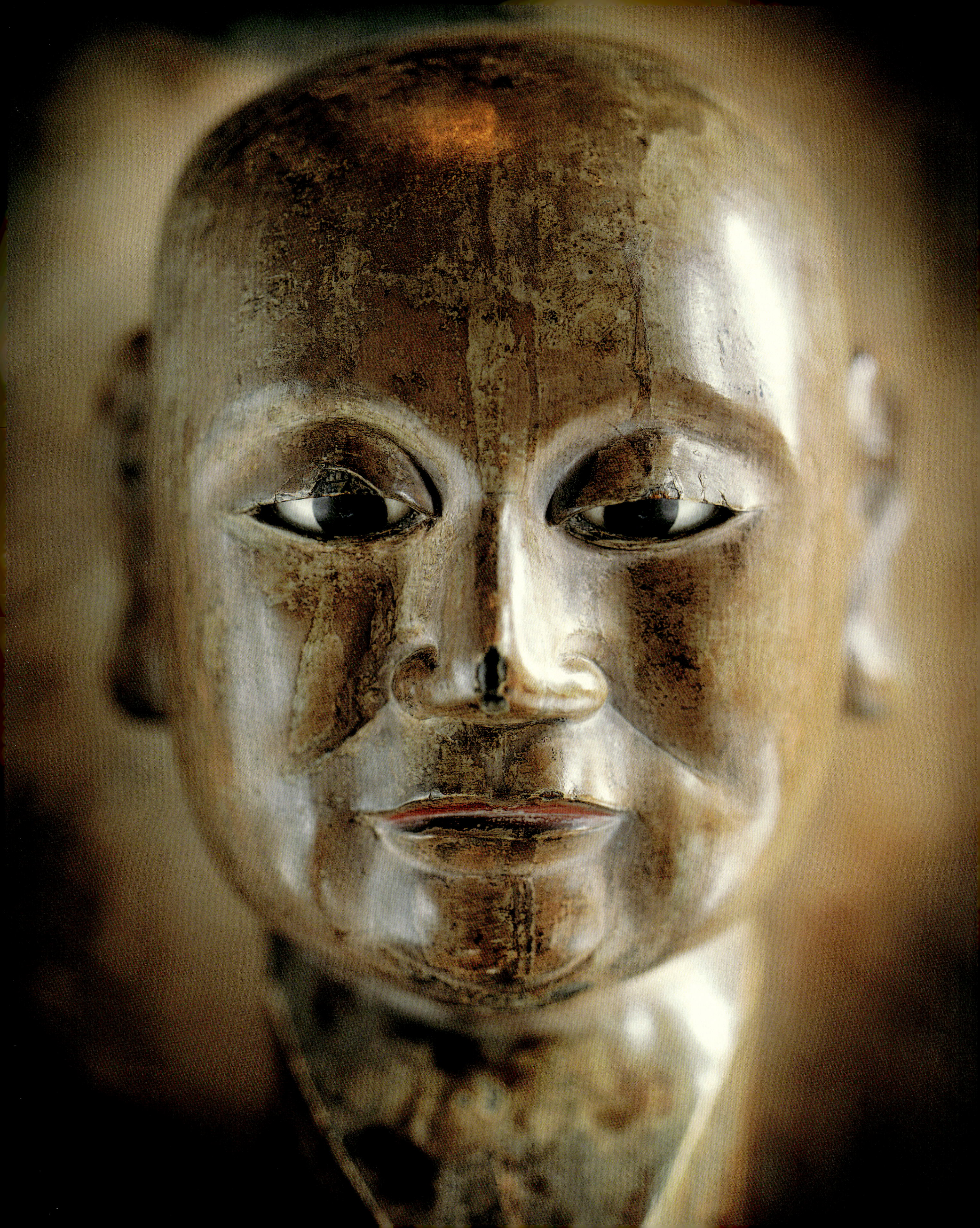

illustrations

12-13. Detail of a piece of mountain furniture from Franche Comté. To me this old piece of furniture becomes contemporary art when taken out of its original context and put in the Kanaal Gallery. It was probably made by a local carpenter who certainly did not consider it a piece of art, but it is, and the circles give me a feeling of the cosmos.

18-19. Jacques-Laurent Agasse (1767–1849), *A Bloodhound, a White Pointer and Four Spaniels,* circa 1808. Oil on canvas (37.5" x 46"). Recently acquired by the Musée d'Art et Histoire in Geneva.

20-21. George Romney (1734–1802), *Portrait of Peter Woodhouse,* circa 1768. Oil on canvas (77.5" x 51").

22. The Vlaeykensgang, Antwerp. We restored many of the houses in this tiny 16th-century street. **23.** Frans Mattheessens was a lawyer and a great friend of my parents. Here, he was dressed for the big Renaissance party we gave in the Vlaeykensgang in 1977. He was one of the people who influenced me a lot; if I needed any advice on law or on the proper way to conduct business I would go to him. In a way, he was one of my spiritual fathers.

24-25. This is how our house looked in 1977-78, in the Vlaeykensgang, it was a lovely room. Under the flooring, we found a beautiful 16th-century poplar floor, with all the original planks, some over two feet wide. We patched, restored, and waxed them. At the back of the room you can see an early gothic table and above that is our favorite Jef Verheyen picture, *Urbino–L'Espace idéal,* painted in 1977. It is now in our bedroom at the castle.

26. Detail of one of our exhibition stands in New York, 1997. **27.** Our Victorian Opera ball at the Reform Club in London, 1997.

182

28-29. May at the Renaissance party, 1977.

30-31. Our attic at the castle. As you see, I like to mix Oriental furniture with shepherd's furniture, because I feel it is in the same spirit; the Oriental and the primitive share a kind of minimalism that existed for hundreds of years.

34-35. The table set for dinner in our small dining room in 's-Gravenwezel: everything is in white. The rock crystal chandelier is 18th century, the silver is mostly Belgian.

36-37. This is the little corridor between our drawing room and our dining room in the Vlaeykensgang, circa 1975, where we'd hung a lovely set of portraits of a Welsh family painted in 1608.

38. A Nautilus cup with Belgian silver-gilts mounts, by Hendrick van Ockerhout, Bruges (1643–44). This is one of the nicest Nautilus cups I have ever seen. It was made in Bruges and the shell is carved with scenes of the sea. The mermaid is carrying a shell and there are a lot of symbols in it. For me, this represents the real renaissance. **39.** A Coconut Cup of an owl with Parcel-gilt Mounts (Antwerp, 1548). The makers mark is a pelican in a shield. H: 6.75". This owl is very interesting because it's one of the oldest known silver mounted coconut vessels used for drinking wine. The collar rim is engraved: "ALS ALLE ANDER FOGELS SIN THOE NESTE SOIS MIN FLIGE BESTE" ("When all other birds are in their nest, my flight is at its best").

40. An example of very simple, pure, late 17th century and early 18th century English silver, which I like very much because the shapes are so simple. It is mainly Britannia Standard silver. When touched, it has a wonderful skin. **41.** This statue of a deacon is early 14th-century French. It was most probably a supporter of a reliquary. I love this figure for its serenity and its almost Buddha-like expression. It is very exciting when I find an expression normally associated with Buddha echoed in early gothic or European art.

42-43. Turned objects of the 15th, 16th and 17th centuries have always been some of my great favorites. This is a wonderful collection of ivory Pokals.

44. This is my favorite piece of turned ivory; it is South German of the early 17th century. There is not one piece in any collection that I would prefer to this one. It's been twisted and turned in an unbelievable way. In spite of all this movement, there is harmony. **45.** Detail of the music room with very interesting architectural furniture. In the back, a Chippendale bookcase, for which we have the original designs. On the table, an architectural cabinet designed for collecting medals. In the cupboard, early pre-Columbian Valdivia sculptures, circa 1500 B.C. On the walls, a series of horse paintings executed for the Fuggers family by Rubens' workshop, They are signed and were commissioned for a house in Antwerp in 1609.

46. This is a collection of Sukothai vases from the 13th, 14th and 16th centuries. I love these particular vases because they were made during the first period of peace in Thailand, after the long Khmer period when Thailand really became Thai. **47.** This is my collection of all kinds of human beings, the family of man. I have put Asians, Africans, and Europeans together; some of them are mad, some charming, some curious people. On the bottom shelf, I have placed my collection of terracotta figures by Daumier.

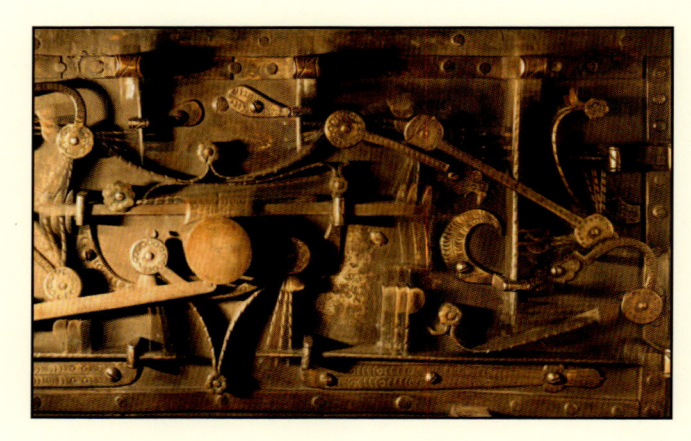

50-51. When I was about 17, I saw an exhibition of Tinguely's work but of course I could not afford to buy anything. Then I found a 17th-century chest with a very elaborate lock in its lid which turned and moved and reminded me of Tinguely.

52-53. A Regency four-pedestal dining table in mahogany, from England, circa 1810. (23.5 feet long, fully extended.) Provenance: Collection of Maureen, Marchioness of Dufferin and Ava; *The Queen Elizabeth Dining Room* in Hans Crescent, London.

54-55. This Bösendorfer piano belonged to my old friend Jos Macken, who can't play it anymore. He was delighted to sell it to me and now it relives its past in the Kanaal Gallery. Sometimes we bring it to the castle when we give concerts there. On the floor lies *Ellipsoid Pietra Serena*, a sculpture by Dominique Stroobant. It looks like a beautiful, natural stone. On the right is an exquisite bronze bust of the Sukothai period, 13th century. I like this because it is both very oriental, but also has a very Roman feeling.

56. An early work by Lucio Fontana (1899–1968) in terracotta, *Concetto Spaziale,* dated 1955. For me this is really very poetic, it is like the first primitive sculpture made by man. It is also in the shape of an egg, you don't know if it's the beginning or the end. **57.** A collection of Pi symbolizing heaven. These are all in jade, and have the very pure shape of a pierced flat circular disk. The square forms are T'sung. T'sung forms such as these symbolize the earth, and were used for meditation. They are very early, about three or four thousand years old.

58. I discovered this wonderful Cy Twombly at a sale in Antwerp. The first time I saw Twombly's work at the Whitechapel Gallery, in 1987, I was totally disgusted, I hated it and I couldn't chase it out of my mind. Then after about three months I changed my opinion and realized why his work was fantastic. **59.** A prayer scroll we bought in Japan. It is a prayer of a thousand prayers (one prayer for every day). Again, this is not made as art, but I find this even more interesting, because it is religious, it has a purpose. The vessels are two-thousand-year-old Chinese bronzes from the Han period.

60. An old wall in the Kanaal Gallery. **61.** We left most of the beautiful walls of the Kanaal in their original condition, old, damaged, and repaired as they were; they are like a contemporary fresco. Construction of the building began in the 1860s, so some of the colors might date from that time. Other patches are repairs from other periods, it's like a fresco in progress for 150 years. The table is minimal, made by shepherds in the mountains. It is interesting what you can do with very simple objects, it is not the money or the rarity that counts, it is the spirit of things.

64-65. The mantelpiece in the library on which, to the left, is a T'sung earth-brown jade vase, representing the earth, from the second millennium B.C. Above, I hung a *Concetto Spaziale* (1959) painting by Lucio Fontana suggesting man's perception and his ascent into the heavens. To the right, a violet Pi jade (770–221 B.C.) representing heaven.

66. A mask-sculpture that Picasso made and painted in 1943 for Dora Maar out of a piece of wood he found. I love this about Picasso, with his magic he makes something very strong out of nothing. **67.** A figure from Valdivia, one of the oldest pre-Columbian cultures, which flourished around 1500 B.C. Human beings have always been in search of great purity of form, shape, and expression. This primitive search— you can call it primitive or you can call it sacred—is very important. It's a search for simplicity throughout history.

68. A Greek mask, most probably from the Greek theatre. What I like about this is you can almost see it expelling breath, it makes time stop. It is like looking through the past, the present, the future, it is timeless. **69.** A nice 18th-century mountain chair seen from the back. It has been left in its original condition, so you can still see where the sun burnt the varnish. I love its patina, and the circle is reminiscent of a Chinese Pi.

70-71. A very simple object made out of wood used by shepherds to crush chestnuts. The little teeth that look like stones are also made of harder wood. It is an organic organization of stones, or pieces of wood that have been used in a very spontaneous way and yet, to me, it is also art.

72. Lucio Fontana (1899–1968), *Concetto spaziale, Attese* (1965). White canvas with ten cuts, signed on the back (39.25" x 52"). This is a beautiful Fontana—rarely do catalogues show the back of Fontana's work, but we were quite excited about this one and wanted to show it. Fontana always writes interesting text or a little poem on the back: "Fontana 1965, Concetto spaziale Attese. Il mese di Febbraio. Inauguro una mostra" (sic). **73.** Simply a collection of old planks we have been collecting all our lives. We put them on trestles to make impromptu tables just as they did in the middle-ages when a table could go anywhere—the proper dining room was only an 18th-century invention.

74-75. This is the first picture we got from Woburn. Attributed to Thomas Gainsborough (1727–1788). The subject is probably one of the daughters of George III.

76-77. One of my favorite screens. It is Japanese, signed by Tanyu Kano and dated early 16th century. For me it has real cosmic power—it's a Zen painting and it is also the first thing that made me understand what action painting really is. It was made by a great painter who perhaps meditated for months before he made it, then he made it in a second…all that power…Next to it is a beehive found in the Auvergne. It is just a hollow piece of wood, the Auvergnats used to put a stone on top to make it into a beehive.

78-79. Canopic Jar, Egypt, Late Period, 26th Dynasty (664–525 B.C.). H: 20.5". A very beautiful, Egyptian Canopic vase in banded alabaster, one of the most beautiful I have ever seen. It is very large with a fabulous expression and an exceptional sculptural quality.

80. Baroque model for a large ewer, late 17th-early 18th century, in alder wood. This large baroque vase is of unbelievable quality. It was probably made by a great silversmith as the model for a gold or silver vase. I sold it to my old client, Mme. Cleiren, a long time ago. Her daughter inherited it and didn't have room for it, so she asked if I could sell it. We took it to the Paris Biennale and sold it to the Metropolitan Museum of Art in New York. **81.** This is the type of Roman sculpture I like because it is a very realistic, strong, masculine portrait. It is made of bronze and the inset eyes are of glass.

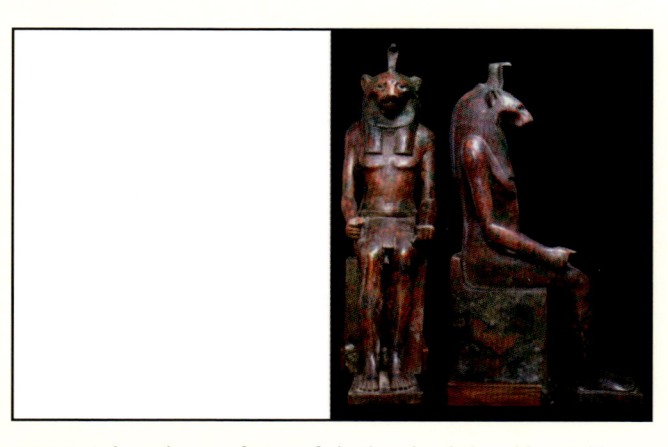

82-83. A large bronze figure of the lion-headed goddess Sekhmet. Egypt, Late Period, c. 690–525 B.C. H. 24". This is one of the first objects we took to the castle but we couldn't find the right room for it—I put it in one room after another. In the end it came to rest in the tower before we sold it to the Miho museum in Japan.

84-85. This is the apartment in the Vlaeykensgang where my son Boris is living now. It is one floor of a house built in 1554. This was the first loft May and I made together in 1972, before we were married.

86-87. Axel Vervoordt in one of his restoration workshops.

88-89. Micael Planer, German baroque five-fold painted screen, oil on canvas, 1653. A beautiful baroque screen which I showed at my first fair in Maastricht in 1976 where I sold it. It then came back to me and I sold it again.

90-91. This was our first workshop in the Vlaeykensgang. We used it for restoring metal locks, clocks, and silver.

92-93. The loft of the Kanaal before restoration.

94-95. Detail of an exhibition stand at the Maastricht TEFAF Fair, 1996.

96-97. Another stand at the Maastricht TEFAF fair, 1993. This entire room is now in Château du Tertre in France.

98-99. A detail of one of our stands at the Paris Biennale. There is a very nice Picasso on the wall, and the chest, one of a pair, is a very good example of the architectural marquetry I have always loved. With this, I put Tang china, Egyptian pieces, and a red porphyry vase. I love red porphyry. In Ancient Rome, only the emperor could possess it, it was rare even in those days.

100-101. Detail from the Brussels Antique Fair in 2001. The painting is by Richard Serra (b. 1939), there is a sculpture by Sjoerd Buisman (b. 1948), a Chinese Ming table, on which stands a Bactrian elongated idol (early second millennium B.C.) and some pre-dynastic Egyptian stone vessels. Boris created this composition and I was very pleased with it.

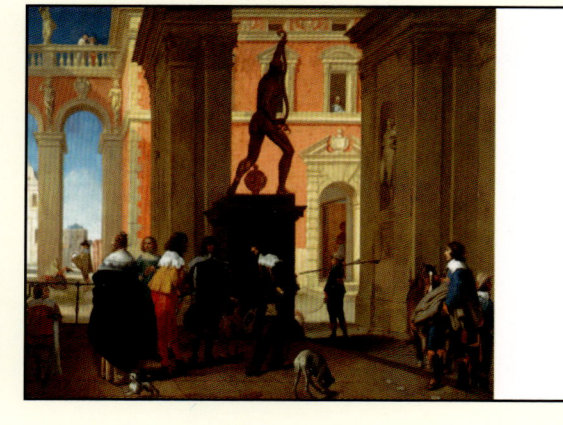

102-103. Jacob van Oost the Elder (Bruges, 1601–1671), *Figures Gathered in a Classical Courtyard around a Sculpture.* Signed and dated "I VAN OOST INVE/1640." Oil on canvas (73.5" x 94.5"). This painting by Jacob van Oost the Elder, a Bruges painter. I especially like it for its scale, the architecture, the inspiration from Italy, and the spirit of Anthony Van Dyck.

104-105. The famous cabinet made for the marriage in 1651 of Eleonora Gonzaga and the Emperor Ferdinand II of Austria. It was probably made in Mantua and has several different marbles, semi-precious stones, and rock crystal, all mounted on ebony.

106. A very interesting, typical Antwerp mirror of the Mannerist period, circa 1560, probably designed by Cornelis Floris. **107.** These are unframed, little drawings by Pablo Picasso, made on matchboxes. I love them because they are so spontaneous. Most probably he was waiting in a restaurant and had an idea for a new picture. Dora Maar kept them all, they came from her collection.

108. A beautiful study of horses by Abraham van Diepenbeeck, circa 1620. By kind permission of His Grace the Duke of Westminster.
109. A terracotta bust of Apollo by Godecharle (Brussels, 1750–1835) signed and dated 1781. One of the pieces from a great Belgian collection we bought.

110-111. *Prometeus* by Michiel van der Voordt (Antwerp, 1704–1777). One of a pair of statues, which are both in the garden of the castle where they have been ever since the 18th century.

112-113. This shows the garden surrounding the castle.

114-115. When we moved in, the park was filled with over 700 pines and many beech trees. Working with Jacques Wirtz, my near neighbor, the pines were taken out and we planted a large beech hedge as a frame for the huge rhododendrons which we cut every five years. The idea, inspired by Zen gardens I have seen, is that they should look like stones in the sand or islands in water.

118-119. A corner cupboard, in the dining room at the castle, by Daniel Marot, I bought in England 15 years ago. The Victorians had totally gilded it and it was terribly vulgar, so I stripped it and painted it white since Marot's architectural furniture was often painted grey or white. We copied the little brackets which we hung on the walls to display the collection of Ming china from the Hatcher collection. In the middle of the table is a Delft *tulipière*.

120-121. This is part of the castle's 17th-century kitchen. The glazed earthenware is made by friends of ours, Kinga and Anatoly Stolnikoff. On the right is a Dutch ceramic tile showing the Duke of Cumberland painted by Jan van Aalmis. We have a whole room of such tiles which were made to commemorate the Battle of Fontenoy (1745). The others are in the dining room and in the kitchen.

122-123. This is the old orangery, which we left as unrestored as possible. When we bought the castle it was a workshop, the walls were totally black and we sanded them by hand with lots of friends one Sunday. We discovered the old plaster but I left some of the black in it. Here we mix the simple and the baroque. There is always a huge sofa to rest and listen to music, and a piano, because this room has wonderful acoustics and is fabulous for opera.

124. The new orangery that we built in the walled garden. **125.** The apple tree under which we have lunch as often as we can.

126-127. The old orangery seen from outside. Sometimes we give dinners there by candlelight or hold concerts.

128-129. A 14th-century stone bas-relief from the Meuse river region. I find it exciting because the style and execution of the clothing's folds are almost like abstract painting or sculpture.

132-133. What we call our oriental drawing room. Here we have mixed contemporary art and oriental objects. It is very serene and quiet and is one of my favorite rooms. When we put the big Tàpies here (see next picture p. 134-135), we realized we had to change the room for it, so we made it totally bare. We scraped off the plaster, took away the carpet, put a big fireplace in it, and painted the walls with paint mixed with earth from the park. The 16th-century Japanese screen represents the 1000 horses.

134-135. Antoni Tàpies, *Grand Marron Troué*, 1972. Signed and dated on the reverse. In front of it is the bronze sculpture *Concetto Spaziale Natura* by Lucio Fontana (1899-1968). It makes you think of the earth and cosmos at the same time.

136-137. I always keep this head in our bedroom because I want to see it in the early morning when I wake up. It is placed just where the first sunlight shines in. This head is of the Borobodur period, 8th century. I am so fond of its expression of youth, intelligence, justice, goodness, and unbelievable serenity. It stands on a gothic Flemish chest.

138-139. I find this arrangement of Chinese Tang horses (8th–10th century) and budding branches very feminine and gentle.

140. The Jef Verheyen picture that used to be in the Vlaeykensgang hangs in our bedroom now. This wonderful ceramic vase I like most of all was made in the old Shigaraki ovens in Japan, the first of the Zen pottery of the 16th century. There has never been more interesting pottery made. The chair is Chinese of the Ming period. The chest is late Romanesque, it's very, very early, I think it may be the oldest piece of furniture we own. **141.** A beautiful 17th-century Brussels tapestry, representing Meleager and Atalanta, made by Gerard Peemans. It is woven from gorgeous wool and silk, with gold and silver threads.

142-143. This is one of a pair of lead reliefs, circa 1750, from the collection of Baron Alphonse de Rothschild. It is by Jacob Gabriel Molinarolo (Vienna, 1721–1780), and represents Adonis taking leave of Venus.

144-145. A little chestnut wood table. I love the design because it is so simple—and it makes you want to have lunch!

146-147. *Vibration,* Jef Verheyen (Antwerp, 1932–1984), 1960, watercolor on paper (22.5" x 29.25"). A very simple bathroom in a turret in the castle with a Jef Verheyen watercolor on the wall.

148-149. My absolute favorite sculpture of our entire collection. It is a 13th-century portrait of a Lohan, a supreme monk who achieved the highest level of meditation. It was a wonderful discovery from a German collection we bought years ago. To me, the expression of serenity is very important.

150-151. The Kanaal.

152-153. An unrestored wall at the Kanaal.

154-155. A fragment of a colossal Roman head (1st century A.D.) seen in the Kanaal.

156-157. A detail in one of the rooms at the Kanaal with an original lock. We left all the old nails, locks, and fittings when we were restoring the Kanaal because we thought it was so interesting that when utilitarian fittings are viewed in a different context they, too, become impromptu art.

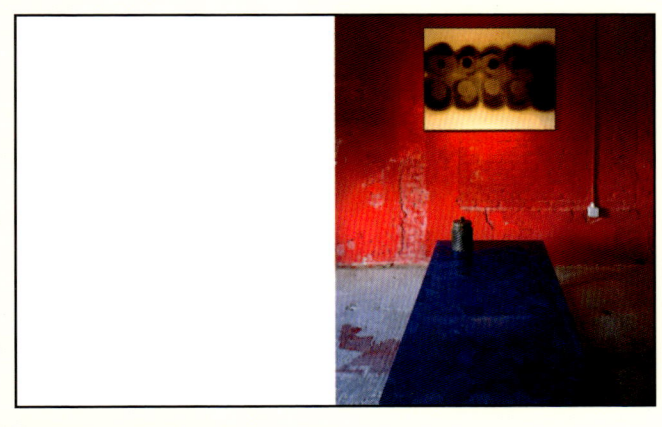

158-159. A smoke picture by Otto Piene (b. 1928), one of the zero artists, in the red room of the Kanaal.

160-161. We called this the museum before we emptied it of all the iron and machinery, leaving a big round room (see **162-63**) where we installed the big work by Anish Kapoor, *At the Edge of the World* (1998).

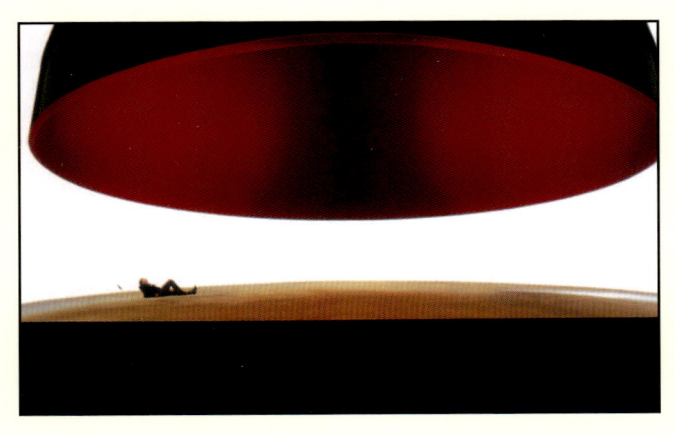

162-163. Anish Kapoor (b. Bombay, 1954), *At the Edge of the World* (1998). The observer has the illusion of a void in which he can lose himself and thereby view the infinite.

164-165. One of the rooms in the Kanaal ready for a large dinner party for one of the art events held here. We call this room the Escher Room because its functional form and architecture remind one of the bizarre fantasies found in this artist's drawings.

166. Our sons, Boris and Dick, in 1984 when they were ten and seven. We had just bought the castle and we were visiting all the attics, trying to discover things amidst the clutter. **167.** A series of minimalistic tables stacked together in the Kanaal.

168-169. A wooden hoop, probably part of a primitive barrel.

170-171. Once we had emptied this room with its huge columns, you could really experience the silence. I decided to bring my whole private collection of Dvaravati sculptures here, works I have been collecting for the last 30 years, and which you almost never see life-sized.

172-173. One of the Dvaravati sculptures.

174. A Sukhotai bronze hand, dating from the 13th century. **175.** A view of the Kanaal.

176-177. In front of an old wall of the Kanaal stands a work by Dominique Stroobant, 1978, made from a camera obscura photograph, of the evolution of the sun with an exposure time of 12 hours.

178-179. An extremely realistic 12th-13th century head of a Japanese Lohan, of lacquer with rock crystal eyes. Its very powerful expression reminds me of a teacher: when I have questions, I sometimes look at it for answers.

photo credits

All photographs by Laziz Hamani, except: © Noel Allum: p. 26; © Congo Blue/Kurt De Wit and Joris Cerstiaens: p. 41, 50-51, 52-53, 66, 67, 79, 92-93, 106, 160-161, 164-165; © Gerald Dauphin: p. 27; © Geralds: p. 23, 28-29, 32-33; © Kees Hageman: p. 22, 24-25, 37, 38, 39, 80, 81, 83, 91, 95; © Image Art/Claude Germain: p. 43, 68, 99; © André Lambrechts: p. 20, 72, 102-103, 107, 108, 142-143, 171; © Cees Roelofs: p. 100-101; © Fritz von der Schulenburg: p. 45, 48-49, 118, 120, 121, 138-139; © Studiopress/Guy Van Grinsven: p. 96-97; © Bernd Urban: p. 40, 57, 104-105; © Jan Verlinde: p. 84-85.

acknowledgments

This book has been a team effort; I would like to thank Robert Lauwers for his invaluable help in every aspect of its research and preparation. My thanks also to Fritz von der Schulenberg and to Laziz Hamani for their extraordinary photographs and to Sébastien Ratto-Viviani for his sensitive design. I would especially like to thank Meredith Etherington-Smith; in writing this book a great friendship has developed. Many people have helped me during my life and, above all, this book is a tribute to them.